Visual Basic and Visual Basic .NET for Scientists and Engineers

CHRISTOPHER FRENZ

Visual Basic and Visual Basic .NET for Scientists and Engineers

ISBN (pbk): 1-59059-017-1

Printed and bound in the United States of America 12345678910

Trademarked names may appear in this book. Rather than use a trademark symbol with every occurrence of a trademarked name, we use the names only in an editorial fashion and to the benefit of the trademark owner, with no intention of infringement of the trademark.

Technical Reviewer: MN, MCSD

Editorial Directors: Dan Appleman, Peter Blackburn, Gary Cornell, Jason Gilmore, Karen Watterson

Managing Editor: Grace Wong

Project Managers: Alexa Stuart, Erin Mulligan

Copy Editors: Jennifer Lind, Nicole LeClerc, Ami Knox

Production Editor: Kari Brooks

Compositor: Impressions Book and Journal Services, Inc.

Indexer: Carol Burbo

Cover Designer: Tom Debolski

Marketing Manager: Stephanie Rodriquez

Distributed to the book trade in the United States by Springer-Verlag New York, Inc.,175 Fifth Avenue, New York, NY, 10010 and outside the United States by Springer-Verlag GmbH & Co. KG, Tiergartenstr. 17, 69112 Heidelberg, Germany.

In the United States, phone 1-800-SPRINGER, email orders@springer-ny.com, or visit http://www.springer-ny.com.

Outside the United States, fax +49 6221 345229, email orders@springer.de, or visit http://www.springer.de.

For information on translations, please contact Apress directly at 901 Grayson Street, Suite 204, Berkeley, CA 94710.

Phone 510-549-5938, fax: 510-549-5939, email info@apress.com, or visit http://www.apress.com.

The source code for this book is available to readers at http://www.apress.com in the Downloads section.

R0178186936
MB

For my beautiful Love, Thao!
You're my inspiration for this book. Thank you for being such a supportive,
caring, loving fiancée, and now wife, through this project and my life.
Anh yêu em!!!

Contents at a Glance

Contents

Chapter 4: Variables, Data Types, and Operators ..73

Chapter 5: Arrays and Loop Structures 95

Chapter 6: Built-in Functions 125

Chapter 7: Writing Your Own Functions and Procedures 157

About the Author

 **Christopher Frenz** holds degrees in biology and chemical engineering from Manhattan College and is currently a graduate student in biochemistry at the Albert Einstein College of Medicine. His past research experience includes examining the role of gap junctions in the development of the inner ear as well as developing mathematical models of tissue-based structural support systems in cacti. His current research interests include performing molecular dynamic simulations on bio-molecules as well as using artificial neural networks to model biological systems. Frenz is also proficient in the programming languages of FORTRAN, Pascal, and Perl, and he has over 10 years of programming experience. When not busy toiling away at his computer, he spends his time enjoying the company of his wife, Thao, and their cat, Little T.

Acknowledgments

THE HARDEST PART about writing the acknowledgment section is determining where to begin. The whole staff at Apress was wonderful to work with and a big help in making the project come together.

I'll begin by thanking the two project managers involved in the book , Alexa Stuart and Erin Mulligan. Although you two often drove me crazy with deadline after deadline, I have you to thank for keeping me motivated and focused on completing this project in a timely manner. Without you, I might still have been working on the first draft.

Next, I would like to thank MN for being such a thorough and dedicated tech reviewer. I appreciate the time and effort he spent reviewing and re-reviewing the code contained within the book as the content changed from a VB 6.0 focus to a focus on VB .NET. MN proved to be invaluable in locating pieces of code that had to be slightly modified as the different alpha, beta, and release candidate versions of VB .NET evolved.

Another invaluable component to this project was Karen Watterson, who always seemed to have a never-ending stream of ideas. In many instances Karen's ideas worked to fill out and expand the usefulness and robustness of the book's content, making it a more valuable resource for all. Additionally, I would like to thank Karen for helping me to navigate my way through the whole publication process as I put together this book.

I would also like to thank Dr. Joseph Reynolds of the Manhattan College Department of Chemical Engineering for his review of Chapter 13 and his insights into mathematical modeling.

Finally, I would like to thank my family, especially my grandparents, Anthony and Angelina Chiodo, for their support and for their bearing with me on the nights I spent more time with my home computer than I did with them.

Preface

IF YOU ARE A NOVICE PROGRAMMER, this book is designed for you. The text begins with an overview of the Visual Basic development environment, its important characteristics, and how the environment can be manipulated to suit your needs. Next, a discussion of forms and their uses ensues. This discussion is followed by coverage of the Visual Basic controls, which are most essential to scientific programming. You then learn how to put controls to work by making use of the different control events.

Once this introductory material has been covered, I show you the different data types that Visual Basic supports, with extra attention being paid to the various numerical data types and their uses. At this point the true heart and soul of the book begins, as you begin to gain insights into the various operators that can be used to manipulate these data types. You get an in-depth look at numerical and logical operators, and their order of operations are clearly spelled out.

Next, I describe the different types of loop structures and provide an explanation of the possible uses of each. Practical examples, such as mathematical iteration, are also given to clearly demonstrate the significance of loop structures in scientific programming. Following this, you learn about the different built-in functions that are available in Visual Basic and how to use them in your own projects. Many of these built-in functions are highly useful in the programming of mathematical routines, and thus are essential tools for any scientific programmer. Despite the extensive list of built-in functions, however, not every function you'll desire to carry out is already worked out for you. Therefore, you also get a chance to explore the different ways in which you can code your own customized functions.

After a firm understanding of the crucial elements of the Visual Basic language has been established, I discuss methods for putting these principles together into a complete and polished program. The basics of file handling and data acquisition are explored along with sophisticated interface techniques that are useful in science, such as programming customized spreadsheets. The usefulness of these interface techniques are then exemplified by an example program that performs calculations on a mathematical matrix. The book then delves into coverage of topics such as scientific graphics and data presentation as well as the all-important topics of debugging and error handling. You discover ways to package and distribute your applications so that the rest of the scientific community can make use of your ingenuity.

By this point, you should have a firm understanding of how to code a scientific program, but this still leaves the question of what to code. Thus, the book next pursues the topic of mathematical modeling. I cover the basic principles of mathematical modeling in depth and use them to illustrate how to mathematically model a chemical plant so that you have a clear idea of how to translate different aspects of your work into Visual Basic code.

The book then presents a brief introduction to the new but rapidly growing field of bioinformatics. Bioinformatics is a powerful new concept in biology that takes advantage of the processing power of computers to help researchers make sense of the ever-growing wealth of molecular biological information. I discuss the major endeavors being made in the field and demonstrate a procedure that could be used to find DNA sequence similarities in order to give you a true appreciation of the vital role that computers play. Finally, the book examines the relevant aspects of the new .NET platform and shows you how to code a scientific Web-based application.

CHAPTER 1

Overview of Visual Basic Programming and the Visual Basic Development Environment

VISUAL BASIC (VB) AND Microsoft's more recent VB .NET are powerful and useful programming tools for the development of applications for the Microsoft Windows operating system. What makes this programming language so special is that the programmer can literally draw out the graphical user interface (GUI). This makes developing a GUI relatively easy instead of daunting. It also makes Visual programming unique from more traditional programming, so this chapter starts off by taking a look at the basics of Visual Basic development and the Visual Basic development environment.

An Overview of Visual Basic Application Development

The first and most important step in developing any sort of application is to establish a firm idea of what exactly you desire your program to do. Do you want to calculate the molarity of a solution or maybe determine the amount of heat produced by a certain chemical reaction? Do you simply want to display raw data you've collected in tabular format? Or, do you want to display it in chart form? In other words, the first step in developing a scientific program usually is to ask yourself, "What kind of problem do I need to solve?"

Once you've identified the problem, the question arises of how to address it. As the programmer, you must ascertain what information to gather to solve the problem, and how to manipulate this information in order to obtain the desired result. What calculations need to be performed? What comparisons need to be made? Finally, it is essential that the desired outputs (results) and their forms are determined. The simplest and most effective way of tackling these issues is through the construction of a flowchart. A flowchart is a highly useful tool in planning well-structured approaches to obtaining problem solutions—yes, even when you use tools that rely on event-oriented programming. (These subjects will be covered in detail in Chapter 13.)

After defining the problem and outlining your approach to solving it, it's time to begin developing your application in Visual Basic. The first step in designing the VB application is to plan and lay out the GUI. The GUI is the component of the program that determines how the program user interacts with the program. Thus, it's essential that the GUI be laid out in a user-friendly way. In scientific programming, the GUI is most often used to collect the data required to perform the programmed calculations and to dictate which calculations are performed.

Data collection is accomplished through the use of controls such as text boxes and command buttons. Controls allow the VB program to respond to different user inputs, such as typed in text and numbers, or mouse clicks. These responses to user inputs are termed *control events*. Control events truly dictate the operations of VB applications because the code in a VB program only really tells the application how to respond to each individual control event. Thus, different segments of program code (event procedures) are initiated in response to different user events, making VB programs fundamentally different from the more traditional top-down designs used with other programming languages. As a scientific programmer, you'll spend most of your time coding event procedures, which perform necessary calculations in response to the different possible control events.

Once you've established the GUI and the different event procedures, the last step in developing sound VB applications is to test the programs out and pinpoint all the sources of error. These errors are then corrected, which computer programmers refer to as *debugging*.

This book will primarily focus on the newer .NET platform. However, the book also covers VB 6.0 in order to transition people already familiar with VB 6.0 to VB .NET, as well as to teach people new to VB the necessary tools to use if they are presented with any VB 6.0 or older code. This feature should come in handy, because more lines of traditional VB code already exist than any other programming language's code. Furthermore, despite all of the enhancements that the new .NET platform offers, VB 6.0 is still expected to remain in widespread use for some time to come.

The Visual Basic Development Environment

Now that you've established an understanding of VB application development basics, let's move on to the VB development environment, which is referred to as the *integrated development environment (IDE)*. The quickest and easiest way to familiarize yourself with the VB IDE is to actually "play around" with the environment and its different options, so launch VB and do just that.

The first screen you'll see once the application has loaded is the New Project dialog box (see Figure 1-1). If you're using VB 6.0, you'll notice that this screen has three tabs. The Recent tab lists the VB projects worked on most recently. The Existing tab brings up a standard File Open dialog box you can use to access any previously created VB project. At this time, however, you are most concerned with the New tab, which allows you to work on a new VB application. When you click on the New tab, you'll see a multitude of different project types that you can create (the exact number depends on your edition of VB). For the purposes of this book, however, you'll only concern yourself with the Standard EXE choice.

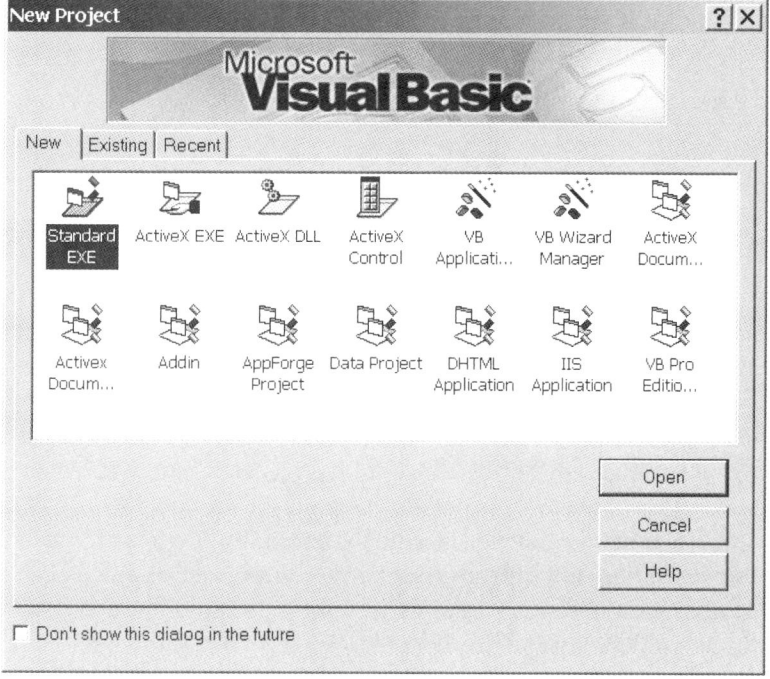

Figure 1-1. The VB 6.0 New Project dialog box

If you're using VB .NET, the New Project dialog box is a little different (see Figure 1-2). It has no Existing or Recent tabs, so you're limited to choosing a project type for a new project. To open an already existing project, you need to use the File menu, which this chapter will discuss in more detail. For now, it is enough to know that you'll work with the Windows Application option, which is the .NET equivalent to VB 6.0's Standard EXE option. Both project types are used to code standard desktop applications for the Windows operating system (OS).

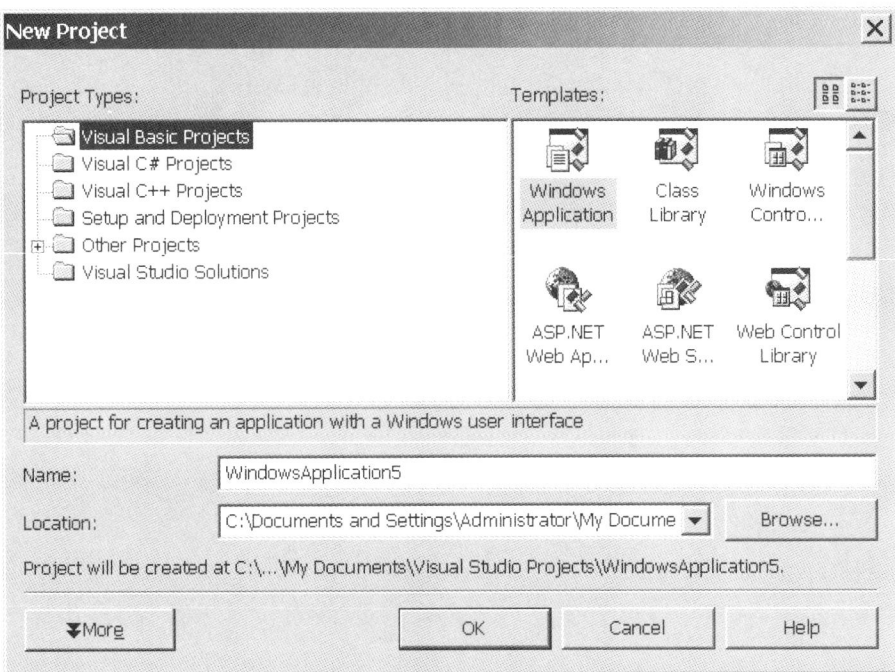

Figure 1-2. The VB .NET New Project dialog box

Some other project types listed are worth mentioning, although this book won't utilize them. As you become a more advanced user, you may want to learn how these other project types can aid in the creation of larger applications. In the VB 6.0 dialog box, the most notable project types are the ActiveX control, with which you create custom controls for your VB projects (for more information on controls, see Chapter 3), and the ActiveX dynamic link library (DLL). A DLL is like a library of functionality that you can add to the application to increase its ability to process data. These libraries are great because they can be used over and over again by multiple applications. In VB .NET, the equivalent project types are the Windows Control Library and the Class Library. Additionally, both development environments allow you to code add-ins for automating repetitive tasks or otherwise enhancing productivity.

Now that you are somewhat familiar with what you can create with VB, select the Standard EXE option or the Windows Application option and take a closer look at the IDE.

The Title Bar

The Title bar is the horizontal strip that runs across the top of the application screen and is common to all Windows applications. The Title bar in VB yields more information than the average title bar. When you first start to work on a VB project, you'll discover that the Title bar gives the project name (Project1 is the default in VB 6.0 and WindowsApplication1 is the default in VB .NET) followed by a dash and the program name, Microsoft Visual Basic. The program name is then followed by one of three options that show the current state VB is operating under. The first option, Design, is present whenever you are busy developing your application. The Run option appears when you're actually running and testing the application. The third option, Break, appears when the application you were running temporarily stops to allow for debugging the code.

The Menu Bar

Directly below the Title bar, you'll find a strip that contains the terms File, Edit, View, and so on. Clicking any one of these terms brings up a pop-up menu. This strip, the Menu bar, provides access to almost all of Visual Basic's features through its various pop-up menus. This rich feature accessibility makes the Menu bar one of the IDE's most important features, and thus all of the crucial elements of the different menus within the Menu bar are explained in this chapter. First, you'll look at the more traditional VB 6.0 menus, and then you'll examine the corresponding new VB .NET menus and how their functionality differs.

The VB 6.0 File Menu

The File menu is one of the most useful menus because it contains all of the tools required to save files, start new projects, and print out all of your source code. The different elements found in the File menu and their important functions are as follows:

> **New Project:** With this menu item, a dialog box appears that is exactly the same as the New tab from VB's New Project dialog box. Selecting this option also unloads any project you're working on, but don't worry; it gives you the option to save the changes first.

> **Open Project:** Clicking on this option brings up a standard File Open dialog box with which you can open up both recent and existing VB projects.

This option also resembles the two rightmost tabs from the New Project dialog box.

Save Project: This menu item is similar to the Save feature in most Windows applications. It creates the project file (.vbp) on the first save, and from there on in saves the active copies of all the files that make up the project, as well as the project file itself.

Save Project As: Similar to the Save As features found in most Windows programs, this option creates a new VB project file that you can then save under a different name. Keep in mind, however, that this feature only copies the project file, not all of the files found in the project.

Save Form: This option creates the form file (.frm) on the first save, and then saves the active copy of the form on all future saves. This option also appears if you choose the Save Project option without first saving your form.

Save Form As: This menu item creates a new form file that you can save under a different name. It is useful in creating backup copies of files.

Print: The print option lets you print out the source code, the forms that make up your GUI, or both. It also gives you the ability to print out an entire VB project or just a certain segment of interest.

Make .exe File: With this option, you can create VB applications that can run independent of the VB IDE or in Microsoft Windows systems where VB isn't installed. However, standalone applications usually require custom control files and DLLs, which won't get packaged with the program if you use this option alone. Thus, it's better to utilize the Package and Deployment Wizard described in Chapter 12.

Figure 1-3. The VB 6.0 File menu

The VB .NET File Menu

It's worth noting several changes to the VB .NET File menu so that the new GUI elements don't confuse anyone. Items such as Print and Save Form, which possess the same meaning and functionality, won't be described again, however.

Open: This is similar to past versions of VB, but with even more options. Instead of just opening past projects from your hard disk or other drive, you now may open projects found on the Web or open other types of Visual Studio files.

Save All: This option is just like the VB 6.0 Save Project option. It saves not only the current form's changes, but also every change made on every form within the project.

Recent Projects: Instead of placing all of the recently accessed projects at the bottom of the File menu like most Windows applications, Visual Studio .NET displays them in a separate pop-up menu. If you choose a project from the menu, your current project will be closed and the selected project opened.

Recent Files: This option works much as the Recent Projects option. This option, however, lets you access files of types other than project files that were recently used.

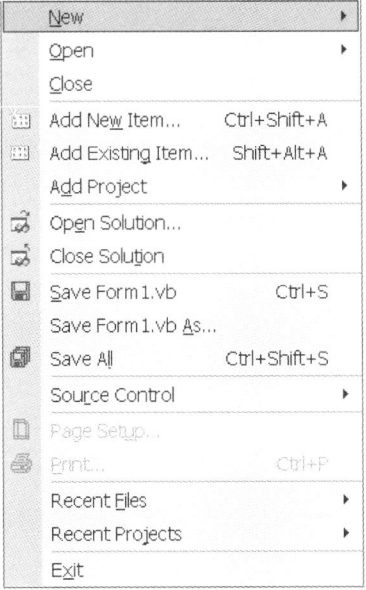

Figure 1-4. The VB .NET File menu

The Edit Menu

The Edit menu contains many useful functions for writing and organizing your code. Several menu items may be familiar because they are fairly common to all Windows programs, but just in case, this chapter will cover all the frequently used options. This menu is basically the same in both VB 6.0 and VB .NET; thus, everything presented in this section applies to both IDEs.

Undo: This option reverses the last editorial change, which is often highly useful if you mistakenly made some sort of editorial change to your project.

Redo: The Redo option puts back the last editorial change that you reversed with Undo.

Cut, Copy, and Paste: Going into detail on these three options is hardly necessary because anyone who has ever used a Windows program has used Cut, Copy, and Paste. In VB, these three options utilize the Windows clipboard in the same way as other programs and are just as useful.

Delete: The Delete option erases all of the highlighted information in your project, but be careful—unlike Cut, Delete doesn't save a copy to the Windows clipboard.

Find: Available when the Code Window is active, this option is a great way to locate a certain piece of code or other text within hundreds of lines of code or more. A Find dialog box asks you to enter the text string that you want to search for. You can specify a search range that allows VB to search the current procedure, current module, current project, or selected text. VB then searches the selected range and places you at the first occurrence of that term. If the text isn't present within the range, a message tells you the text wasn't found. Use Find Next to locate other instances found further down in the code.

Replace: Like the Find option, this option is available when the Code Window is active. Replace works much as the Find option in that it seeks out the text string of your choice. However, the Replace command not only seeks out the sought-after text, but also changes it to the new text string.

Indent/Outdent: It's definitely easier to follow and understand code when the author has indented well. One way to add a good indentation pattern to your code is to use the Indent and Outdent commands; however, using the Tab key is much quicker.

> **NOTE** *Good indentation patterns will be exemplified throughout the book's sample code.*

Bookmarks: The Bookmarks option is extremely useful for large projects because it lets you mark a certain location in your code. Later on, you can use the Bookmarks command to jump to that region of code and spare yourself from scrolling through numerous lines of code.

Figure 1-5 shows the VB 6.0 Edit menu, and Figure 1-6 shows the VB .NET Edit menu.

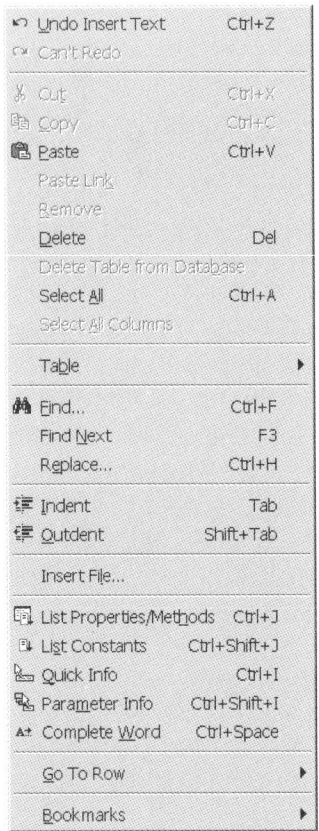

Figure 1-5. The VB 6.0 Edit menu

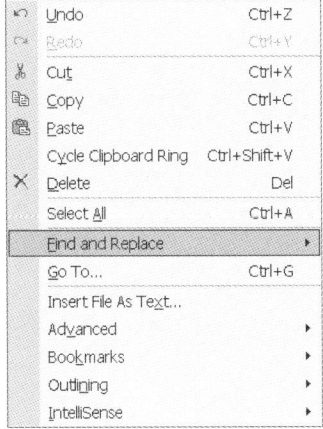

Figure 1-6. The VB .NET Edit menu

The VB 6.0 View Menu

The View menu lets you display and hide various features of the VB development environment. With it, you can customize the IDE and keep handy the features you use most often.

Code: Use this option to view all of the code for the form you're currently working on.

Object: View the form that corresponds to the code that you're currently working with.

Definition: View the code that corresponds to the procedure located near the cursor.

Last Position: Go back to your cursor's prior location. Jump back and forth between regions of code that are far away from one another.

Object Browser: View information regarding the objects found in your VB project. This option is of great use if you are coding an object-oriented program.

Project Explorer: With this menu item, a window displays all of your VB project's files. This window is normally visible by default and is found in the top right corner of your screen.

Properties Window: View and set many properties that contribute to the appearance and functionality of your forms and controls. This feature is extremely useful when it comes to designing your GUI. This window is also normally visible by default and is found on the right side of the screen just below the Project Explorer window.

Form Layout Window: This window will help you set where the form will appear when your application runs.

Toolbox: Display and hide the toolbox, which you'll normally find on the left side of your monitor. (This chapter will discuss the toolbox in more detail later.)

Toolbars: Select and customize the toolbars you want visible.

Figure 1-7 displays the VB 6.0 View menu.

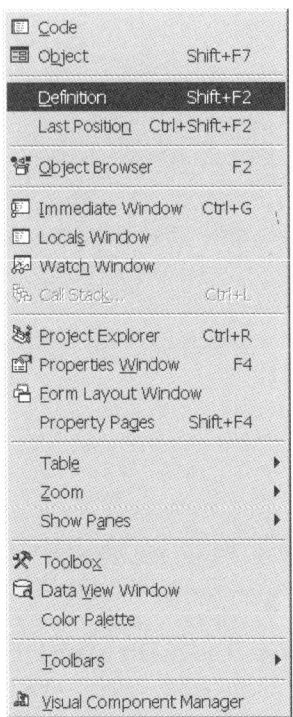

Figure 1-7. The VB 6.0 View menu

The VB .NET View Menu

As with the File menu, the base functionality of the View menu is unchanged. However, the new .NET IDE presents us with some GUI changes.

Designer: As with the Object option in VB 6.0, this option allows you to view the current form. The rationale behind this new terminology is that when you view the graphical representation of the form and its components, you are considered to be in design mode.

Solution Explorer: Basically the same as the Project Explorer, this option lets you view all of the files associated with your project. A new feature of the Solution Explorer, however, is that it also allows you to view your project's references. Later in the book, you'll see that VB .NET derives much of its functionality from references to different namespaces in the .NET Framework. You can view a namespace simply as a collection of procedures that add functionality to your applications. If you're familiar with Java, you'll instantly recognize this as the .NET equivalent to the Java notion of a Package. As with the Project Explorer window, this window is generally present in the upper right corner of the screen.

Figure 1-8 shows the VB .NET View menu.

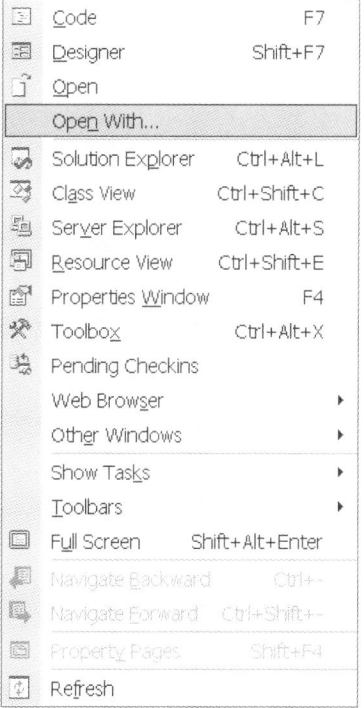

Figure 1-8. The VB .NET View menu

The VB 6.0 Project Menu

The Project menu is crucial in more sophisticated projects; you can enhance your projects by adding forms and other modules to them.

Add Form: Add additional windows (forms) to your application.

Add MDI Form: Add a Multiple Document Interface (MDI) form to a project to create a form that behaves as a "child" window to the initial "parent" form. A child form is seen only within the boundaries of the parent form.

Add Class Module: Class modules are used in object-oriented programming and are required to define the class that will be used throughout your project.

Add File: Add the code found in another file to your current VB project.

Components: Add more controls to your toolbox. This is often important because the basic controls are not always suitable for all programming needs.

Project Properties: Get information about your project, and set various project options.

Figure 1-9 displays the VB 6.0 Project menu.

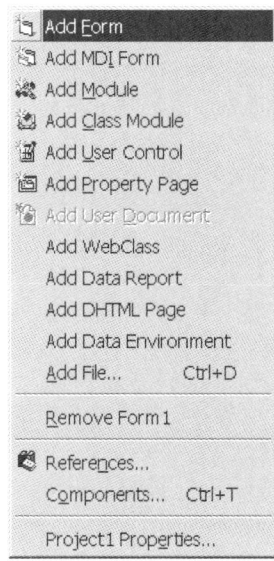

Figure 1-9. The VB 6.0 Project menu

The VB .NET Project Menu

For your purposes, this menu is basically the same as in VB 6.0 except for two small differences. First, the Add Class Module option now is changed to Add Class. Second, the Add MDI Form option is no longer available. This is because the WinForms in VB .NET are more robust than the forms in VB 6.0 in that they are more functionally flexible. In VB .NET, you can turn any form into an MDI form by changing one of the form's properties, as you'll see in Chapter 2. Figure 1-10 displays the Project menu in VB .NET.

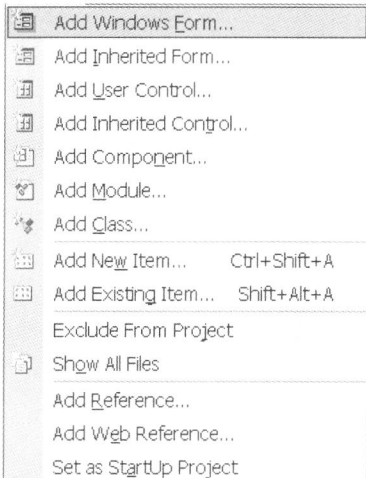

Figure 1-10. The VB .NET Project menu

The Format Menu

Use the Format menu, which you can find in both VB 6.0 and VB .NET, to accurately position your form's controls. This can be useful when you lay out your GUI. The different menu items are pretty self-explanatory, however, so no detail is required.

The VB 6.0 Debug Menu

The Debug menu (see Figure 1-11) contains several tools you use when testing your applications for errors.

Step Into: When VB goes into Break mode, this tool lets you execute the next line of code and enter into any subprogram that is called.

Step Over: When VB goes into Break mode, this tool lets you execute the next line of code, but will skip over any subprogram that is called.

Step Out: When VB goes into Break mode, this tool lets you get out of any subprogram you entered before VB went into Break mode.

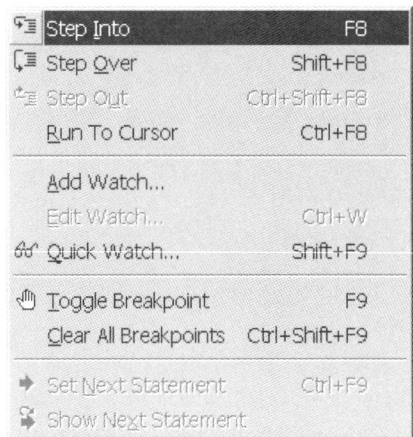

Figure 1-11. The VB 6.0 Debug menu

The VB 6.0 Run Menu

You'll use the Run menu quite frequently when you test and debug your applications. The Run menu actually initiates your application and its source code.

> **Start:** As the name indicates, Start begins the execution of your program code and runs the application.

> **NOTE** *The application will go into Break mode if a bug or an error is encountered.*

> **Start With Full Compile:** When you select Start, VB initially compiles only the code required to get the application up and running, and then compiles the remainder of the code as needed. By selecting this option, you compile all of the code before running the application. This option is recommended for larger projects.

> **End:** Use this option to shut down the application when you're done testing it and are ready to continue coding.

Figure 1-12 shows the VB 6.0 Run menu.

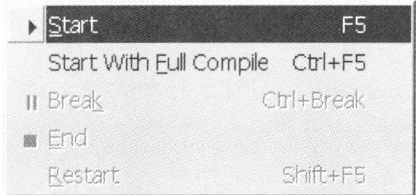

Figure 1-12. The VB 6.0 Run menu

The VB .NET Debug Menu

The VB .NET Debug menu (see Figure 1-13) encompasses elements found in both the VB 6.0 Debug and Run menus. For example, from this menu you can begin the execution of your program by clicking Start, or you can make use of the tools Step Into, Step Over, and Step Out. In addition to combining the two menus, one change is worth noting.

Stop Debugging: This option works exactly the same way as the End option found in VB 6.0—it just has a different name. If you want to quit the application's execution, this is the command for you.

Figure 1-13. The VB .NET Debug menu

The VB 6.0 Add-Ins Menu

You can use the Add-Ins menu to integrate separate tools into VB to enhance its functionality. Third parties commonly produce add-ins to increase VB capabilities in specialized areas. VB .NET has no Add-Ins menu. Instead, you access add-ins by going to the Tools menu and choosing the Add-In Manager option.

The VB .NET Build Menu

With the Build menu in VB .NET, you can build your applications. "Building an application" is basically the technical terminology that describes the process of creating a compiled executable. Use the Configuration Manager to choose between two types of builds. The first type is a Debug build, in which the code is not optimized and symbolic debugging information is produced to aid the developer in eliminating errors. In a Release build, compiler optimizations are applied and symbolic debugging information isn't generated. This results in a faster and smaller executable.

Figure 1-14 shows what the VB .NET Build menu looks like.

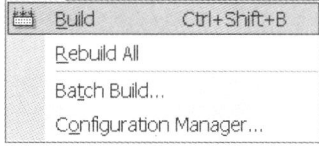

Figure 1-14. The VB .NET Build menu

The Help Menu

The Help menu behaves much as the Help menus of most Windows applications and is extremely useful. To take full advantage of it, make sure to install your Microsoft Developer Network (MSDN) library. Also, VB comes with an online help capability, which is useful because the online help is updated frequently. You can access the online help system at `http://msdn.microsoft.com`. In VB .NET, you also can turn on a feature, Dynamic Help, that many beginners may find extremely useful. This feature opens a window that presents all of the help topics related to what you're currently working on. Thus, most of the information you need is at your fingertips.

The Toolbars

Located directly below the Menu bar is a strip that contains a series of icons. This default strip, the Standard toolbar, is of great use because it provides shortcuts to many of the Menu bar's pop-up features.

> **TIP** *You can customize the toolbars through the View menu or by right-clicking the toolbar and selecting Customize. Customizing the toolbars is a great way to keep the icons you use most frequently right at your finger-tips. Also, if you don't like the toolbar at the top of the screen under the Menu bar, you can drag and drop it someplace more convenient.*

The Visual Basic Toolbox

The toolbox is a rectangular box that runs vertically down the left side of the screen and contains a set of icons. This box contains the VB controls you add to the forms to develop your GUI and to add functionality to your program. Controls allow VB programs to respond to different user events, such as typing in text, and thus are essential for the development of VB applications.

> **TIP** *Familiarize yourself with some of the different controls in the tool-box by pointing the mouse over the different icons. A tool tip will inform you what each control is.*

The Form Window

Next to the toolbox is a window that takes up the majority of the VB window. In this region, the Form window, you add controls to the forms to develop your GUI (see Figure 1-15). This region also transforms into a coding window when you are ready to add code to the VB application. In fact, you'll spend most of your time working in Visual Basic in either the Form window or the Code window, so the next chapter will begin to explore forms and their functionality.

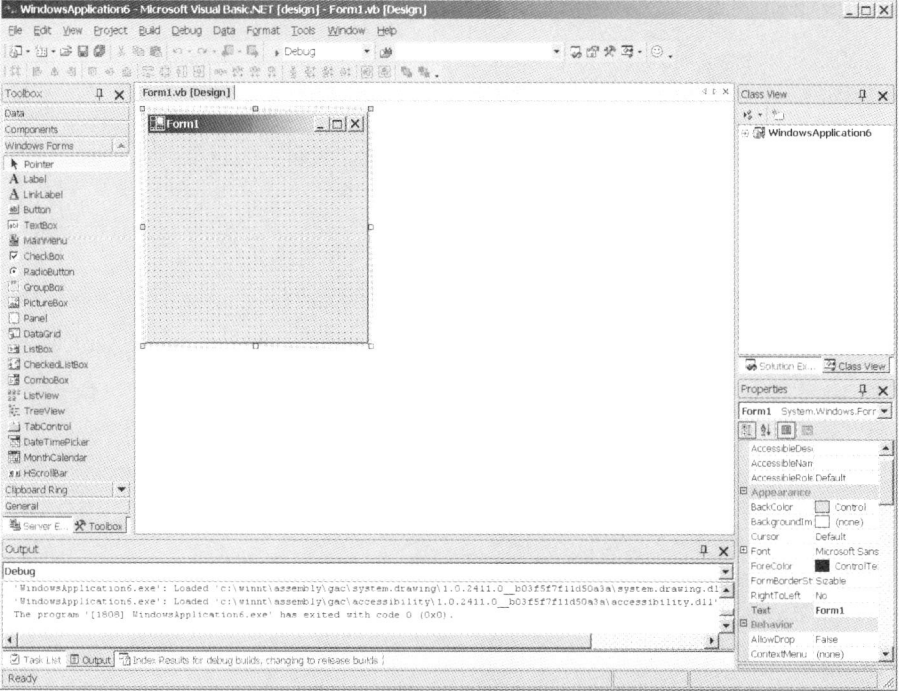

Figure 1-15. The VB .NET IDE

Working with WinForms

NOW THAT YOU UNDERSTAND the basics of VB application development and are familiar with the VB IDE, you can begin to look at WinForms. WinForms form the foundation of an application's GUI and are essential to developing VB applications. WinForms are basically blank containers in which you add different controls and events in order to add functionality to your VB program. Previous versions of VB simply referred to WinForms as "forms," and the two terms are used synonymously throughout this chapter.

If you're familiar with past versions of VB, keep in mind that WinForms are much improved, with even more flexibility. One downside to this enhancement is that many form events and methods found in VB 6.0 are modified. Thus, even experienced VB programmers should browse through this chapter to get up to speed on all of the important modifications. In this chapter, you'll examine and learn how to manipulate forms and their properties. You'll also look at how different form methods and form events enable the forms and the application being developed to interact with one another in response to different user actions. In addition, the chapter discusses single document interface (SDI) applications and multiple document interface (MDI) applications.

WinForms and the .NET Framework

WinForms are no longer VB-specific forms, as were past versions of VB, but instead are accessible to all Visual Studio programming languages. In fact, this uniformity across development languages is one reason why WinForms received their name. WinForms are the first time a completely Windows-based forms package existed for Visual Studio. Technically speaking, WinForms are a component of the .NET Framework's namespace that is dedicated to developing a GUI for desktop applications. This namespace, System.Windows.Forms, contains the classes necessary for creating Windows-based applications, including the classes required to utilize forms in your applications. It also contains many other essential building blocks, such as controls (see Chapter 3 for more information on controls).

Within this namespace, however, you must consider a hierarchy of classes before arriving at the class that defines the WinForms that you'll interact with in the VB IDE. As these classes move up the hierarchy, they inherit from a more base class, and then add some functionality of their own. In this way, higher classes are more generic than the classes down the hierarchy, which are more specific and, hence, provide increased functionality.

Control class: The first important class in the WinForms namespace is the Control class, which inherits from the .NET Object class. The Control class gives basic functionality to forms and controls by doing the following:

- Enables a VB .NET program to define a rectangle on the screen, and thus provides the visual foundation for the WinForms and their associated components.

- Forms the basis for the appearance properties of forms and controls, such as Font, BackgroundImage, and BackColor.

- Plays an essential role by possessing the functionality required to process messages relayed from the Windows operating system (OS). This ability to relay OS messages forms the basis of the program's acceptance of keyboard and mouse click input.

RichControl class: The next important class is the RichControl class. It inherits the Control class and further enhances the base functionality by increasing the graphical display capabilities. RichControl forms the basis for the appearance properties of forms and controls, such as Font, BackgroundImage, and BackColor (discussed later in the chapter).

ScrollableControl class: This next member of the hierarchy inherits from the RichControl class and, as its name suggests, adds scrolling functionality to elements of the user interface. This class forms the basis for properties such as AutoScroll.

ContainerControl class: This class inherits from the ScrollableControl class, and adds the abilities required to successfully utilize child controls. This class tracks which control on your form has the focus, and also allows you to tab from control to control. For more information on focus, peer ahead into the next chapter.

Form class: The last class is derived from the ContainerControl class. The Form class adds the ability to display caption bars and system menus, as well as to create nonrectangular windows. In other words, this class puts the finishing touches on the WinForms that you'll interact with in the VB IDE.

WinForms are also a crucial component of the .NET Framework's aim of unifying the skills required to create both desktop and Web-based applications. In previous versions of VB, programmers often had to develop user interfaces for Web-based applications differently than they did with desktop applications. In .NET, however, many of the component classes of the WinForms and Web Forms namespaces have compatible functionalities, thus VB programmers can apply these development skills more easily to both desktop and Web-based applications. Chapter 15 discusses Web Forms further.

The Structure of a Form

Anyone with a fair amount of experience using the Windows operating system (OS) should be familiar with a form's basic structure; any application that runs visibly on your computer is based on some type of form. However, to ensure that you understand VB-relevant forms, examine the basic form structure in Figure 2-1.

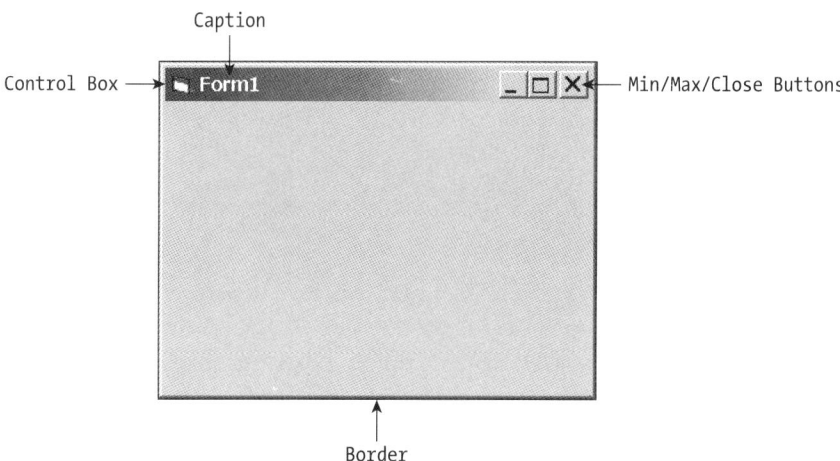

Figure 2-1. A blank WinForm

The Border

The Border property works just as you'd expect; it defines the form's boundaries. In VB, you can make this boundary resizable by the user, or you can make the border one of fixed dimensions. These characteristics can be set at design time by using the BorderStyle property.

The Title Bar and Caption

Similar to the VB Title bar described in Chapter 1, your form's Title bar will be the strip (most likely blue) located at the top of the form. The Title bar provides you with that particular form's name, the caption, which is found on the left side of the Title bar.

The Minimize, Maximize, and Close Buttons

There's no need to go into detail on these items; the buttons should be familiar to anyone who has ever used a Windows application. It's nice to know, however, that any form you design has certain features in common with other Windows applications. This familiar look and feel is helpful to your program's users.

The Control Box

The control box is a short menu that appears when you click on the top left corner of a form. This menu gives you the option to restore, move, minimize, maximize, or close a form. Individuals who prefer to control programs using the keyboard instead of a mouse often use the control box.

The Form Properties

To list all the initial properties of a form, click once on the Form1 form to select it as the active object. Next, look over to the Properties window on the right side of the screen. There you'll see a listing of all the properties that define the appearance and some of the functionality of the form. You'll examine the most commonly used properties and their responsibilities.

> **NOTE** *Feel free to experiment with each of these properties along the way. Doing a task is often the most effective way of learning it.*

The Name Property

You usually use this property in larger projects because it defines the name to which you'll refer the form in your code. The default for this property is Form1. Keep in mind that this property is different than the Text property, and that changing one won't change the other.

The Appearance Properties

This group of properties lets you specify how program users will view this particular form, including the color, font, and even the border.

The BackColor Property

This property lets you change the form's background color from default gray to a more aesthetically pleasing color. To do this, click on the arrow next to the current color selection. You'll see a dialog box that contains two color palettes. Then, browse through the palettes and choose a color.

The BackgroundImage Property

This property allows you to create forms that are a little more eye-catching than a plain monochrome backing. When you adjust this form's property, a File Open box appears (see Figure 2-2) that allows you to choose a graphics file to serve as the form's background.

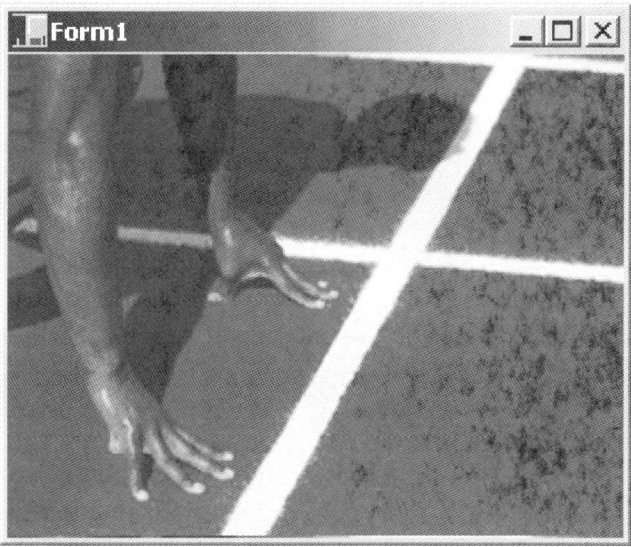

Figure 2-2. Choosing a BackgroundImage file allows you to place graphics in the form's background.

The BorderStyle Property

As mentioned earlier, the BorderStyle property dictates the appearance and behavior of the form's border. You can choose among six different types of borders to use in your applications.

None: This option means that the form has no border. It also lacks a Title bar, including the Minimize, Maximize, and Close buttons. Select this option only when you wish to give the application a splash screen upon start-up.

FixedSingle: With this setting, the form can't be resized by dragging its borders, but it will have a Title bar, along with the Minimize, Maximize, and Close buttons.

Fixed3D: The Fixed3D option is new to VB .NET. It's similar to the FixedSingle setting in that the form can't be resized, and that it does possess the standard Title bar. The only difference is that if this option is selected, the border has a raised three-dimensional (3-D) look.

FixedDialog: This option creates a form that has a Title bar, but no Minimize or Maximize buttons, only the Close button. Also, the user won't be able to resize the form.

Sizable: This default setting for BorderStyle gives the form a Title bar complete with all of its buttons. In addition, the user can resize the form by dragging the borders.

FixedToolWindow: This option is rarely used. It creates a form that is similar to the FixedDialog setting, except the font and the Close button in the Title bar are smaller. Also, this type of form won't appear in the task bar.

SizableToolWindow: The last setting, SizableToolWindow, is almost exactly like the FixedToolWindow. In fact, the only difference between the two is that with this setting the user can resize the form by dragging the border.

The Font Property

This property lets you set the font that displays information on the form. When you change this property, the standard Windows Font dialog box appears (i.e., similar to what you see when changing a font in Microsoft Word).

The ForeColor Property

The ForeColor property doesn't influence the form's color itself, but instead influences the color of the form's text and graphics. The default color for this property is black.

The Text Property

You can probably guess that you use the Text property to give the form a caption or a title. This caption appears in the Title bar above the form, as well as in the application icon that Windows places in the task bar at the bottom of your screen. The default caption is Form1. For users of past versions of VB, this property is similar to the Caption property. Remember, however, that the Text property is a completely distinct entity from the Name property.

The Behavior Properties

The following properties control how forms function and respond to different program events.

The Enabled Property

The Enabled property determines whether or not the form responds to different user events, such as mouse clicks. With the default value, True, the form can respond to different user events. This form property usually isn't set to anything but True at design time, and is usually only changed, under special circumstances, during program execution.

The Visible Property

The default value for this property is True, which means that the form is visible to the program user. If you set it to False, the form becomes invisible to the user and can't be manipulated. Forms are generally only made invisible when you are working with MDIs, and you want to hide one or more of the forms. Furthermore, this property is usually only set to False at runtime and not during the design phase.

The Design Properties

The following design properties are extremely useful when you add controls to the VB form because they will help you position the controls properly.

The DrawGrid Property

When this property is set to True, a positioning grid is placed on the form. This grid is similar to the grids used in most graphic drawing software. It makes it easier to align and position controls on the form.

The GridSize Property

The GridSize property controls the spacing between the dots that make up the grid. The property accepts values in an X,Y type format where X controls the horizontal spacing and Y controls the vertical spacing. In both cases, the larger the value, the greater the spacing.

The SnapToGrid Property

When this property is set to True, it ensures that each element placed on the form is aligned with the closest row and column of the grid. This makes it extremely easy to perfectly align controls.

The Layout Properties

The layout properties determine the size of the form and where the form appears on the computer screen.

The Height Property

As is evidenced by its name, the Height property sets the form's height. The default unit for form height is pixels. One pixel is the smallest unit of resolution that your monitor can achieve, but that isn't really worth worrying about right now because we aren't discussing graphics programming. In VB 6.0 and earlier versions, the default unit of measure wasn't pixels but twips, which are equivalent to 1/1440 of an inch. The Height property controls the form height by allowing you to set how far down from the top the form extends. The Y property sets the placement of the top of the form.

The Width Property

This property functions similarly to the height property in that it controls the width of a form. It allows you to set, in pixels, how far the form extends from the left edge. The X property sets the placement of the left edge.

The X (Left) Property

The X property is one of the properties that affect the form's placement on the screen. This property dictates the distance of the form's left edge from the screen's left edge. As with height, the default unit for X is also pixels.

The Y (Top) Property

As with the Left property, the Top property controls the start-up position of the top edge of the form. The default unit for this property is also pixels.

The StartPosition Property

This property gives you an easy way to determine the start-up position of your form on the screen. The default value, WindowsDefaultLocation, positions the form in the upper left corner of the screen. This property works independently of the user's screen resolution, so it is a much easier way of controlling start-up position than altering the X and Y properties.

The WindowState Property

This property controls the state in which the form appears, such as whether the form appears normal (i.e., as you laid it out), in a minimized state, or in a maximized state. The default is the normal state. State is only usually changed through code as the application runs.

The Window Style Properties

These properties give you further control over the form's appearance, as well as some control over the form's functionality.

The ControlBox Property

The ControlBox property determines whether or not your form possesses a control box, and it has only two choices: True, the default value, means that the form does possess a control box, and False means that a control box is absent.

The Icon Property

This property is used to choose an icon for display on the desktop of any computer on which your VB application is installed. The icon you select also appears as the icon on the control box. VB has a wide variety of icons, but you can design your own with the professional and enterprise editions.

The IsMDIContainer Property

Setting this property to True enables the form to behave as a parent form for an MDI application. This chapter discusses MDIs in greater detail later.

The MaximizeBox and MinimizeBox Properties

These two properties work exactly the same. If you want Maximize and Minimize buttons on your form, leave these two properties set to True. To eliminate these buttons, set them both to False.

The Opacity Property

This interesting new property lets you control the form's degree of opacity or transparency. The form is transparent at the 0 setting and opaque at the 100 percent setting. You can set a median degree of transparency by choosing a number between 0 and 100.

The ShowInTaskBar Property

The default value for this property is True; upon loading, your form will be shown in the Windows task bar. If set to False, the form won't appear in the task bar, even if it is the active form.

> **NOTE** *Before moving on to the topic of form events, it's important to mention one last fact. For any property not covered that you are interested in, or if you forget a certain property's function, click on the property's name in the Properties window. Once you've selected the property name, a very brief description of the property will appear inside the bottom portion of the box.*

The Form Events

Now that you have an in-depth understanding of all of the essential form properties, it's time to learn about the different form events. Understanding form events is crucial to getting your forms to dynamically respond to different user actions. As your programming abilities improve, you'll find that by adding code to different events your VB application will behave exactly as you want it to. You'll see examples of this in the solution calculation program that starts at the end of this chapter.

For now, though, let's discuss the most commonly used form events.

The Activated Event

After a form loads into memory, this event sets the form to be the active form. This is similar to when you click on a window in any Windows application, in order to set that window as the active window.

The Click and DoubleClick Events

As you can probably guess, these events allow you to write code that defines the application's response to a mouse click. The Click event works for a single mouse click, while DoubleClick requires two. These events can be called upon with forms, but they are more often used with controls, which you'll see in the next chapter.

The Deactivate Event

The Deactivate event is the opposite of the Activate event. This event occurs when the form stops being the active form.

The Layout Event

This event occurs when a control has to lay out its child controls. Form is a ContainerControl that hosts other child controls.

The Load Event

The Load event is probably the most frequently called upon of all events. It occurs when the form is loaded into memory from the disk, before it becomes visible on the screen. It specifies some of the form's contents and properties.

The Resize Event

This event allows you to instruct your program's response to a user's attempts to resize the form. For example, if the user makes the form bigger, you might want to make all of the controls on the form bigger as well to keep the size ratios consistent.

The Closed and Closing Events

These events occur when the form is removed from memory and disappears from view. You may add code to these events to remove open files from memory before a form closes, which prevents your program from wasting system memory. The major difference between the two events is that Closing occurs while the form is unloading, and Closed occurs immediately after the form closes. These two events work much as the Unload event found in VB 6.0, and are the most commonly used form events. As the book progresses, however, you'll learn about other events that are crucial to any VB application.

Form Methods

In addition to form events, form methods get your forms or other VB objects, such as controls, to behave dynamically. A method is a VB command that tells an object what to do. Methods are written in code with the following syntax:

```
Object.Method
```

This concept should become clearer as the most common methods are defined.

The ResetText Method

ResetText allows you to remove all of the text found in the form's Text property. In some ways this is like the Cls method in VB 6.0, with the exception that it doesn't clear the form of text, but rather the Title bar. To invoke this method you add the following line of code to your project:

```
Me.ResetText
```

The Hide Method

With this method, you remove a form from view without removing it from memory. This is often used to temporarily hide a form that will be needed later; keeping a form in memory often speeds up an application.

The Activate Method

Use the Activate method to call up a form from the disk and load it into memory. The form will be visible, unless the visible property is set to False.

The Show Method

This method brings a hidden form into view. Remember, however, that to use the Show method, the form must already be loaded into memory.

The Close Method

When a form is closed, it is removed from memory and the system resources acquired during the form's lifetime are freed.

A Simple VB Application

By now you probably are wondering how to use this voluminous information, so let's code a simple VB application that is centered on a single form. Begin by starting up VB and choosing the Standard EXE option (i.e., Windows application). Now, double-click on the form in the Form window. Notice that the Form window changes to the Code window, which lets you begin to program your first VB application. At this point, add the following lines of code to this window:

```
Private Sub Form1_Activated(ByVal sender As Object, ByVal e As System.EventArgs) _
Handles MyBase.Activated
        Me.Text = "Visual Basic Programming is Fun"
End Sub
Private Sub Form1_Click(ByVal sender As Object, ByVal e As System.EventArgs) _
Handles MyBase.Click
        Me.Text = "I'm On My Way To Becoming a Pro"
End Sub
```

Now that you've added the code, go to the Debug menu and select Start. Notice that the code added to the Activate event took your originally blank form and, via the Text property, added the text "Visual Basic Programming is Fun" to the Title bar (see Figure 2-3).

> **NOTE**   *The _ (underscore) at the end of the code line is called a* code break *or* line continuation character. *It allows you to break a line of code in the middle so you can type it on two or more lines for easier viewing. The VB IDE allows for much longer code lines than the typeset of this book, however, and most of the broken code lines in this text can be easily viewed and written as a single line of code in the VB IDE.*

Figure 2-3. The result of the Activated event being invoked

Now, click on the form once to invoke the Click event. Notice that the text added in the Activated event is replaced with the text "I'm On My Way To Becoming a Pro" (see Figure 2-4).

Figure 2-4. When the Click event is invoked, your code changes the Text property.

This simple application should start to give you a basic understanding of how VB applications work and how they are coded. Also, it should let you see how forms are utilized within an application.

Single Document Interface Applications

Now that you have a good understanding of forms and how they work, you can look at how they come into play in a VB application. You'll first consider a single document interface (SDI) application, which you just finished coding. This application consists of one or more forms, each of which is a full-fledged window. In other words, each window is independent of other windows.

Multiple Document Interface Applications

A multiple document interface (MDI) application consists of a main parent form and one or more child forms. The parent form acts as a container for all of the child forms. This is similar to the setup found in applications such as Microsoft Word or Excel, where the main program itself is a parent form, and all of the open documents are child forms contained inside this main parent form. These forms are considered to be dependent because the child form can only exist within the parent form.

To get a better idea of what this means, start a new project (solution). One form should already be present, but for this example you'll need to add a second form to your project by going to the Project menu and selecting Add Windows Form. Select the Windows Form option from the top left corner of the dialog box that appears. Now, switch to the Code window of Form1 and add the following code to your application:

```
Private Sub Form1_Load(ByVal sender As System.Object, ByVal _
e As System.EventArgs)  Handles MyBase.Load
        Me.IsMdiContainer = True
        Dim child As New Form2()
        child.MdiParent = Me
        child.Show()
End Sub
```

If you ran this application, you'd see that you first establish Form1 as the parent form. You then create an instance of Form2 and set its MdiParent property equal to Me (i.e., Form1). Finally, make the child form visible using the Show method discussed earlier.

If you play around with the Maximize, Minimize, and Close buttons, you'll see that Form1 acts as a container for Form2. In other words, the child form can be smaller than the parent form, but can never exceed the parent form's dimensions. Also consider that the child form can't exist without the parent form. If you close Form2, Form1 remains unchanged. However, if you closed the parent form, you'd find that any and all open child forms would close as well.

Figure 2-5 illustrates how the parent and child forms comprise an MDI application.

Figure 2-5. A multiple document interface application

NOTE *By this time, you should have a firm understanding of forms and how VB applications use them. However, a solid VB application requires more than forms to obtain any really useful functionality. The next chapter discusses controls and the wealth of functionality they can add to any VB application.*

In the next chapter, you'll also get a taste for scientific programming in VB. You'll code a simple VB application that tells you exactly how to make a solution of a certain molarity, if you provide it the molecular weight of the solute and the final volume you desire.

Controls and Their Uses

As you found out in the previous chapter, forms are the foundation of virtually any Visual Basic application. But this basic foundation leaves a lot to be desired in terms of functionality. Thus, controls were created. Controls form the building blocks of a VB application by giving the program a variety of ways to interact with its user. For example, text boxes allow program users to enter information into a program, while radio buttons allow users to choose one of many possibilities. Furthermore, these two examples only scratch the surface of what controls can do. You can add probably thousands of different controls to a VB application, many of which are available from third-party sources.

This chapter, however, only familiarizes you with VB's most commonly used controls, in order to give you a basic understanding to start developing applications. You will use many of these controls to build a program to perform solution calculations (i.e., molarity based). As the book progresses, though, it covers more advanced controls and utilizes them to develop applications. Finally, the chapter describes some third-party controls that are extremely useful to the scientific programmer.

Controls and the .NET Framework

The beginning of Chapter 2 described a class hierarchy that helped define the functionality contained within WinForms. You learned that this hierarchy of classes existed in the System.Windows.Forms namespace, and that the Form class put the finishing touches on your WinForms. In this namespace, however, one more element of the hierarchy should be discussed: the UserControl class.

The UserControl class inherits its base functionality from the ContainerControl class. This class provides an extendable set of visual form elements that programmers can use in their applications. The controls discussed in this chapter are built on these visual form elements. A more advanced use of this class is that advanced programmers can utilize it to create controls with custom functionality. This topic is beyond the scope of this book, however, so this chapter focuses on controls that already exist.

Adding Controls to Your Forms

Remember the toolbox in Chapter 1 that was on the left side of the VB IDE? Well, that's where you can access all of the most basic VB controls. The easiest way to add a control to a form is to go over to the toolbox and double-click the control that you're interested in (see Figure 3-1). A default-sized control will appear in the top left corner of the form in VB .NET (the control is placed in the middle of the form in VB 6.0 and earlier versions). This method's only difficulty, however, is that after the control is added to the form you must then position it on the form to resize it to the desired dimensions.

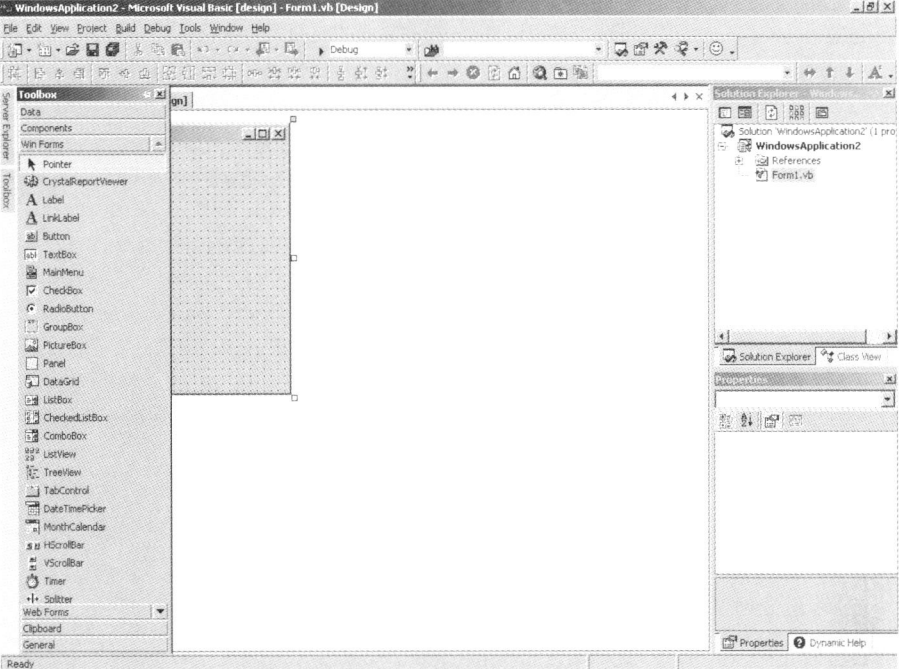

Figure 3-1. Getting ready to add a control from your toolbox

Thus, another fairly simple and straightforward method exists for adding controls to your form, and simultaneously positioning and sizing them.

1. First, go to the toolbox and select the control of your choice.

2. Next, single-click that control's icon. After you do this, notice that the icon takes on a "sunken" and "depressed" appearance, showing that the control has been selected.

3. Now, move the mouse pointer to the position on the form where you'd like to place the top left corner of the control.

4. Next, left-click the mouse, but don't let go. Instead, keep the button depressed.

5. Drag the mouse pointer over the position where you want to place the bottom right corner of the control, and then release the left mouse button.

As you were dragging the mouse, you probably noticed a rectangular shape form between where you initially depressed the mouse button and the then-current pointer position. This rectangular box indicates the control's size and position, because the control will fit inside the dimensions of that box.

Moving Controls on a Form

The method previously described makes it fairly easy to place a control exactly where you want it, but as your project progresses you'll find that you must slightly change the position of a few controls. It's easiest to do this by placing the mouse pointer over the control and clicking the left mouse button. Then, while keeping the button depressed, drag the control over to its new location. You also can use Ctrl and the arrow keys to move the control around, but the most precise method is to manually adjust the X and Y properties of the control.

When working with more than one control, you also can move them all simultaneously by holding down the Shift key and using the mouse to select all of the controls you desire to move. You can drag all of the controls the same direction and distance from the start position using the mouse. This method is often useful because it allows you to move all of the controls as a block, and thus maintains the initial spacing and relative positioning found between the controls.

> **NOTE** *Control positioning is especially critical for developing applications for PDAs and other mobile devices, because of their greatly restricted user interface. Thus, good GUI design is even more important.*

Once you're happy with the controls' positions, you may want to lock them in place to avoid an accidental repositioning. You can do this easily by going to the Format menu on the toolbar and selecting Lock Controls.

Locked controls cannot be repositioned, but if repositioning becomes necessary, just go back to the Format menu and select Unlock Controls.

Resizing Controls on a Form

As with moving controls, resizing a control is easy with a mouse. Click the left mouse button once on the control you desire to resize. After doing this, you should see eight squares around the control's border. Place the mouse over one of these handles, called *sizing handles,* and you'll see an arrow (see Figure 3-2). The arrow indicates the directions the control will expand when that particular sizing handle is adjusted. To use a sizing handle, click the desired handle. While holding the button down, drag the sizing handle in the desired direction until you reach the sought-after size. Then, release the mouse button and the control will be resized.

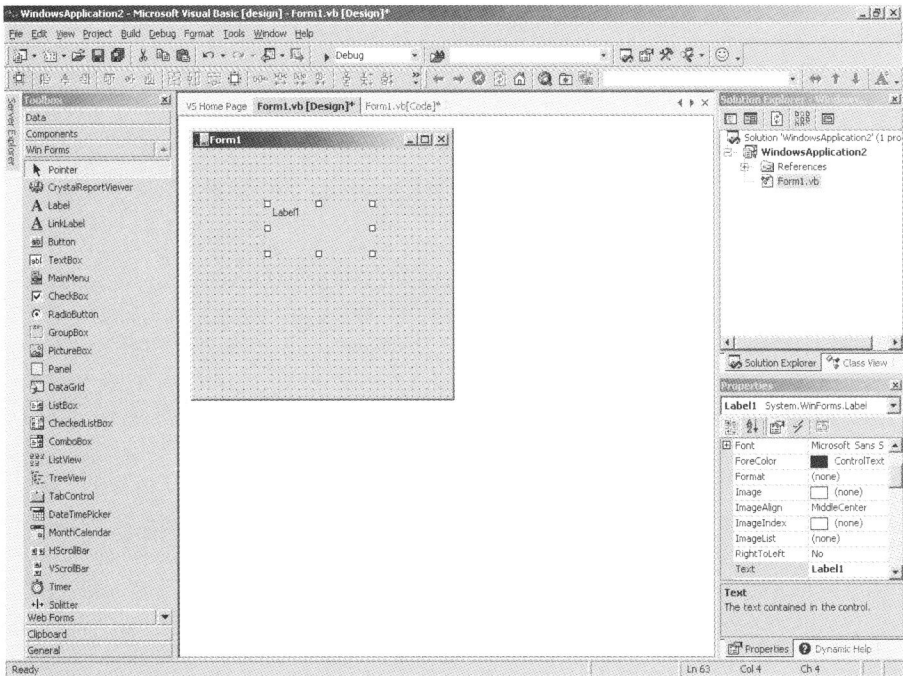

Figure 3-2. Control sizing handles

Labels

The Label control is one of the most straightforward and easiest to use controls in VB because, as its name suggests, the label's predominant function is to display some type of information. Often this information is some type of identification for another control, or helps make the application more user-friendly. You can access the Label control from the toolbox by choosing the large boldfaced capital letter **A**.

Label Properties

As with the form properties, you'll find that after you add a Label control to your project and set it as the active control, the label's properties will appear in the Properties window. Many properties that the label control possesses are similar to some of the form properties. For example, X, Y, Height, and Width determine the label's size and position, as they do for the form. The only difference is that the size and location refer to the form (and its scale) and not the screen. Another example is that BackColor sets the background color of the control and not the form. Thus, these properties won't be covered again for each individual control because you should already be familiar with their function. This chapter, however, covers properties that are unique to each control and are crucial to implementing its functionality.

The TextAlign Property

This property determines the alignment of the text within the label (i.e., the Text property). The default option for this property is TopLeft, but you can also have the options TopRight, TopCenter, MiddleLeft, MiddleCenter, MiddleRight, BottomLeft, BottomCenter, or BottomRight. This property is equivalent to the VB 6.0 Alignment property, but it provides more options than the Alignment property of VB 6.0.

The AutoSize Property

In VB 6.0, this property, if set to True, allows the label to grow horizontally in order to encompass all its text, as represented by the Caption property. When the WordWrap property is turned on, AutoSize also enables vertical growth.

In VB .NET, this property, if set to True, allows the label to grow horizontally in order to encompass all of its text, as represented by the Text property. However, VB .NET doesn't support the WordWrap property.

The WordWrap Property (Applies to VB 6.0 and Earlier Versions)

If this property is turned on, your label will behave like a word processor; it ensures that no words in your text break in order to fit the label's dimensions.

Label Events

Labels can respond to several user events, including mouse clicks (Click) and double-clicks (DoubleClick), but labels rarely respond to such events. Instead, their only true function is for informative purposes. The Click and DoubleClick events work exactly as they did in the previous chapter on forms, except that they respond to the label being clicked.

Text Boxes and Rich Text Boxes

Text boxes are undoubtedly one of the most useful controls you'll find in VB (see Figure 3-3). Text boxes are the most commonly used way of entering data into an application and receiving the application's output. For example, say that you wrote a program that performs the calculation Mass/Volume=Density. Two text boxes could read in the Mass and Volume and output the Density to a third text box. The only difficulty with using text boxes for mathematical calculations is that anything (even numbers) entered in a text box is treated as a string of text. But don't worry; VB easily solves this with several built-in functions, covered in Chapter 6, that convert strings into numerical values. Rich text boxes function similarly to text boxes, but they have the added ability to display multiple fonts and aren't limited to a maximum number of characters. Rich text boxes, however, come with most, but not all, versions of VB.

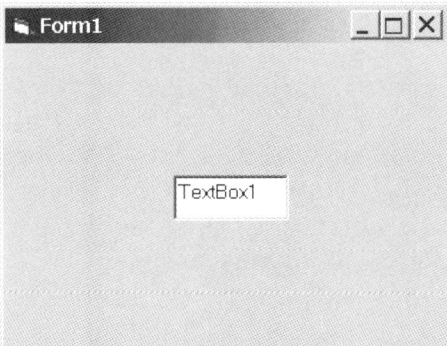

Figure 3-3. A text box

Text Box Properties

As with labels, many text box properties are quite similar to properties you've already seen. Some properties, however, are unique to text boxes.

The ReadOnly Property

If set to True, ReadOnly prohibits program users from changing any text contained within the text box. However, the user can scroll down in the text box to view the entire contents and can even highlight text. The default setting for this property is False. In VB 6.0 and earlier versions, the equivalent of this property is the Locked property.

The MaxLength Property

The default value for this property is 0. This means that the user can type in as many characters as he wants, as long as he doesn't exceed VB's inherent limit of a little over 32,000 characters. If you change this number to anything but 0, however, that number will become the maximum number of characters that the user can type in the box.

The Multiline Property

As the name suggests, setting this property to True lets the program user enter multiple lines of text into a single text box. The text entered in the text box is automatically word-wrapped if it exceeds the box's horizontal limits. Furthermore, the user will be able to move through the box.

The ScrollBars Property

When this property is changed from its default value of 0, the text box control will possess scroll bars that let the user navigate throughout the entire text box. You can make the text box possess either horizontal scroll bars or vertical scroll bars, or both.

The Text Property

This property controls the text inside the text box when the application loads. By default, this property equals TextBox1; if you desire the text box to be completely empty upon the start of the application, make sure you delete this default text string.

Text Box Events

As you've seen, both forms and labels can respond to certain events, such as the Click event. Like forms and labels, text boxes also possess certain event procedures that they can respond to. The Click event is one such event, but it isn't among the most commonly used events for working with text boxes. Thus, the most important events needed to work with text boxes are now described.

The TextChanged Event

The TextChanged event is triggered every time any type of change is made to the contents of the text box, such as a character insertion or deletion, or a string pasted into the text box. This event often performs simple data entry validation. For example, a program that requires numerical input into a text box can't function properly if any non-numerical text is entered. You could solve this problem by using the TextChanged event to set off some type of warning message if non-numerical text is entered (there are also more advanced ways of doing this). In earlier versions of VB, this event was referred to as the Change event.

The Enter Event

The Enter event occurs when the user enters the control. This occurs in a text box when the user clicks inside the control and the text box becomes ready to accept typed-in text. You can also initiate the Enter event by tabbing into the text box. This event is similar to the GotFocus event discussed next.

The GotFocus Event

You've probably noticed that when you click the mouse over a form or a control in almost any Windows application, that item becomes the active item. In VB, the active item is the item that possesses the program's focus. Thus, this event is triggered when the text box becomes the active control, and thereby the control that receives the program's focus.

The Leave Event

The Leave event is the opposite of the Enter event. This occurs when the user shifts the focus away from that particular control and the control is no longer able to accept user input.

The LostFocus Event

The LostFocus event is simply the reverse of the GotFocus event. It occurs when the focus is shifted from the active text box to some other control on the form.

Illustration of Text Box Events

Now that you're familiar with several new events, take the time now to write a short program that illustrates how the Enter and Leave events operate.

1. First off, add two text boxes of equal size to a blank form. Name the text boxes Text1 and Text2, respectively, using the Name property of the TextBox control found in the Properties window.

2. Next, position the text boxes so they are side by side on the form, with Text1 box on the left and Text2 box on the right.

3. Now, blank out the text properties on both text boxes so no text is initially found within them.

4. Next, switch from the form window to the code window and add the following four subroutines:

```
Private Sub Text1_Enter(ByVal eventSender As System.Object, ByVal eventArgs As _
System.EventArgs) Handles Text1.Enter
    Text1.Text = "This Is Text Box 1"
End Sub


Private Sub Text1_Leave(ByVal eventSender As System.Object, ByVal eventArgs As _
System.EventArgs) Handles Text1.Leave
    Text1.Text = " "
End Sub


Private Sub Text2_Enter(ByVal eventSender As System.Object, ByVal eventArgs As _
System.EventArgs) Handles Text2.Enter
    Text2.Text = "This is Text Box 2"
End Sub
Private Sub Text2_Leave(ByVal eventSender As System.Object, ByVal eventArgs As _
System.EventArgs) Handles Text2.Leave
    Text2.Text = " "
End Sub
```

Once you've entered the code, run the application and observe what happens. First off, when the application loads you'll find that the words "This Is Text Box 1" are inside the first text box (see Figure 3-4). This is because when a VB program loads, the focus is automatically placed on the first control created. Shifting the focus to this control also causes the control to be Entered, and thus the control's Enter event is invoked. Now, click once over the second text box. Notice that the Text2 Enter event is invoked and the text box's Text property is changed to "This is Text Box 2" (see Figure 3-5). Thus, keep in mind that changing the Text property demonstrates how properties can be defined at runtime as well as at design time. Also, notice that as the focus shifts from Text1 to Text2, the Text1 Leave event is invoked and the text within Text1 is blanked out. If you then click on text box 1, you'd see that the Text1 Enter event is induced along with the Text2 Leave event.

Figure 3-4. Before the first TextChange event is triggered

Figure 3-5. After the TextChange event

Finally, remember that the mouse isn't the only way to change the focus within a Windows application; so is the Tab key. VB automatically enables the Tab key to switch between controls. By default, tabbing through controls always shifts the focus between controls in the order in which they are created. You can alter this by adjusting the TabIndex property. Thus, to make the Text2 control receive the initial focus, you could alter the program code by adding the following:

```
 Private Sub Form1_Load(ByVal sender As Object, ByVal e As System.EventArgs) _
Handles MyBase.Load
     Text2.TabIndex = 0
 Text1.TabIndex = 1
End Sub
```

If you run the application, Text2 will be the first control to receive the program's focus. It's important to remember that in VB the TabIndex list begins with 0.

Text Box Methods

In addition to the different events that text boxes can respond to, one method can be invoked occasionally. This method is the Focus method. As is evident from the name, this method sets the focus on a particular control regardless of TabIndex. For example, you could set the initial focus on Text2 by using the following code:

```
Protected Sub Form1_Activated(ByVal sender As Object, ByVal e _
As System.EventArgs) Handles MyBase.Activated
  Text2.Focus()
End Sub
```

You noticed, most likely, that this method is coded in the same way as the form methods.

Buttons

Like text boxes, buttons (known as command buttons in VB 6.0) are one of the most widely used controls in VB (see Figure 3-6). Almost any application you develop will possess one or more command buttons because they are commonly used for initiating some type of program action, such as calculation or mathematical analysis in scientific programming. The chapter will demonstrate the use of command buttons later when you code your solution program.

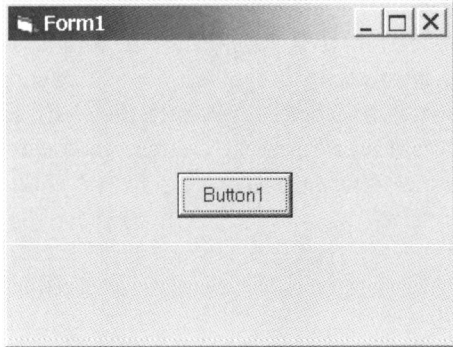

Figure 3-6. A Button control

Button Properties

This chapter described the vast majority of button properties, but a few properties are unique to command buttons.

The DownPicture, Picture, and Style Properties (Applies to VB 6.0 Command Buttons)

These three properties should be discussed together because they are interrelated. First, VB lets you choose between the default standard plain background or a graphical command button background. To choose a graphical background, you must change the Style property to the graphical setting. Now, you can choose a graphic image file for the background by using the Picture property. When you alter the Picture property, a standard File Open dialog box appears in which you select the graphics file. Similarly, if you want the picture to appear (or change) after the user depresses the command button, you can use the DownPicture property.

In VB .NET you can explore the Button control's Image, ImageAlign, ImageIndex, ImageList, and TextAlign properties that control the application buttons' look and feel.

The Cursor Property

You know that the normal mouse pointer is an arrow. However, you can change the arrow to another pointer type using the Cursor property. This can visibly demonstrate the programmatic significance associated with clicking on a button. Past versions of VB referred to this as the MousePointer property.

Button Events and Methods

The Click event is the most widely used button event. It's also, by far, the most important of all the command button events; the action of clicking usually triggers some type of program action. Clicking, however, is not the only possible command button event; so are the GotFocus and LostFocus events. Finally, remember that the Focus method can be used with buttons.

List Boxes and Combo Boxes

List boxes and combo boxes (see Figure 3-7) have some slight differences in functionality, but share most features. Use list boxes when the program user needs to select from a list of choices that is, for all practical purposes, fixed. Combo boxes, on the other hand, allow the user to not only view choices on the list, but also to input data.

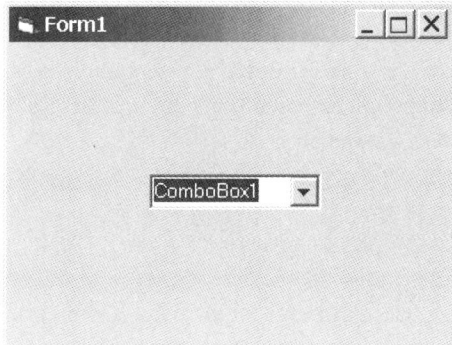

Figure 3-7. A ComboBox control

List Box and Combo Box Properties

Although both controls share certain properties in common with the controls mentioned earlier, these two control types have several unique properties.

The Columns Property (Applies to VB 6.0 and Earlier Versions)

This property is possessed by list boxes but not by combo boxes, and controls the number of list box columns. The default value of 0 yields a single column list box with vertical scroll bars (if required). If you change the property to 1, the list box will be single-columned but with horizontal scroll bars. If changed to a number greater than 1, the list box will be able to support that number of data columns.

In VB .NET, the ListBox control's ColumnWidth and MultiColumn properties define the columnar features of the list box. Try it out and see how it works.

The Items Property

List boxes and combo boxes possess this property, which contains all of the elements listed in the controls. You can easily add items by typing them into the String Collection Editor, which is invoked when you click the ellipsis button next to the Items property in the Properties window. Also, you can add items to the list by using the Items.Add() method, discussed later in this chapter. In fact, this property is a collection of items in the list box.

The Items.Count Property

List and combo boxes share this property, which usually is invoked only at runtime. Its purpose is fairly straightforward; as the name implies, it tells you how many items are stored in the control's List.

The Items.Item Property

Each item stored in the list of either a list box or a combo box is given an index number, the ListIndex, that represents the order of that item on the list. The index numbering starts with zero. For example, the first element of a list box named List1 can be referred to in code as List1.Items.Item(0). Thus, this property gives you a way to refer to a specific item on the control's List. If you look at older VB code, you'll find this property referred to as the ListIndex property instead.

The Sorted Property

This property, common to both types of controls, orders and arranges the items located in the list (Item property). When set to True, all of the list items are arranged in their ASCII character order, which for the most part is alphabetical. To test this property, add a list box and a button to your form, and add a collection of unordered random strings to your Items property. Now add the following line of code to your button's Click event:

```
ListBox1.Sorted = True
```

When you run the application and click the command button, you'll see all of the strings placed in alphanumeric order.

> **CAUTION** *This property can't handle the Unicode character sets that are becoming more prevalent. These sets are outside of the ASCII character range and will result in program errors.*

List Box and Combo Box Events

You're already familiar with the most commonly used list box and combo events, the Click and DoubleClick events. These events generally allow the user to select a specific item from the list within the control. Other events include KeyUp, KeyDown, and KeyPress. These events occur when the user presses (KeyDown) or releases (KeyUp) a key while an object has the focus, or when the user presses and releases (KeyPress) an ANSI (American National Standards Institute) key. Chapter 9 covers these events.

List Box and Combo Box Methods

List boxes and combo boxes are often used with several methods that enable you to lay out or alter their contents at runtime. These methods are different from the ones you've seen, but operate in exactly the same way.

The Items.Add Method

As the name suggests, this method allows you to add items to your control's List. Earlier versions of VB referred to it as the AddItem method. To examine the syntax for this method, momentarily imagine that you are writing a chemistry program that performs calculations using the different gas laws. You want your program to perform only one type of gas law calculation at a time, and you want the user to select the calculation type from a drop-down box (combo box). You could use the following code to add the different gas law choices to the combo box. Set the Name property of the combo box to Combo1 and execute the application (see Figure 3-8):

```
Protected Sub Form1_Activated(ByVal sender As Object, ByVal e _
As System.EventArgs) Handles MyBase.Activated
  Combo1.Items.Add("Ideal Gas Law")
  Combo1.Items.Add("Boyles Law")
```

```
    Combo1.Items.Add("Charles Law")
    Combo1.Items.Add("Partial Pressures")
    Combo1.Items.Add("Van der Waals Equation")
End Sub
```

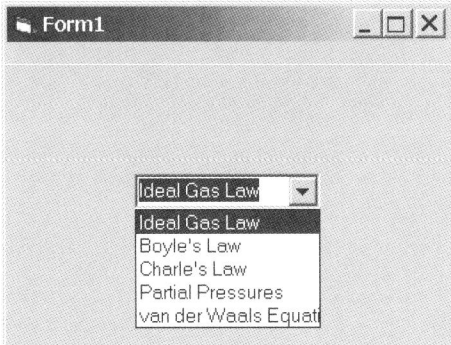

Figure 3-8. Displaying the items added to the combo box

The Items.Remove Method

This item uses the exact same syntax as the Items.Add method, only this method doesn't add items to the control's List, but removes them. It is equivalent to the RemoveItem method found in past versions of VB.

The Items.Clear Method

Say that you want to remove all of the items from your control's List. You could repeatedly use the Items.Remove method, but this could become very tedious and time-consuming if the list is long. Luckily, VB makes this task quite easy with the Items.Clear method. By entering the code `Combo1.Items.Clear` you'd be able to completely remove all of the items from the combo box named Combo1.

Radio Buttons

Radio buttons (option buttons in VB 6.0) are controls that let you select one option from several possible choices (see Figure 3-9). These controls aren't used individually but in groups. By default, all of the radio buttons placed on a single form are considered in the same group. When one radio button in a group is selected, the others are automatically turned off. However, if the user must make several choices, where each choice has its own options, you can take advantage of the GroupBox control (referred to as Frame in earlier versions of VB). The GroupBox control usually isn't actively used within an application, but generally only serves as a container for other controls. To group items inside of a GroupBox, you first draw the GroupBox, and then add the required controls to the region within the GroupBox. Remember not to create the controls before the GroupBox because it will lead to the controls not being grouped properly.

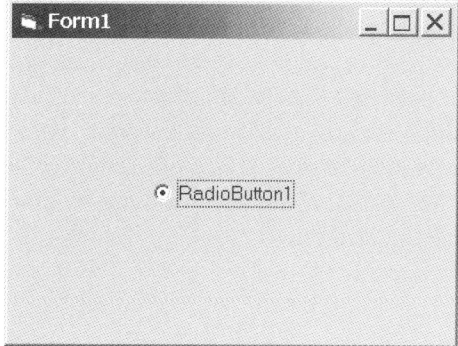

Figure 3-9. A radio button

Radio Button Properties

For the most part, radio buttons possess the same properties as other controls you've seen. However, understanding the Checked property is crucial to correctly using both radio buttons and check boxes.

The Checked Property

Remember that when you select one radio button all of the other radio buttons in the group are set to False. This on-and-off switching is made possible by the Checked property. If the value is set to True, that particular radio button is turned on (i.e., selected), and the other buttons are turned off or set to False. Thus, use the Checked property with a conditional (If) statement to distinguish which option was selected. Earlier versions of VB referred to this as the Value property.

Radio Button Events

Radio buttons can respond to different user events, including Click, DoubleClick, GotFocus, LostFocus, and the various Key events. However, these controls aren't generally used in this manner, and are almost always utilized for their Checked property characteristics.

Check Boxes

Like radio buttons, check boxes allow users to select from a list (see Figure 3-10). However, check boxes are different in that they enable users to select multiple items. For example, suppose you were creating some type of computerized medical survey about a new medication that is currently undergoing clinical trials. One question to ask the test subjects is "What side effects, if any, are you suffering from?" Because multiple side effects are possible, you'd want to use check boxes instead of radio buttons so the survey-taker could check all that apply. Like radio buttons, check boxes keep track of the selected items by utilizing the Checked property. Check boxes also respond to the same events as radio buttons, but these events aren't often used.

Figure 3-10. A check box

Timers

Timers are a useful control if you want an event to occur periodically. This is most often observed with the AutoSave feature: When turned on, the program responds to a Timer event and asks you if you want to save your data. Another common use of timers is to add a clock to your application so users can keep track of elapsed time. Keep in mind, however, that the Timer event is only triggered after the set time interval has passed, and not always exactly at the specified time interval, because the CPU might be busy processing something else. Thus, the Timer event will be triggered fairly accurately to the nearest tenth of a second or so, but not down to the theoretical millisecond timescale. Also, keep in mind that the Timer control is visible at design time but not at runtime, so the placement of a timer on a form is completely irrelevant.

Timer Properties

The most important of all the Timer properties is the Interval property. This property dictates the period of time VB waits before calling the Timer event. Theoretically, this interval can range from 1 millisecond (ms) to ~65,000 ms, but due to hardware limitations, the 1 ms interval time isn't practically feasible. For the hardware-oriented among you, the hardware timer in your PC (IBM compatible) ticks about 18.2 times per second, which works out to a timer resolution of 55 ms.

Timer Events

The event used with timers is quite simple to remember: The Tick event. After the interval time has passed, this event triggers some form of program action. Another way to use a timer is to keep track of elapsed time. For example, say you want to know how long your application has been running. You could determine this by adding a timer and text box to a form and writing the following code:

```
Public I As Integer
Private Sub Form_Load(ByVal sender As Object, ByVal e As System.EventArgs) _
 Handles MyBase.Load
    Timer1.Interval = 1000
    Timer1.Enabled = True
End Sub
Private Sub Timer1_Tick(ByVal eventSender As System.Object, ByVal eventArgs As _
System.EventArgs) Handles Timer1.Tick
    I = I + 1
    TextBox1.Text = CStr(I)
End Sub
```

Don't worry about the Public statement yet; the next chapter discusses variables. For now, just concern yourself with the fact that in the form's Load event the timer interval is set to 1000 ms or 1 second. Thus, every second the Tick event is called upon, the value of I (which starts at zero) is increased by 1. The value of I is then displayed in the text box (see Figure 3-11). This means that as I increases every second, so too does the number displayed in the text box. Therefore, the number inside the text box is the elapsed time that the application has been running.

Figure 3-11. Three seconds have passed since the timer was initialized.

New .NET Controls

VB .NET introduces several controls that weren't present in past versions of VB. Every control discussed in the previous sections is a VB application building block, and should be familiar to users of past VB versions. The controls discussed now are new to the .NET Framework and should interest old and new VB programmers alike.

The CheckedListBox Control

This control features all of the properties, events, and methods associated with the standard ListBox control, except for one minor change. This control places a check box next to each item contained within the list, and displays a check next to each selected item. This control can be useful when multiple selections are required; it easily allows the user to recall which items he/she has already selected.

The GroupBox Control

This control most closely resembles the frame control from past versions of VB in that it consists of a simple wire frame border (see Figure 3-12). It gives you no access to changing its BorderStyle property, and thus you cannot deviate from this style. You can however, add some text to the control's Text property to title the frame.

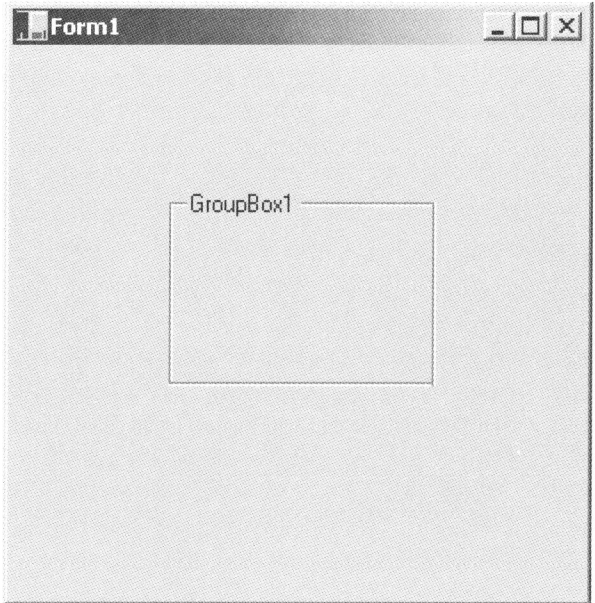

Figure 3-12. A GroupBox control

The Panel Control

This control is a little more stylistically flexible; you can change the BorderStyle property to your liking. In addition, with the Panel control's AutoScroll property you can add scroll bars to your frame. However, this control doesn't have a Text property, so you can't give your frame a title.

The LinkLabel Control

The LinkLabel control behaves much like a hyperlink on a Web page (see Figure 3-13). You use it to navigate to another window in your application or to a Web page, thus connecting your user to pertinent information. Using the control's Image property, this control can be displayed as text in a hyperlink format or as graphical hyperlink. The linking actions are generally used with the control's Click event. As applications continue to become more and more Web centric you'll probably see more uses of this control.

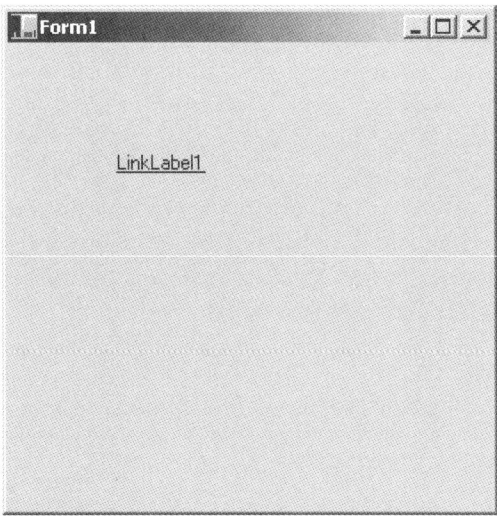

Figure 3-13. A LinkLabel control

The DateTimePicker Control

This is an excellent control for any application that requires your user to select dates and/or times. Users can enter in dates and times in a variety of different formats, and the control has the look and feel of the Windows Date/Time Properties window (see Figure 3-14).

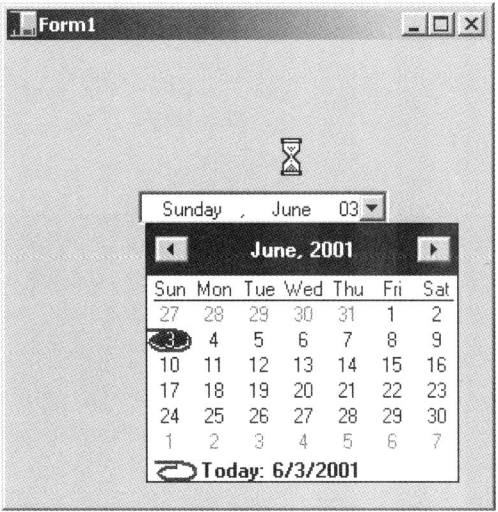

Figure 3-14. A DateTimePicker control with a date display

The DateTimePicker Properties

This control possesses several properties that haven't been examined yet. Therefore, you'll now examine some of its essential functionality properties.

The Format Property

This property controls the format of your date and time information. It offers four possible selections. With the first choice, Long, your control displays a date as follows:

Saturday, June 02, 2001

The second choice, Short, also allows the control to display a date, but the date is presented in an abbreviated format as

6/ 2/2001

With the Time option, the control displays a time instead of a date. The default format for the Time option is

2:48:40 PM

The last option is Custom, which lets you specify your own unique Date/Time display format.

The Value Property

This property's use is fairly straightforward; it stores the date and time information that the control displays. Changing the value of the property results in the new date/time information being displayed.

The ShowUpDown Property

This property affects how the user interacts with the control; it dictates how the user modifies the control's Value property. If this property is set to False, the user will adjust the date and time in a drop-down window. If the property is set to True, then up and down buttons will be used to adjust the date and time values (see Figure 3-15).

Figure 3-15. A DateTimePicker control set to display time

The ToolTip Control

This control is somewhat unique in that its functionality depends on the presence of other controls. When you add it to the project, you'll find that each control on the form now has a new property called ToolTip on ToolTip1, assuming you were using the VB default name ToolTip1. If you enter text into this property, the text will show when you place your mouse over that particular control (see Figure 3-16). If you examine the ToolTip control's inherent properties, you can adjust how long it takes for the tool tip to appear (InitialDelay) and how long the tip remains visible (AutoPopDelay). For those of you familiar with VB 6.0, this control works much as the ToolTipText property, only you now have even greater control over the tool tip's timing.

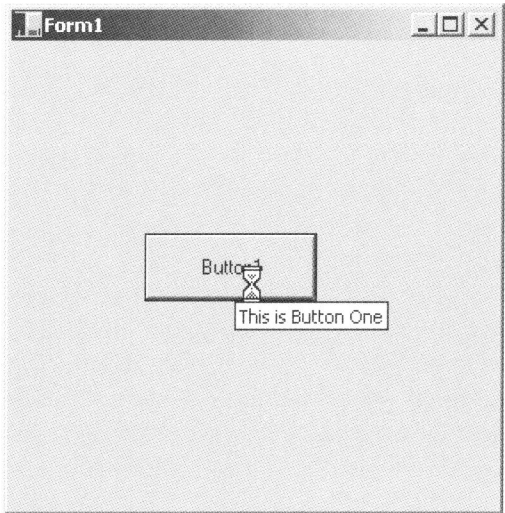

Figure 3-16. A ToolTip control

The ErrorProvider Control

This control is a great way to let users know that an error is associated with one of your controls. Like the ToolTip control, this control adds an additional property to each control on your form. In this case, the property is called Error on ErrorProvider1, assuming you were using the default name ErrorProvider1. If you enter any sort of text into this property, a tool tip along with an error icon will be placed next to the control when an error occurs (see Figure 3-17).

Figure 3-17. An ErrorProvider control

Message and Input Boxes

Message boxes and input boxes aren't really true controls, but function in much the same way as controls. For example, input boxes can collect information while message boxes can display data. These "controls" differ, however, in that they aren't really defined at design time, but are called and defined by code at the application's runtime.

Message Boxes

Message boxes, like labels, display information to the program user. Message boxes differ from labels in that they aren't designed into a form, but consist of a dialog box that appears over the form. The advantage to this type of construction is that the message can't be ignored. To get rid of the message box and continue using the program, the user must first address the dialog box. This architecture makes message boxes ideal for issuing important warnings to program users, as well as short important messages.

Message Box Types

Ten different types of message boxes can be utilized in VB. The first type is the OKOnly box. This is the default if you don't specify a type, and as the name implies, it displays a dialog box that possesses a command button with OK written on it. Similarly, an OKCancel box displays both an OK button and a Cancel button. Likewise, the YesNo and YesNoCancel boxes display Yes and No buttons and Yes, No, and Cancel buttons, respectively. Following this same trend, the RetryCancel box displays Retry and Cancel buttons, while the AbortRetryIgnore displays Abort, Retry, and Cancel buttons.

The remaining four types don't specify the command buttons that appear, but rather the icon symbol, if any, that appears on the message box.

> **NOTE** *Keep in mind that these types can be used with any of the previous six types.*

The first type, the Critical box, displays a circular red icon that contains a white X.

The Exclamation box displays a yellow triangle that contains a black exclamation point.

The Information box displays a white bubble, similar to those used in comic strips. This bubble contains a blue lowercase i.

The last type is the vbQuestion box, which displays that same white bubble, only with a question mark inside of it instead.

These last four types are good to remember when you want to emphasize the importance of your message.

Message Box Syntax

The syntax of using message boxes is quite simple, and in fact, a single line of code calls them up. The code for a typical message box is as follows:

```
MsgBox ("The message", MsgBoxStyle.Information, "Message Box Title")
```

For example, if you needed a number input into a certain text box, you'd write code so that if anything other than a number were inputted, a warning message box would appear. The message would display the message "Enter numbers only" and the Exclamation icon. You'd also want the message box to display an OK button and to have the title warning. This could be easily accomplished with the following code (see Figure 3-18):

```
MsgBox ("Enter Numbers Only", MsgBoxStyle.OKOnly + MsgBoxStyle.Exclamation, _
"Warning")
```

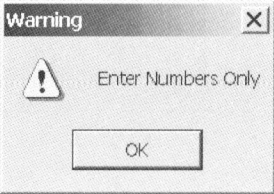

Figure 3-18. A typical warning displayed in a message box

> **NOTE** *You could also accomplish this type of warning with the new ErrorProvider control, which you'll get to later in the book.*

In actuality, however, you could leave out the OKOnly code, since this is the automatic default, but it's used here anyway to demonstrate the syntax.

Input Boxes

Text boxes are by far the most common means of collecting data for a VB application, but sometimes input boxes are necessary alternatives. For example, say you code a password-protected application, and upon start-up you want the user to enter his password. This is an ideal situation for an input box because the program won't function until the user addresses the input box. This immediate need is what makes input boxes valuable in certain situations.

Input Box Syntax

The syntax of input boxes is slightly different than message boxes, however, because they do read information into the program. This information is in the form of a string (alphanumeric text). The next chapter covers strings and variable types, but for now just know that a string variable called "X" must be set equal to the input box to make the data usable to the program. The program can't directly manipulate the input box, so X is made to equal the input box string so X can be manipulated in its place. The syntax for input boxes is demonstrated by displaying the code required to create the password input box described in the previous section. The code is as follows:

```
X = InputBox("Enter Password", "Security Feature")
```

This code produces an input box entitled "Security Feature," and asks the user to Enter Password. The text the user enters is set equal to X (see Figure 3-19).

Figure 3-19. An input box

Using Multiple Controls Together: A Sample Application

Now that you are familiar with the most commonly used controls, it's time to learn how to use multiple controls in conjunction with one another. You'll do this by coding your first scientific application.

It's OK if you can't always follow the code used in this application; some of the coding methods haven't been discussed. The important thing to remember is how the different controls are called upon and utilized to provide the building blocks required to create this application. This application is simple, yet may be quite handy for anyone who works in a laboratory setting because it can assist in the making of solutions of different molarities. The program asks users the desired molarity of the solution, the desired final volume, and the molecular weight of the solute. Based on this information, the program then calculates the mass of solute required to make the solution.

For starters, create a form similar to the one shown in Figure 3-20. This form uses labels to ask all three questions, and text boxes to receive the user's numerical responses. The text boxes' Name property is set to Text1, Text2, and Text3, respectively. The molarity and volume questions also use combo boxes to provide drop-down lists of the different unit choices. The combo boxes' Name property is set to Combo1 and Combo2, respectively. For molarity, the choices are Molar, mMolar, and uMolar, while for volume the choices are Liters, mLiters, and uLiters. These unit choices are added by taking advantage of the Items property at design time. Molar and Liters are entered in the Text properties of their respective combo boxes to provide a default setting. Next, a button with the caption "Calculate" and Name property set to Command1 is added to the form, along with a fourth text box with the BorderStyle property set to none and Name property set to Text4. Next, add the following code to the command button's Click event:

```
Private Sub Command1_Click(ByVal sender As Object, ByVal e As System.EventArgs) _
Handles Command1.Click
  Dim Mol, Mass, MW, V, Vol As Single
  Mol = CSng(Text1.Text)
  MW = CSng(Text2.Text)
  V = CSng(Text3.Text)
  Vol = V
  If Combo1.Text = "Molar" Then
   Mol = Mol
  ElseIf Combo1.Text = "mMolar" Then
   Mol = Mol / 1000
  ElseIf Combo1.Text = "uMolar" Then
   Mol = Mol / 1000000
  End If
  If Combo2.Text = "Liter(s)" Then
   V = V
  ElseIf Combo2.Text = "mLiter(s)" Then
   V = V / 1000
  ElseIf Combo2.Text = "uLiter(s)" Then
   V = V / 1000000
  End If
  Mass = Mol * MW * V
  Text4.Text = "To make a solution of this molarity add " & Mass &
" grams of solute and bring volume up to " & Vol & " " & Combo2.Text
End Sub
```

In this code, Mol is the desired molarity, MW is the molecular weight (grams/mole), and V and Vol are units of volume. As you can see after the variables are declared (the Dim statement), the variables are set equal to the numbers found in their respective text boxes. You can use the CSng function to convert the text found in a text box into a numerical value. Next, the If statements detect which option in the combo box was selected and make the appropriate adjustments, since the upcoming calculation is based on Molar and Liter(s) as units. Finally, the mass is calculated and the results displayed in the fourth text box (see Figure 3-20). Also, keep in mind that all this code is only triggered after the user has invoked the command button's Click event.

This short application should make it obvious that no one control creates useful applications, but that each individual control plays an essential role. The labels provide the users with the questions they need to address, while the text boxes provide a means to input and to display data. The combo boxes provide the users with a drop-down menu that adds functionality to the application, while the command button triggers the whole calculation routine.

NOTE *In the interest of brevity and simplicity, this program hasn't incorporated error handling code. See Chapter 11 for coverage of this topic.*

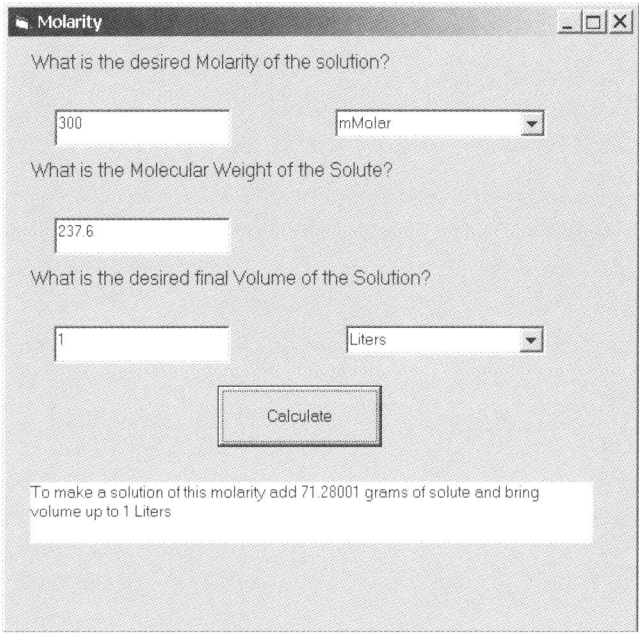

Figure 3-20. The molarity program GUI

Third-Party Scientific Controls

Now that you have an understanding of the most commonly used controls and how they work, it's time to talk about third-party controls. Many companies, other than Microsoft, create specialized controls that VB programmers can use to add even more functionality to their applications. In fact, thousands of third-party controls are in existence. Several highly useful third-party controls for scientific programming are now described. This book doesn't go into depth about their use, but you can download the demos and check them out for yourself using the provided company Web addresses.

Graphics Server

This software package allows you to add sophisticated graphing abilities to any application that you code, including 2-D and 3-D line graphs, scatter plots and log/log graphs, and numerous other graph types. It's one of the most complete graphing packages on the market today. The package also incorporates analytical functions, such as curve fitting, error bars, and basic statistical analysis of your graphed data. In addition, graphs can even be generated in real time, as your data is collected. For more information go to the Graphics Server Web site (`http://www.graphicsserver.com`). The cost of this product as of November 2001 was $599.

MathLibX

This is a small, inexpensive ($79.95 as of November 2001) suite of five scientific controls produced by Newcastle Scientific. The first control in the suite allows for linear and non-linear fitting of curves by the least squares method. The second control allows you to perform fast Fourier transforms and inverse fast Fourier transforms on data sets. The next two controls allow the filtering of data that is collected in real time. The filters include highpass, midpass, lowpass, and Kalman filtering. The final control allows you to sort arrays of data. You can find information on these controls at `http://www.mathfunctions.com`.

Measurement Studio

These controls, produced by National Instruments, provide an ideal method for linking your VB application to any sort of data acquisition or instrumentation system (National Instruments DAQ boards required). These controls allow the interaction of the VB application with analog and digital devices, and enable programs to make use of a computer's serial and I/O ports. The package also allows acquired data to be graphed (2-D and 3-D) in real time. Additionally, you can create a user interface with dials, gauges, knobs, meters, thermometers, and so on for professional-looking instrumentation panels that monitor and interact with equipment. The ActiveX controls in Measurement Studio support events are multithreaded, and include a LabWindows/CVI 5.5 server. The top-of-the-line NI Developer Suite Professional Edition cost about $4,000 as of November 2001. You can find more details at `http://www.ni.com/mstudio/prod_info.htm`.

Spread 3.5

Spread 3.5, produced by Farpoint Technologies, is a great product for programming powerful spreadsheet and database applications. With this control you can create spreadsheet programs that have advanced formatting and printing options, which is a big plus to the application user. Furthermore, the spreadsheet control inherently supports 74 different mathematical functions that the program user can use to perform calculations within the spreadsheet cells, as well as sorting capabilities. Finally, one of the most useful benefits of this control is it is compatible with spreadsheets that are saved in Excel 97 format. Information on Spread 3 is available at `http://www.fpoint.com/products/spread/spread.html`. As of November 2001, the retail price was about $400.

Total VB Statistics

This product is available from FMS and is a very thorough statistical analysis program. It allows you to perform field and group analyses, as well as to calculate frequency and percentile distributions. The program allows for data regressions and probability calculations. As of November 2001, the cost for this product was $599. For more information, visit `http://www.fmsinc.com`.

AppForge

Though particularly scientific in function, this suite is currently a hot topic in the VB community. AppForge created the AppForge Booster runtime engine that allows you to run VB applications (must use their controls in development) on Palm-enabled devices. You probably won't be using your Palm Pilot for any heavy-duty number crunching, but it's still a good idea to familiarize yourself with such products because mobile computing is here to stay. One interesting scientific application of such programs is field research, where the investigators cannot always bring a more powerful computing environment with them. As of November 2001, its cost ranged from $69 to $695 depending on which edition you select. For more information, visit the AppForge Web site at `http://www.appforge.com`.

By now it should be pretty obvious that most third-party controls provide specialized capabilities. Don't let this fact, however, diminish the importance of the basic VB controls; these controls form the building blocks of most VB applications. The next chapter discusses the different data types found inside VB and the different operators that are used with these data types. Thus, after completing Chapter 4, you should be well on your way to coding mathematical routines with VB.

Variables, Data Types, and Operators

Variables are character representations of the data values that your applications will use. Each variable holds data that belongs to a certain data type. Programming languages use the term *data type* to classify the information that their applications deal with. In VB, for example, data types can handle strings of text or Boolean operators, as well as a variety of different numeric data types. You used some of these different data types in the previous chapter's solution calculation program.

This chapter discusses the different data types and how they apply to coding scientific routines. Even if you're familiar with the basic VB data types, you still should read through this chapter; VB .NET introduces several new data types and some modified ones. Also, you'll learn about the basic operators that can act on these data types and the usefulness of the operators by coding a short program.

Data Types in VB .NET

The changes in VB .NET data types mainly are due to the common language runtime (CLR) and cross-language capabilities that Microsoft is introducing in VS .NET and the .NET platform (if you're familiar with Java, it's worth mentioning that the CLR is similar to the JVM). In other words, every .NET-based programming language uses the same basic data types. For example, every language has a 16-bit integer as a data type (i.e., a Short in VB .NET) and a double-precision floating point type, to name a few. This is because the data types are all laid out in the System.Object namespace, one of the namespaces that provides the base functionality for the entire .NET platform. The subsequent sections examine these universalized data types, called the *Common Type System*.

Strings

Strings are the type of variable (defined by the System.String class) that stores textual information. This is, in fact, the reason for the term *string*; you can consider a line of text as a string of characters. Thus, strings store alphanumeric characters. You can identify them in VB 6.0 by placing a dollar sign ($) after the variable name, though it's preferred to explicitly declare a variable as String. In VB .NET, appending the identifier type character $ to any identifier forces it to the String data type. For example, say that your application needs to access a chemical name that a program user entered in a text box. You could easily accomplish this with the following lines of code:

```
Dim ChemName As String
ChemName = TextBox1.Text
```

In science, though, strings are important for more than storing and accessing simple textual information. Consider the explosion of the fields of molecular biology and bioinformatics: The large volume of DNA and protein sequence data generated is often recorded as character strings. DNA sequences consist of repeating units of A, G, C, and T, while amino acid sequences are recorded as a sequence of 20 letters that each represent one of the amino acids. Chapter 14 covers this subject in depth.

In VB programming, the standard string holds anywhere from 0 to 2 billion characters of information. These characters, traditionally in either ASCII (American Standard Code for Information Interchange) or ANSI (American National Standards Institute) code, are each represented by a number between 0 and 255. This is because any item stored in a computer's memory must be stored numerically. VB .NET, however, differs from past releases of VB in that Unicode now replaces the ASCII code. Unicode allows for storing characters as any numerical value between 0 and 65,535—a much larger range than the ASCII code, which also allows for storing a wealth of different characters. In fact, Unicode was created to facilitate the use of non-English languages in computer programs and Web sites. The good news for scientists and engineers is that many characters available under Unicode correspond to a wide array of mathematical and scientific symbols.

The Chr and Asc Functions

If this discussion of numbers representing characters makes you wonder what number represents what character, then the Chr function might interest you. You can find the corresponding character for any number simply by using the function

```
Chr(n)
```

where n can be any number between 0 and 255. For example, to display the letter G in your text box you'd code the following:

```
TextBox1.Text = Chr(71)
```

because G is assigned the numeric value 71 in the ASCII character set. This function doesn't utilize Unicode characters numbered beyond 255, but you can use non-ASCII, Unicode characters through the Char data type, which this chapter discusses later.

> **TIP** *For more information on Unicode characters, look under the Char data type.*

The Asc function works in the opposite manner of the Chr function. The Asc function takes a string's first character and returns its ASCII number. Just be cautious to avoid executing this function on a null string (an empty string) because it generates a runtime error.

String Constants

String constants are a great way to format the textual output that your program generates. If you neglect to add some type formatting to your text strings, especially longer ones, VB probably won't display your text in the most eye-pleasing manner. For example, you might find unnecessary line breaks or text displayed in one huge line.

To fully understand the basics of string constants, look at them in action. As you've seen, a message box can display text. In this application, it will display the text "Visual Basic Programming is Fun." However, "Visual Basic Programming" must be on one line and "is Fun" on a second line. You easily could accomplish this with the following code:

```
Line1 = "Visual Basic Programming"
Line2 = "is Fun"
Message= Line1 & vbCrLf & Line2
MsgBox (Message)
```

vbCrLf is a string constant, which tells VB to insert a carriage return and a line feed. Similarly, if you want to Tab any of your text, you can use the string constant vbTab.

String Concatenation

Looking back to the previous code's line that defines Message, notice that an ampersand (&) is between Line1 and the string constant, as well as Line2 and the

string constant. The ampersand is one of the most commonly used string operators because it joins two strings together. The technical term for this process is
concatenation, but it may be easier to think of it as a ligation. When concatenat-
ing two or more strings, remember that the strings are joined in the order in
which they're written. For example, if you reversed Line1 and Line2 in the
Message definition, you'd end up with

```
is Fun
Visual Basic Programming
```

Thus, don't get into the habit of viewing concatenation as "string addition."

The Char Data Type

New to VB .NET, this data type testifies to the growing importance of database
data. The Char data type, defined by the System.Char class, provides a direct
method of storing and utilizing Unicode characters in VB projects. The global use
of computers and Internet-based applications has generated a need to support
thousands more character types than ASCII is capable of. Many scientists and
engineers will find these Unicode code characters greatly useful because they
extend beyond language and include a large number of mathematical and scientific characters. A great source of Unicode information is the Unicode
Consortium Web site (`http://www.unicode.org`). This consortium is a collabora-
tive effort between software manufacturers to create internationally accepted
Unicode standards. One of the Web site's most useful features is its Unicode
Character Database, which gives you a graphical representation of each character
and its numeric Unicode ID.

The Unicode data type itself is a 16-bit quantity (as opposed to 8-bit ASCII)
that stores the numerical values of Unicode characters. This data type can
hold integer values ranging from 0 to 65,535. For example, consider the following code:

```
Dim Uni as Char
Uni =  CChar (ChrW(90))
TextBox1.Text  = Uni
```

First, define Uni as a variable of type Char, and then set Uni equal to the
character represented by the value 2245. Finally, print the character in a text box
that corresponds to the numeric Unicode Id 90, which is the letter Z. Just be careful, however, that the numeric ID corresponds to an actual Unicode character.
Setting a Char variable equal to a nonexistent character may result in a hard-to-
find error.

Numerical Data Types

Many different kinds of numerical data types are available to VB programmers and are among the most important data types to scientific programmers. A large part of your programming will be modeling mathematical systems or solving complex mathematical problems. This section first explores the three different data types that store integer values.

The Short Data Type

The smallest of all Integer data types, it can hold a 16-bit integer value. Thus, a variable of the type Short can hold any integer value between –32,768 and 32,767. This data type is new to VB .NET (System.Int16 class) and corresponds to the old Integer data type. Integer arithmetic with Short variables is extremely fast, but keep in mind the data type's minimum and maximum limits to avoid errors. Besides integer arithmetic, Short variables are often used as counters to keep track of how often some event occurs.

The Integer Data Type

Like the Short data type, Integer variables only hold integer values. Integer variables, however, aren't limited to 16-bit values, but can hold 32-bit values. That means that an Integer variable (System.Int32 class) can hold any variable between –2,147,483,648 and 2,147,483,647. As with Short variables, integer arithmetic is extremely fast. One important difference, though, is that Integer variables use twice the memory of Short variables. Therefore, if you don't need the enhanced range provided by the Integer data type, you're better off with the Short data type. This data type is changed in VB .NET and is equivalent to the Long data type of past VB versions.

The Long Data Type

This data type isn't equivalent to the Long data type found in past versions of VB, but is new to VB .NET (System.Int64 class). The Long data type is a 64-bit Integer data type that is capable of holding integer values from –9,223,372,036,854,775,808 to 9,223,372,036,854,775,807. It takes up twice the memory of the Integer data type and four times the memory of the Short data type. Still, integer arithmetic is quite fast. As with Short and Integer data types, consider the range of integer values you're working with and choose your data type accordingly.

The Single Data Type

Variables of the Single data type are single-precision floating point variables (System.Single class). This basically means that single-precision numbers store approximations of real numbers. Because of this ability, you'll use this data type quite often. In fact, you used it in Chapter 3's molarity program. Keep in mind with single-precision variables that they can store real numbers with up to 38 places, but only the first seven places are guaranteed to be accurate. Thus, in a calculation that yields an answer of 436.783478, only the 436.7834 is guaranteed to be accurate. The remaining 0.000078 might be accurate, or it might be slightly different than the exact answer. Single-precision math is slower than integer math, but you benefit from manipulating real numbers.

The Double Data Type

The Double data type (System.Double class) is a double-precision floating point variable for applications that require great accuracy. The Double data type can hold data values over 300 places in length and has a guaranteed accuracy of 16 decimal places. Just remember to consider the accuracy your application requires. If a Single variable's accuracy is sufficient, avoid using the Double data type; it only results in a slower calculation speed and a greater use of system resources.

> **NOTE** *For newer 32-bit processors, this isn't always true because double-precision floating points are often the native type used in floating point calculations.*

Also, consider the number of non-zero digits at the end of a number, after its decimal point. For example, if you set X = 12.54, VB would store 12.54 as a single-precision variable even if X can hold double-precision numbers. Thus, X would equal 12.54000. If you instead set X = 12.54# X would equal 12.54000000000000, which is a lot more precise. The number sign (#) works like the dollar sign ($) used with strings and lets VB know that it's dealing with a double-precision number.

The Decimal Data Type

New to VB .NET, this data type shares some features with the Currency data type found in VB 6.0. The Decimal data type (System.Decimal) was designed to accurately calculate decimal fractions, since computers make use of binary fractions, which aren't exactly equivalent. The Decimal data type does this by using a 96-bit integer that can be scaled by a power of 10. This scaling factor represents the number of digits to the right of the decimal point with a value of 0, meaning no decimal places. The largest possible decimal value is 79,228,162,514,264,337,593,543,950,335 and the smallest possible non-zero value is 0.0000000000000000000000000001. Decimal variables are therefore extremely valuable for applications that require a high degree of accuracy within the data type's specified range, since the data type is accurate to 28 decimal places. Just as with the Double data type, if you have a value of 0.05 that's accurate to more than 28 places, you can avoid writing out every additional 0 by placing the type identifier D after the value.

Guidelines for Choosing the Appropriate Numerical Data Type

As mentioned in the data type descriptions, a higher data type precision or larger integer value requires more system resources. This greater use of system resources results in a longer processing time. While this is a valid consideration, also note that a more robust data type better serves some situations.

For example, say you want to code an iterative math technique that uses a counter variable to count the number of iterations. If the application performs exactly 1,000 iterations every time it runs, then it definitely makes sense to use a Short over an Integer or a Long. The application will never require the Integer and Long data types' enhanced ranges. However, if you don't know how often the iteration performs because it's left to the user, then a Short might not be the best option. The user may want to perform 5 iterations or 500,000. In this case, it's wiser to choose either the Integer or Long data type; it makes your application more robust. The very tiny processing time increase is a small trade-off for preventing application crashes during a large number of iterations.

Also, consider your application's length. For example, this chapter will demonstrate a Reynolds number calculation to classify fluid flow through a pipe. The Single data type sufficiently generates an accurate answer for this very short and simple application.

However, consider an application with thousands of lines of mathematical code. In this situation, you're strongly discouraged from using Single data types, even if your final answer requires only single-precision accuracy. Think of the problem this way: Each time you use a Single, every place past the seventh is not accurate. Thus, with each new calculation you build on this inaccuracy. By the end of this long mathematical routine, you'd probably find a discrepancy between the final answers if you performed the calculation with both Singles and Doubles. Instead, the Double answer would be more accurate and appropriate because in scientific programming your data's integrity is a prime concern.

Numerical Operators

As a scientific programmer, this section should interest you because you'll finally be given some tools to manipulate numerical data. In fact, by the end of this section you'll have learned all of the skills necessary to write simple mathematical routines. The best part is that you already should be familiar with most of the mathematical operators in VB—multiplication, division, addition, subtraction, and exponentiation—which are summarized in Table 4-1.

Table 4-1. Mathematical Operators

NUMERICAL OPERATOR	MATHEMATICAL OPERATION
^	Exponentiation
*	Multiplication
/	Division
+	Addition
-	Subtraction

As you can see, none of these operators are strange or foreign; even better, you use them just like any normal mathematical equation. For example, to multiply the numbers 2 and 3 you only need to code 2 * 3.

In addition, VB has two operators that let you perform integer divisions. The first operator, the backslash (\), divides one number by another to produce an integer answer. It does this by throwing away the decimal portion of the answer. Thus, the calculation 9\4 returns 2 for an answer. The second operator, the Mod operator, addresses the obvious question of what happens to the remainder; it shows you the remainder that results from an integer division. Consider the same 9\4 example. You already know that 4 goes fully into 9 twice, but now use the Mod function to determine the remainder. If you execute the code 9 Mod 4, you discover that the remainder is 1.

The Order of Operations (Operator Precedence)

You're familiar now with the various numerical operators and what they do, so consider the order in which they act. VB doesn't prioritize all of the operators equally. In any line of code, certain operations execute before others. Luckily, VB's order of operations is, for the most part, similar to the order used in algebraic equations. First, parentheses divide sets of operations into groups, and thus the operations found within a set of parentheses always have priority over all other operations. For example, the mathematical routine (2+3) * 5 yields an answer of 25 because 2+3 executes first. Next, all exponentiation operations will execute. Thus, in the equation 5 * 2^2, the answer is 20 because 2 is squared before it's multiplied by 5. If there is more then one exponentiation operation they execute as they occur, from left to right.

The multiplication and division operators execute next. Both are of equal weight (priority), so they execute from left to right. Therefore, the code 5 * 4/2 would first multiply 5 by 4 to receive 20, and then would divide 20 by 2 to receive the final answer of 10. Next, the integer division (\) operator executes, followed by the Mod operator, and finally addition and subtraction, which are of equal weight. Thus, like multiplication and division, addition and subtraction execute in the order in which they occur (left to right).

Now, consider the following mathematical equation in a stepwise fashion.

$$(3 + 2 \, / \, 1) \, \wedge \, 2 * 4 + 6 * 2 - 4 \, / \, 2$$

First, find the operation or set of operations with the highest priority. In this case, the highest priority operations are inside the parentheses. Thus, the operator inside the parentheses with the highest priority turns out to be the division operator of 2 by 1, which leaves you with

$$(3 + 2) \, \wedge \, 2 * 4 + 6 * 2 - 4 \, / \, 2$$

After executing the next highest operator inside the parentheses, the plus sign, you have

$$5 \, \wedge \, 2 * 4 + 6 * 2 - 4 \, / \, 2$$

Now that you've addressed the parentheses, notice that in the remainder of the equation the exponentiation is the next highest priority. After squaring 5, the equation looks like

$$25 * 4 + 6 * 2 - 4 \, / \, 2$$

After exponentiation, you'll execute the multiplication and division operators from left to right to yield

$$100 + 12 - 2$$

Finally, the addition and subtraction operations execute, leaving a final answer of 110.

For a more detailed and formal treatment please refer to VB .NET documentation under the heading "Operator Precedence and Associativity."

The Boolean Data Type

The Boolean data type (System.Boolean class) is probably the simplest of all the data types because it only holds two possible values. All Boolean variables must be either True or False. Despite their seeming simplicity, however, Boolean variables often are quite useful in scientific applications because they apply to many programs that use logical and/or conditional statements.

Conditional Statements

Conditional statements often use Boolean expressions; conditional statements allow your program to choose an execution pathway based on preexisting conditions, the simplest being the Simple If . . . Then statement of the form `If this condition Then take this action`.

This statement checks to see if the "condition" results in a True value. Therefore, if Boolean value, B, was set equal to True and replaced "this condition" with B, your "action" would execute. If B equaled to False, however, the "action" wouldn't execute. A great thing about conditional statements is that although they are Boolean expressions, a Boolean variable doesn't have to be the condition. You also can use a mathematical expression, such as $X = 1$. If X equals 1, VB treats this condition as being True, the same as if B were true. If X doesn't equal 1, then the condition would be False. To illustrate this conditional statement's syntax, code the following simple routine to print out the number 1 in a text box if $X = 1$.

```
If X = 1 Then
    TextBox1.Text=CStr(X)
End If
```

The Simple If . . . Then statement is useful, but does have limitations. For example, suppose you need other actions to execute if X doesn't equal 1? Well, you can easily address this by using Block If . . . Then statements. Block conditional statements can respond to two or more conditions, and can make use of the conditional ElseIf. Adding to your previous example, you don't just want to print out X when it equals 1, but to add 2 to X when it equals 2. You'd accomplish this with the following code

```
If X = 1 Then
    TextBox1.Text=CStr(X)
ElseIf X = 2 Then
    X = X + 2
End If
```

You also could easily extend this code to add extra conditions if X = 3, 5, or 105 by incorporating additional ElseIf statements.

The Else statement is another highly useful conditional statement. You can add it to the end of a Simple If . . . Then statement or a Block If . . . Then statement to dictate what action executes if none of the previous conditions are met. Taking your previous example, say that for all numbers other than 1 and 2 you want X to be multiplied by 3. You'd accomplish this with the following code:

```
If X = 1 Then
    TextBox1.Text=CStr(X)
ElseIf X = 2 Then
    X = X + 2
Else
    X = X * 3
End If
```

Now that you've been exposed to the three types of conditional statements used in VB, don't let their simplicity fool you. The subsequent sections illustrate how to form complex statements by combining relational and logical operators with these conditional structures.

Relational Operators

If . . . Then statements are often used in conjunction with relational operators, just like the = sign you just saw in the previous sample. VB offers the following relational operators, shown in Table 4-2.

Table 4-2. Relational Operators

RELATIONAL OPERATOR	OPERATION
<>	Not Equal To
<	Less Than
>	Greater Than
<=	Less Than or Equal To
>=	Greater Than or Equal To

Remember, however, that the relational operator in an If . . . Then statement won't define any of the variables according to that relation, but tests to see if that relation is True or False. For example, if you code

```
If X >= Y Then
```

the action executes if the relation is correct. If X is less than Y, no action executes and X remains less than Y (unless the coded action changes the value X).

Logical Operators

Just as some operators work with numerical expressions, so too do some operators work with Boolean expressions. These operators, listed below in Table 4-3, function like the relational operators just examined.

Table 4-3. Logical Operators

LOGICAL OPERATORS	OPERATION
AND	Checks to see if both conditions are true
OR	Checks to see if at least one condition is True
XOR	(Exclusive OR) Checks to see if one but not both conditions are True
Not	Checks to see if the specified condition is not met
EQV	Checks to see if both conditions are True or False

Now that you know the different logical operators, take a closer look at how they actually work. For example, in the code

```
If X = 5 AND Y <> 5 Then
```

the action only executes if X actually equals 5 and Y equaled any number but 5. If X didn't equal 5 or if Y did equal 5, the action wouldn't execute. In other words, the AND operator requires that both conditions be True. If one condition is required to be True, then you can use the OR operator; this operator allows the action to proceed as long as at least one condition is met. An OR operator also functions if both conditions are met (True).

If the action must execute if only one condition is True, but not both, then use the XOR operator. With XOR, which stands for Exclusive OR, the action only proceeds under the circumstance that an either-or condition exists. Thus, only one condition can be True for the action to proceed.

The Not operator negates whatever condition is found in the conditional statement. For example, assume that X really does equal 5. If you run the code

```
If NOT (X = 5) Then
```

you find that the action doesn't execute because X really does equal 5. This is because X = 5 is True but the NOT operator makes it Not True, or False. Similarly, if X doesn't equal 5, the action executes because the overall conditional is Not False, or True.

The last logical operator is the EQV, or equivalent. This operator checks to see if both conditions are True or both conditions are False. If both are True (or False) the conditions are equivalent, and thus the overall condition is True and the action executes.

The Order of Operations Revisited

Just as numerical operators operate in order, so too do relational and logical operators. This order of operations, however, is much less complex than the numerical order of operations. First, parentheses separate operations and give precedence to certain operations. Thus, in the conditional

```
If X = 5 AND (Y - 1 > 6 OR Z < 15) Then
```

VB first checks to see if either the Y or Z condition was True, and then executes the AND operator. As you can then see, the relational operators execute next to see if each individual condition is True or False (i.e., does X = 5, is Y-1 > 6). Finally, the logical operators execute to determine whether or not the overall conditional statement is True or False. If no multiple logical operators are of the same precedence (i.e., no parentheses), such as

```
If X = 5 AND Y - 1 > 6 OR Z < 15 Then
```

then the operators execute from left to right.

Select Case Statements

Using Block Ifs and multiple logical operators can become confusing, so VB provides you with an alternate logical structure. This structure uses Select Case statements that behave like more traditional conditional statements. Consider the following code:

```
'X is your variable
Select Case X
Case Is < 5
    X = 10
Case 5 to 9
    X = X + 1
Case 11, 14, 17 ,20
    X = 0
Case Else
    X=100
End Select
```

First, select the case (i.e., the current state of your variable X) and compare it to the following criteria. Check to see if X is < 5, and if so, set X equal to 10. Next, check to see if the Case contains a value ranging from 5 to 9, and if so, add 1 to X. As you can see, the "To" construct is easier to write out than

```
If X>=5 AND X<=9
```

In another scenario, Case statements are easier to use than If statements. In this particular line of code, you can check if X has a value of 11, 14, 17, or 20 by separating the values with a comma. This spares you from typing an awful lot of "X=s" and "ANDs." Finally, you can use a Case Else statement, which works just like the Else statement in the If structures. In other words, if no previous statements are True, then the statement X=100 executes.

Declaration of Variables

Now that you have a firm understanding of VB's different data types and their operators, you're almost ready to code useful mathematical and logical routines. In fact, you'll do just that in the next section. But first, consider one last thing about the data types used in your applications. Each data type has one or more variables associated with it. How does VB know what variable corresponds to what data type? The answer is easy. All variables must be declared, or set to a certain data type, before they can be utilized.

The Dim keyword, commonly known as the *Dim Statement*, easily accomplishes this declaration of variables. Basically, the Dim keyword is placed before the variable name and its corresponding data type. For example, to declare X as a Short you use the following line of code:

```
Dim X as Short
```

If you want X instead to be a Double, you easily declare it as such by simply replacing Short with Double, or any other data type. Also, remember that multiple variables of the same type can be declared on the same line. For instance,

```
Dim var1, var2, var3 as Boolean
```

declares var1, var2, and var3 as Boolean variables. This is a new feature in VB .NET. Earlier versions of VB would declare only var3 as a Boolean variable, and would treat var1 and var2 as Variant data types, the earlier VB's default data type. If you forget to declare the data type of a variable, VB assumes it to be of Object data type, discussed later in the chapter. It's best to avoid this and explicitly declare all variables with a specific data type because this "universal" data type often leads to unwanted program behavior. In fact, in VB 6.0 you can add the declaration Option Explicit, and VB will force you to declare every variable you're going to use. This option is turned on by default in VB .NET.

Example Problem: Reynolds Number Calculation

If you've ever dealt with fluid mechanics you're probably familiar with the Reynolds number concept. The Reynolds number is a dimensionless quantity used to determine if fluid flows are laminar turbulent. For fluids flowing through a pipe or tube, the Reynolds number is defined as

$$N_{RE} = \frac{DV\rho}{\mu}$$

where D is the pipe's diameter in meters, V is the fluid's average velocity in m/s, ρ is the density of the fluid in Kg/m^3, and μ is the fluid's viscosity in Kg/m-s.

For fluids flowing through a pipe, a Reynolds number of less than 2,100 means that the fluid is flowing in a laminar fashion. For a number 4,000 or greater, the flow is turbulent. If it's between 2,100 and 4,000, then the flow is in a transition state between laminar and turbulent flow. You'll code a short application to calculate the Reynolds number of a fluid flowing through a pipe, to determine whether that flow is laminar or turbulent. This example demonstrates many of the skills covered in this chapter so far, including numerical operators and conditional statements.

First, add five text boxes and four labels to your form as shown in Figure 4-1.

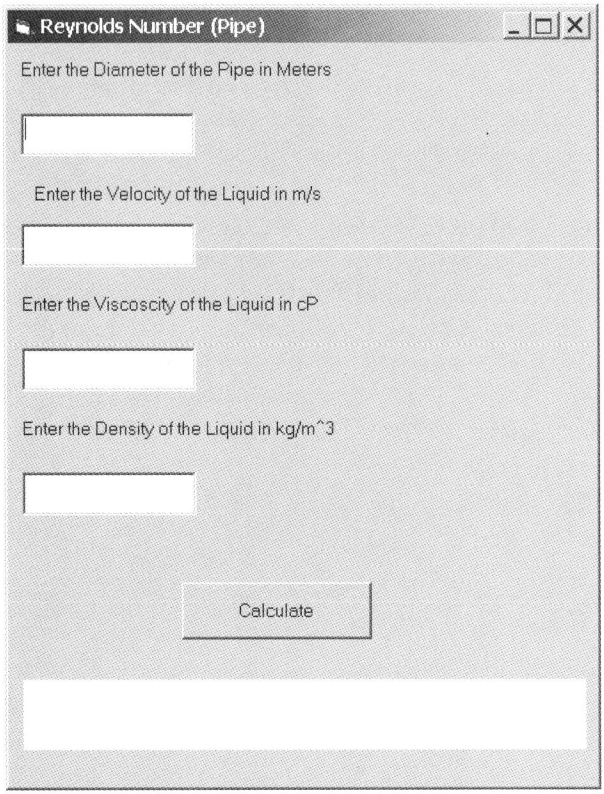

Figure 4-1. The GUI for your Reynold's number calculator

Next, add a command button and the following code to the command button's Click event.

```
Private Sub Command1_Click(ByVal eventSender As System.Object, ByVal eventArgs As
System.EventArgs)
          Dim D, V, u, p, NRE As Single
          Dim Flow As String
          D = CSng(TextBox1.Text)
          V = CSng(TextBox2.Text)
          u = CSng(TextBox3.Text)
          p = CSng(TextBox4.Text)
          NRE = (D * V * p) / (u * 0.001)
          If NRE < 2100 Then
                  Flow = "Laminar"
          ElseIf NRE >= 2100 And NRE <= 4000 Then
                  Flow = "Transitional"
          Else
                  Flow = "Turbulent"
          End If
       TextBox5.Text = "The Reynolds Number is " & NRE & " Therefore the
Flow is " & Flow
End Sub
```

Following the code line by line, notice that the first step declares all of the variables utilized in the routine. The program deals with real numbers, and the accuracy of double-precision variables is unnecessary because 2,100 and 4,000 are the only really critical values. Thus, single precision variables are preferable. They take up fewer system resources and execute faster. The variable Flow is declared as String because it stores textual information. Next, these single-precision variables are set equal to the information entered in their corresponding text boxes. CSng is a function that converts the text in the text box to a single-precision number. Chapter 6 describes this conversion function and others like it.

Now that each initial variable is defined, the numerical operators perform the required calculation. The resultant value is then set equal to NRE. Next, a series of conditional If . . . Then statements determine if the flow in the pipe is laminar, turbulent, or transitional. Notice how this set of conditional statements uses some of the relational and logical operators previously discussed. If the Reynolds number (NRE) is less than 2,100, Flow is set equal to laminar. If it's greater than or equal to 2,100, but less than or equal to 4,000, then Flow is set equal to transitional. Finally, for all other cases (i.e., NRE greater than 4000) Flow is set equal to turbulent. The final line of code then displays the results in the fifth text box, shown in Figure 4-2.

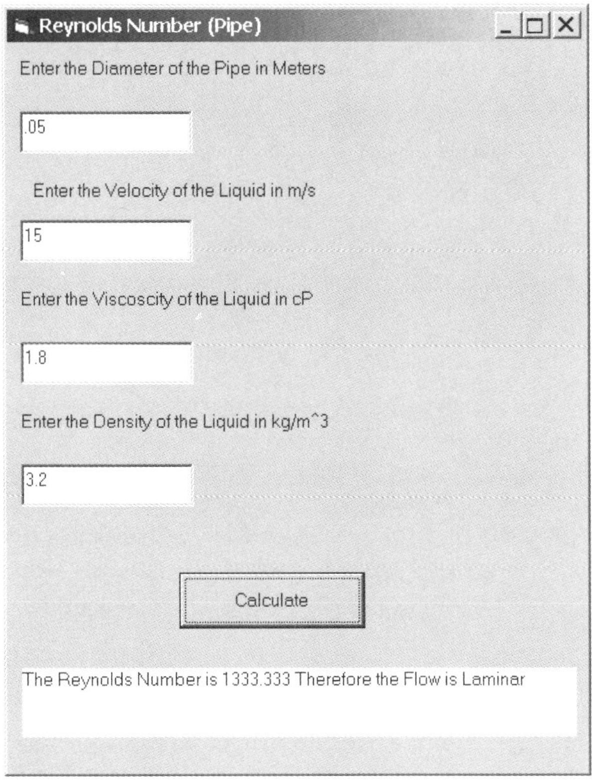

Figure 4-2. Sample Reynolds number calculation

This application clearly illustrates how data types and the different operators can play a crucial role in controlling a program's flow and output. As the book progresses, you'll see that more complex architectures can easily handle more complex situations. But for now, make sure you thoroughly understand how these data types, operators, and conditionals work because they are crucial building blocks to even the most powerful scientific applications. The above code doesn't handle runtime errors because it assumes the user always enters valid data. For a real productivity application to be "well behaved," extensive error capability must be built into the code. Error handling in VB 6.0 and earlier versions was handled with On Error GoTo statements or On Error Resume Next statements. The VB .NET platform dispenses with the On Error constructs in favor of try-catch-finally blocks, similar to Java's method of exception handling.

The Byte Data Type

A few more data types that VB supports aren't as commonly utilized as the ones previously described. This section briefly describes these remaining data types, however, to give you an understanding of their purpose. The first is the Byte data type, which can store an integer value between 0 and 255. This data type is most often used to deal with the handling of binary files.

The Sbyte Type

The Sbyte data type is short for signed byte because some of the values within its range are negative. The Sbyte data type holds integer values that range from –128 to 127.

The Date Data Type

As the name suggests, this variable can hold date and time information. Variables of this type can hold any value between midnight January 1 in the year 100 to midnight December 31 in the year 9999. This variable is defined by placing the value of the variable between two number signs (#), as follows:

```
D = # January 5, 2001 10:15 AM#
```

> **NOTE** *Other date formats are possible. Find more information on these formats using VB's help feature.*

The Object Data Type

The Object data type, which replaces the Variant data type found in VB 6.0, can be thought of as the universal data type. That is, the Object data type can hold information that corresponds to any other data type. Thus, a variable of this type could hold a string just as easily as a real number. While this sounds like a great feature, the Object data type doesn't always accurately interpret a data type, which can lead to program errors. It's better to explicitly declare all variables so that they belong to a set data type. Advanced systems programming, such as OLE (Object Linking and Embedding) automation and COM (Component Object Model) applications, use Object data types.

Private and Public Variables

So far, you've seen variable types that can only be seen by code contained within the same procedure in which they are declared. VB allows for variables to be considered as Private and Public, as well (see Table 4-4). Private variables aren't just viewed in a single procedure, but can be viewed (and/or changed) by any procedure on that form. Code can view Public variables, on the other hand, anywhere in the application, even on another form. These variables aren't declared inside a procedure, and are usually written at the top of the code window. The following syntax declares Public and Private variables:

```
Public Variable Name As Data Type
Private Variable Name As Data Type
```

Thus, remember to use the Public or Private keyword in place of the Dim keyword. You generally use Public variables when multiple procedures in different modules require access to the same information. For example, say you're writing a program that calculates the thermodynamic quantities of change in enthalpy, entropy, and Gibb's free energy, and wanted to use a separate function/procedure to calculate each value. Each calculation requires information pertaining to the system's initial and final temperature, so you might declare two public variables as follows:

```
Public TI, TF As Single
```

All three procedures could call on these variables to access this information without reading it three different times. Chapter 7 demonstrates this use of Private variables, when you write the code necessary to transpose a matrix. Keep in mind that these variables are often the source of program bugs because they can be accessed in so many different places. Thus, if they pose no benefit to your application, it's best to stick with variables declared within a procedure or subroutine.

Table 4-4. Private and Public Variable Types

PRIVATE VARIABLES	PUBLIC VARIABLES
Can be accessed by any code contained on the same form as the variable declaration	Can be accessed by code anywhere in the program, regardless of which form the code is contained in

Static Variables

Normally, every time a VB procedure is initialized, all of the variables within that procedure are set back to zero (or "" (null value) in the case of strings). Thus, the values from the last time the procedure was run don't persist. You can avoid this reinitialization, however, by using the Static keyword. If a variable is declared as Static, its value persists even when the routine is reinitialized. For example, code a simple program that counts how often a command button is clicked. To do this, add a command button named Command1 and a text box named Text1 to a new project form (see Figure 4-3).

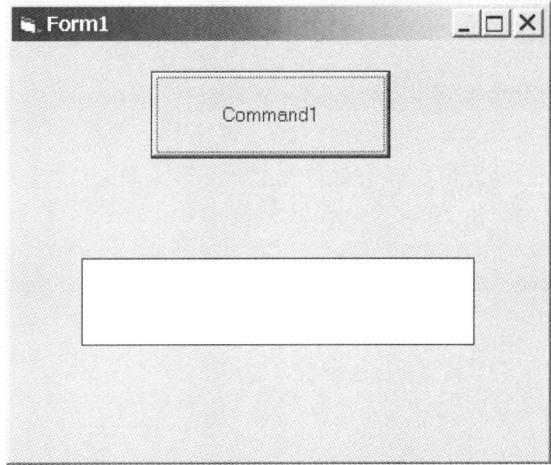

Figure 4-3. The form layout

Now, add the following code:

```
Private Sub Command1_Click(ByVal eventSender As System.Object, ByVal eventArgs As
System.EventArgs)  Handles Command1.Click
  Static NumClicks As Integer
  NumClicks = NumClicks + 1
  Text1.Text = "The Button Has Been Clicked " & NumClicks & " Times"
End Sub
```

As you can see, when the procedure is first invoked, the variable NumClicks is initialized to zero. However, every time the procedure is reinvoked, the variable isn't reinitialized, but instead retains it value.

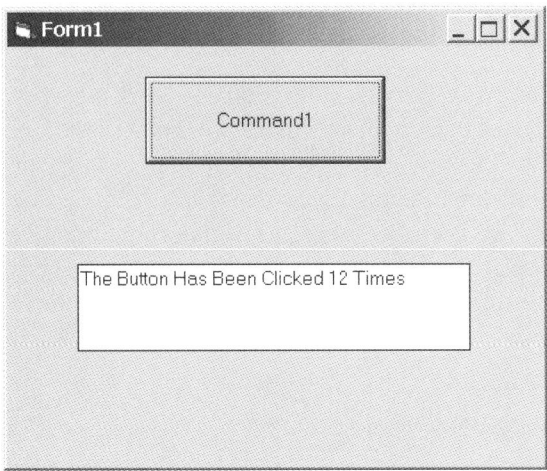

Figure 4-4. The number of times the command button was clicked

Now that you understand the different data types that Visual Basic offers, the next chapter examines more complex data structures, such as arrays. You'll also start to explore some more complex program architectures such as loop structures, which are highly useful in manipulating arrays and performing iterative techniques.

Arrays and Loop Structures

THIS CHAPTER HAS TWO FOCUSES, the first of which is arrays. Arrays are a "higher order" of data structure that can be used in conjunction with the data types the previous chapter discussed. The second focus of this chapter is on loop structures. Loops are highly useful in performing mathematical iterations, as well as manipulating an array's different elements. As the chapter progresses, you'll see that while these focuses are extremely useful on their own, you can also combine them to program powerful matrix math routines. This chapter provides numerous program examples of these concepts, so make sure you understand the basic elements of VB programming that the first four chapters introduced.

One-Dimensional Arrays

The simplest way to picture a one-dimensional array is to view it as a list, or even a vector, because a one-dimensional (1-D) array is really nothing more than a collection (or list) of variables of the same type. For example, consider a chemical inventory list. It lists, in order, NaCl, H_2SO_4, and ethanol. Also assume that the lines on the list are numbered starting with zero, so that the item on line 0 was NaCl, line 1 was H_2SO_4, and line 2 was ethanol. If you think of the numbered lines on the list as storage spaces, such that H_2SO_4 is stored in storage space 1, then you have a basic understanding of an array. Only, instead of storing chemical inventory items, an array will store items that correspond to any of VB's data types. For example, each chemical inventory item name is a string, so you could express your list in VB as an array of strings, as shown in the following example.

```
Chemicals(0) = "NaCl"
Chemicals(1) = "H2SO4"
Chemicals(2) = "ethanol"
```

In this case, the name of the array is Chemicals, and the number in parentheses is the Index, or the position of the item on the list. In VB, the 0 position is the first position of any array (this differs from other popular scientific programming languages such as FORTRAN, which start their array indexes from 1). Thus, any item in the array can be used or referred to by giving simply the name of the array and its index position. Therefore, to enter the item stored in position 0 into a text box named Text1, you'd write a line of code that looked like this:

```
Text1.Text = Chemicals(0).
```

It's also useful to view an array as a vector, especially when dealing with certain mathematical routines. For example, say you had a list of three numbers, 8, 12, and 5, which represent the X, Y, and Z components of a force, respectively. The X component of your vector would equal 8. In the same way, you could place these three components in an array, only now the X component would be in the 0 position of the array. Examine how this would work by considering the following example that calculates the magnitude of the previous force vector.

```
Dim Vector(3) As Short
Dim Magnitude As Single
Vector(0) = 8
Vector(1) = 12
Vector(2) = 5
Magnitude = Math.Sqrt(Vector(0) ^ 2 + Vector(1) ^ 2 + Vector(2) ^ 2)
```

You call on each component of the vector in order to incorporate each directional component into the resultant magnitude, which is stored in the Magnitude variable.

> **NOTE** *An interesting side note is that arrays were first introduced in 1959 with the development of the programming language COBOL.*

Arrays in the .NET Framework

As the last section mentioned, arrays are basically a listing (or vector) of different elements that correspond to a certain data type. These lists are created using the functionality laid out in the System.Array class of the .NET Framework and are also part of the common language runtime (CLR). This functionality not only allows for the creation and manipulation of arrays, but also the creation of customized arrays with special boundary conditions. These capabilities are examined later in the chapter. For now, let's examine some of the useful methods that are associated with the System.Array class.

The Clear Method

The Clear method sets all of the elements of an array equal to zero in the case of a numeric array or in the case of a string array, all elements are set equal to the null string. This method is invoked by using the following code:

```
System.Array.Clear(ArrayName, Index, Length)
```

ArrayName corresponds to the name of the array you want to clear, Index corresponds to the index of the element where you want to begin, and Length corresponds to the number of elements you want to clear.

The Copy Method

Use this method to copy the elements from one array into a second array. When you use this method, conversion functions aren't necessary because the Copy method automatically makes type conversions where possible. This method is used as follows:

```
System.Array.Copy(Array1, Index1, Array2, Index2, Length)
```

Array1 is the source of the data and Array2 is the destination array. Length specifies the number of elements to be copied. Index1 and Index2 correspond to the starting indexes where respective cutting and pasting operations will initiate. Index1 and Index2 are optional arguments; if you leave them out, copy and paste functions will begin at the first element of each array.

CAUTION *Be careful with automatic type conversions. Make sure that you don't try to perform impossible conversions, such as converting Longs into Bytes.*

The IndexOf and LastIndexOf Methods

Use these methods to find the first and last occurrence of a given value within a one-dimensional (1-D) array. The methods will return the element's index that contains the desired value. These methods are used as follows:

```
System.Array.IndexOf(ArrayName, Value)
System.Array.LastIndexOf(ArrayName, Value)
```

ArrayName specifies the name of the array to search and Value specifies the element to search for.

The Reverse Method

This method reverses the order of all of the elements in an array. In other words, the first element becomes the last, and the last element becomes the first. This method is invoked by the code

```
System.Array.Reverse(ArrayName)
```

where ArrayName is the name of the array to be reversed.

The Sort Method

This method can be highly useful for turning an array of elements into an ordered list of elements. The Sort method places the elements of string arrays alphanumerically, and orders numeric arrays from least to greatest. This method is invoked by the code

```
System.Array.Sort(ArrayName)
```

where ArrayName is the name of the array to be sorted.

You now have a good understanding of some of the functionality provided by the System.Array namespace. The next section discusses how arrays operate in VB.

Fixed Arrays

VB supports two distinct types of arrays: fixed arrays and dynamic arrays. The main difference between them is that with fixed arrays, the amount of available memory (i.e., storage spaces) is set at design time, whereas with dynamic arrays this is set at runtime. Fixed arrays are simpler to work with than dynamic arrays, and they're ideal for when you know exactly how many storage slots your array needs.

The downside to fixed arrays, however, is that you can't add information to the array beyond what was allotted at design time. This often leads to error within applications when the program code tries to assign data to a storage allocation unit that doesn't exist. The other downside, although not usually quite as serious, is that when an array length is declared, it sets aside an amount of memory that corresponds to the specified number of allocation units. Thus, if a fixed array is bigger than need be, resources that could otherwise be used elsewhere are wasted because they're storing nothing but empty space.

Declaring Fixed Arrays

By now you should be familiar with declaring variables in VB, so you won't find the code used to declare an array mysterious at all. You simply make use of the previously seen keywords, such as Dim, Private, Public, or Static. Thus, an array declaration would have the following syntax:

```
Dim Name of Array (Length) As Data Type
```

For example, if you needed an array called "A" to hold 34 integer values, you could declare it using the following code:

```
Dim A(33) As Integer
```

The array's length is 33—even though the array needs to hold 34 values—because arrays begin their memory allocation units by starting at 0. Thus, array A has allocation units that number from 0 to 33, for a total of 34 storage spaces.

If it's difficult to get used to this default convention, an alternate way in VB 6.0 declares an array so that it begins at 1. VB also allows you to specify an index (length) range when you declare your array. Thus, you also could code the previous example as follows:

```
Dim A(1 To 34) As Integer
```

This time the array would also possess 34 allocation units, only now they would number from 1 to 34 instead of 0 to 33. Please note that the syntax <lower bound> To <upper bound> is no longer natively supported for specifying the array bounds in VB .NET. This is because in VB .NET, all arrays are zero-based. However, as mentioned previously, you can bring about these same boundary conditions by using the System.Array class to generate a custom array. For example, you could create the previous array with 1 to 34 bounds in VB .NET using the following code:

```
Dim NumElements() As Integer = {34}
Dim LowBound() As Integer = {1}
Dim CustomArray As Array = _
Array.CreateInstance(GetType(Integer), NumElements, LowBound)
```

You can see that you use the functionality of the System.Array class to create a custom array. To do this, invoke the CreateInstance method to lay out a user-defined array type. Specify that the custom array will contain data of the Integer data type, and then specify the number of elements, as well as the value of the lower bound. Then, declare the custom array using the user-defined array type just laid out. Doing this for every array probably isn't worth it, but it may be useful where specifying boundary conditions helps to simplify program logic, especially where the array index differs greatly from some other index needed to describe the data point.

Dynamic Arrays

Unlike fixed arrays, dynamic array lengths aren't set at design time, but at runtime. Dynamic arrays are highly useful because they are much more flexible than static arrays: Their lengths can adjust to suit the application's needs, and so, theoretically, they should never take up unnecessary system resources. The downside is that one program bug could make the array grow too large and demand more resources than are available, causing the program to crash. This is a rare occurrence, however, because Windows memory management does a fairly good job of allocating the needed resources.

For example, say you want to code a program that calculates the mole fractions for all of the components in any solution. You might use dynamic arrays in this application because you have no idea how many components are actually in the solution. Thus, the user would enter the number of components and the required data for each component, and the dynamic array would be sized to hold the data that corresponds to that number of components.

Declaring Dynamic Arrays

At this point, you're probably curious as to how this dynamic resizing works, so let's look at how these arrays are declared. As you saw with fixed arrays, a Dim (or other keyword) statement is used when they are initially declared, but with one minor modification: The parentheses are left empty because a length is not yet specified. This is accomplished as follows:

```
Dim A( ) As Single
```

For example, say your application reads the number of components, called "N," for the mole fraction application just discussed. You can now take advantage of the ReDim statement, which allows you to redeclare the array length. Thus, you set A to possess N storage units as follows:

More Traditional VB 6.0 Method

```
ReDim A(N - 1) As Single
```

In VB .NET, the preceding statement would be just `ReDim A(N-1)` because VB .NET disallows the use of As construct in ReDim statement. This gives an array with 0 to N − 1 storage units for a total of N storage units. Alternatively, VB 6.0 could use the following code:

```
ReDim A(1 To N) As Single
```

VB .NET doesn't support this code because the usage of To and As in a ReDim statement is illegal. In either case, you now can work with an appropriately sized array.

Table 5-1. Advantages and Disadvantages of Fixed and Dynamic Arrays

	FIXED ARRAYS	**DYNAMIC ARRAYS**
ADVANTAGES	Set array length so you don't have to account for changing upper and lower bounds.	Variable length can preserve resources by adjusting array to ideal size for the situation.
DISADVANTAGES	If not sized appropriately when declared, it can be either too small to hold all of the data, or too large and waste system resources.	Must be careful to code all of your loop structures (and the like) so that they can work with the changing boundary conditions.
WHEN TO USE	Exact number of elements is known, and this number of elements remains unchanged throughout the application.	Exact number of elements is not known at design time and/or the number elements changes throughout the lifetime of the application.

The LBound and UBound Functions

After all of this talk of changing lengths and changing boundary conditions, you may be wondering how to determine an array's upper and lower bounds at any point in your application. You easily can accomplish this by using the LBound function to return the array's lower bound, and the UBound function to return the upper bound. These functions return integer values that correspond to the index value of the first and last elements. The syntax for these functions is as follows:

```
'Returns Upper Boundary Value
UBound(arrayname)
```

In VB .NET, however, it's generally unnecessary to apply the LBound function to noncustom arrays, since all VB .NET arrays are zero-based. Thus, under these circumstances, the LBound function should always return zero. Later on, this chapter discusses how these two functions and Determinate loop structures are used together. You can cycle through all of the elements of a dynamic array by going from `LBound(arrayname) To UBound(arrayname)`.

The Preserve Keyword

Keep in mind when utilizing the ReDim statement that every time an array is redeclared, all of the data previously stored in the array is lost. That is, arrays of any of the numerical data types are set back to zero, and arrays of the String data type are set back to "" (null value). Thus, to make multiple ReDim statements while keeping all of your previously stored data, you must employ the Preserve keyword. This keyword lets you to adjust the length of the array while maintaining any data that is already stored in the array.

For example, assume you have a dynamic array of Shorts, X, that you've already "ReDim"ed to have five allocation units. The application also has read data into the array, so that all five storage units are filled. Now you need to redeclare the array to hold seven pieces of data, but it's critical that you don't lose any of the previously stored values. VB 6.0 accomplishes this as follows:

```
ReDim Preserve X(6) As Short
```

In VB .NET, it is just `ReDim Preserve X(6)`. If you examine the contents of this array, you find that X retains its data in the allocation units 0 to 4, and two new allocation units, 5 and 6, are added. Allocation units 5 and 6 initially possess the default value of zero, just like any newly declared variable.

Keep in mind, however, that all of the data may not be retained if an array is redeclared to have fewer allocation units than the original array. For example, if you coded

```
ReDim Preserve X(3)
```

you'd discover that although the data stored in slots 0 to 3 was left untouched, the data stored in allocation unit 4 was lost because that storage unit no longer exists.

Multidimensional Arrays

Up to this point, the chapter has dealt with different types of 1-D arrays. These types of arrays are useful for storing and organizing information into a list-like format, but scientific applications often require more sophisticated data structures, such as when dealing with mathematical matrices. Here, multidimensional arrays become increasingly useful and important.

For example, consider a two-dimensional (2-D) array, which is the simplest form of multidimensional arrays. Two-dimensional arrays store data in what you easily can picture as a tabular format. Think of the first dimension as the number of rows, and the second dimension as the number of columns. Thus, you could refer to the individual allocation unit and the data stored within it simply by specifying the row number and the column number. Two-dimensional arrays are of great use in scientific programs because they allow for the manipulation of mathematical matrices. In fact, later in this chapter you'll use such arrays to code the powerful mathematical routines of Gaussian elimination and Gauss-Siedel iteration.

Arrays can extend well beyond two dimensions, however. In fact, VB can support up to 60 dimensions in a statically declared array (with a normal Dim statement), and up to eight dimensions in dynamically declared arrays (ReDim statement). The total number of storage elements present in an array is equal to the product obtained from multiplying the number of storage slots in each dimension. Thus, many of these arrays can hold an extraordinary amount of information. For example, an array with 60 dimensions and only two storage units in each dimension can hold an astounding 2^{60} or approximately $1.2 * 10^{18}$ entries. However, don't feel intimidated by this; it's rare to see more than two- or three-dimensional arrays in most applications.

> **TIP** *If you plan to use the second and third dimensions to store a variety of descriptors for a particular item, you may want to choose a database structure. A large number of descriptors are often better suited for a database record format. For example, a contact database holds a name, address, phone numbers, email addresses, etc., for each name in the database.*

Declaring Multidimensional Arrays

Luckily, declaring multidimensional arrays isn't much different from declaring the one-dimensional arrays you've already seen. In fact, the only difference is that you must specify a length or index range for each dimension. For example, say you need a three-dimensional (3-D) array of Doubles with ten elements in each dimension. You could declare such an array as

```
Dim X(9, 9, 9) As Double
```

or you could use the alternate declaration method and write (in VB 6.0)

```
Dim X(1 To 10, 1 To 10, 1 To 10) As Double
```

In either case, you'd end up with your desired 3-D array. VB .NET doesn't support the previous syntax. It's worth reiterating that VB .NET arrays are all zero-based. However, as with the earlier 1-D array, you can create custom arrays using the System.Array class. To accomplish this, just add the extra dimensional descriptors to the NumElements and LowBound arrays as follows:

```
Dim NumElements() As Integer = {10, 3}
Dim LowBound() As Integer = {1, 1}
```

The rest of the code remains exactly the same. In this particular case, you would have declared an array that goes from 1 to 10 in the first dimension and 1 to 3 in the second dimension.

Dynamic arrays work similarly. First, declare the array using open parentheses, and then use the ReDim statement, as follows:

VB 6.0 Code
```
Dim A( ) As Double
ReDim A(N, N+1) As Double
```

In VB .NET, the equivalent of the above pair of statements is

```
Dim A( , ) As Double
ReDim A(N, N+1)
```

Please pay particular attention to the comma in the first statement. It's placed between the parentheses, in contrast to the empty parentheses in the VB 6.0 version. This is because VB .NET doesn't allow you to change the rank in a ReDim. Thus, for a 3-D array, a typical declaration and subsequent ReDim would be

```
Dim A( , ,)
ReDim A(9, 9, 9)
```

This time, notice the two commas between the parentheses.

The Preserve keyword also would retain any information previously assigned to the array. Furthermore, remember that multidimensional arrays can be Private, Public, or Static.

The Erase Statement

With all of the talk of arrays and memory management, you may want to know how to free up the resources that an array possesses, but that are no longer in use. This can be accomplished simply by using the keyword Erase. For example, to reclaim some memory from a dynamic array A, you use the following code:

```
Erase A
```

This statement then reallocates all of the memory space set aside for array A so that the space is used for other purposes.

> **NOTE** *Keep in mind that the Erase statement will work only for dynamic arrays. Using an Erase statement with a fixed array won't reclaim any resources, but instead will set the elements of the array back to their default values (such as zero).*

For...Next Loops

This chapter will digress from arrays in order to introduce the concept of loop structures. While loop structures can be used for many purposes other than arrays (as you'll see), they're invaluable for manipulating the different elements found within an array. For...Next loops first establish a counter variable, which is almost always of one of the integer data types. This counter variable is assigned a starting value and an ending value. A coded action contained within the loop then is executed, and the counter variable's value is modified by some set increment (normally one). This action and variable modification then repeats until the ending value of the counter is reached. At this point, the action no longer repeats and the loop terminates. Most programmers use I as the counter variable. The syntax for such a loop is as follows:

```
Dim I As Short
For I = Start Value To End Value Step Counter Increment
      Some Action
Next I
```

As you can see, the For...Next loop gets its name because the two words are vital to the coding of such a loop structure. Also, note that not all For...Next loops possess the Step keyword. Step is required only if the counter is modified by an increment other than +1. A change of +1 is the default increment in VB, so any loop in which I changes by +1 doesn't require this. It's optional to use a counter variable adjacent to the Next keyword, as in Next I, but it is a good programming practice whose utility stands out, particularly when working with deeply nested For...Next loops.

> **NOTE** *When working with For...Next loops, keep in mind that the most common error is to have the loop either execute one too many times or one too few times. Be careful that the loop structure that you need to repeat 10 times does not repeat 9 or 11 times, instead.*

A Factorial Calculator

Now that you have a basic understanding of For...Next loops, you'll code a simple example program. First, add two text boxes and a command button to a new VB .NET project form, as shown in Figure 5-1.

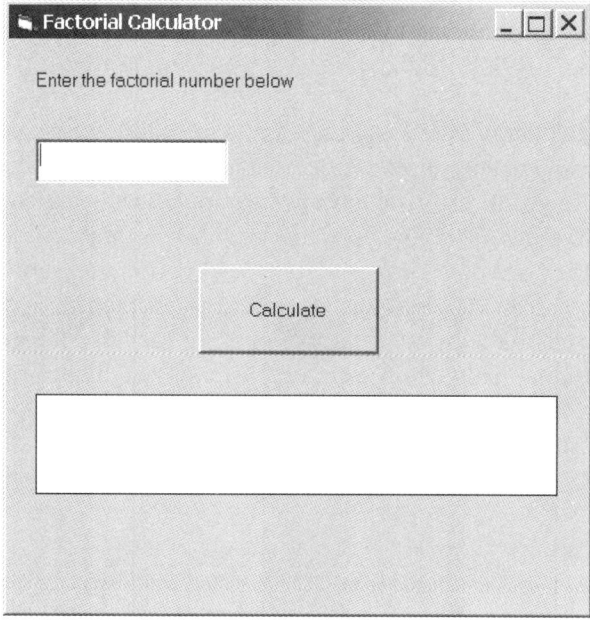

Figure 5-1. The factorial calculator GUI

Now, add the following code to the command button's Click event:

```
Dim Num, I As Short
Dim Ans As Double
Num = CShort(TextBox1.Text)
Ans = 1
    For I = Num To 1 Step -1
            Ans = Ans * I
    Next I
TextBox2.Text = Num & "! is equal to " & Ans
```

Run the application to examine what happens in the program and, especially, the loop structure (see Figure 5-2).

1.   Declare the variables and read in the required data, as you've seen before.

2.   Set the Ans variable equal to 1. This is critical to the application's success because the default value for any variable is equal to 0.

3.   Move on to the first loop statement, which states that the loop counter starts at the same value as Num.

4.   The loop repeats until I is equal to 1 and 1 will be subtracted (Step –1) from I with each loop execution.

5.   As you move into the loop itself, notice that the variable Ans is set equal to 1 (its current value) multiplied by I.

6.   The loop then repeats and Ans is set equal to Num (its new current value) multiplied by I (Num – 1). The loop then continues to repeat.

7.   Finally, when I equals 1, the loop terminates and the value of Ans is outputted in Text2.

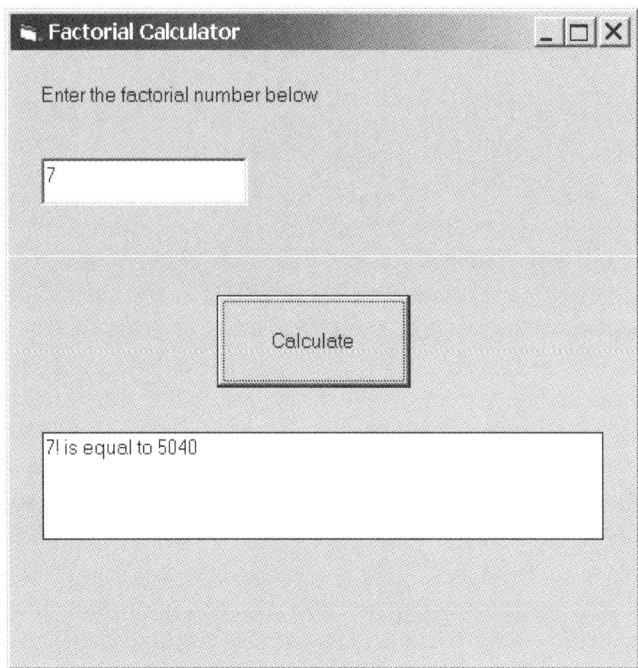

Figure 5-2. The factorial calculator in action

Nested For...Next Loops

Single For...Next loops, you can imagine, are of great use to the scientific or engineering programmer. However, nested loops allow for coding even more powerful mathematical routines. A nested loop is a simple concept: They're really nothing more than a loop(s) within a loop. Nested For...Next loops are especially useful for manipulating multidimensional arrays because you can use each loop within the nested structure to iterate through one of the array's dimensions, as you'll see in the upcoming Gaussian elimination routine. The syntax of such loop structures is generally as follows:

```
Dim I, J As Short
For I = Start Value 1 To End Value 1
    For J = Start Value 2 To End Value 2
        Some Action
    Next J
Next I
```

These loops can have different starting and ending values, and each loop can even have a different Step value attached to it. Also, most programmers usually use the notation of I for the outermost loop and counter names such as J and K for the more interior loops. Use a different counter name for each loop, however; multiple loops modifying the same counter variable will likely lead to program errors. Also, make sure that all of your counter variables' bounds are accurate. One of the most common errors in the programming of loop structures is the "off by one" error. In other words, one of the loops cycled one too many times or one too few times, and led to errors. These errors often can be very tough to track down, especially with heavily nested loops.

Gaussian Elimination

With this example you'll see several important objectives of this chapter in action. First, you'll see a nested For...Next loop, as well as the use of one-dimensional and multidimensional arrays. Second, the program will show you how to use For...Next loops to manipulate arrays in order to create powerful analytical tools. Before you get into the coding of Gaussian elimination, however, take a look at what Gaussian elimination is and how it operates.

How Gaussian Elimination Works

Gaussian elimination is a highly useful mathematical routine that allows users to solve for N unknowns in N distinct linear equations. The routine sequentially eliminates unknowns until it obtains an equation where only one unknown remains. It then solves for this unknown and back-substitutes it into a previous equation to solve for a second unknown. The back-substitution then repeats until all of the unknowns are solved for. To clarify, consider the following system of distinct linear equations:

$$\text{Equation \#1: } X1 + X2 + X3 = 6$$
$$\text{Equation \#2: } 2X1 + X2 + 3X3 = 13$$
$$\text{Equation \#3: } X1 + 5X2 + 2X3 = 17$$

The first step of a Gaussian elimination is to eliminate the variable X1 from equation 2 as follows:

$$2X1 + X2 + 3X3 = 13$$
$$-2(X1 + X2 + X3 = 6)$$
$$\overline{ 0 - X2 + X3 = 1}$$

This elimination process repeats to also remove the variable X1 from equation 3, and leaves us with the following set of equations:

Equation #1: X1 + X2 + X3 = 6
Equation #2: 0 – X2 + X3 = 1
Equation #3: 0 + 4X2 + X3 = 11

After the first round of eliminations is complete, a second round of eliminations begins to remove the variable X2 from equation 3. This elimination occurs as follows:

$$4X2 + X3 = 11$$
$$\underline{4(–X2 + X3 = 1)}$$
$$0 + 5X3 = 15$$

This second round of eliminations yields the following equations:

Equation #1: X1 + X2 + X3 = 6
Equation #2: 0 – X2 + X3 = 1
Equation #3: 0 + 0 + 5X3 = 15

As you can see, the variable coefficients in the equations form a triangular matrix, and the last features only one unknown variable (X3). The Gaussian elimination routine then solves for this unknown:

$$5X3 = 15$$
$$X3 = 15/5 = 3$$

Now that you know the value of X3, you can back-substitute it into equation 2 and solve for X2.

$$–X2 + X3 = 1$$
$$–X2 + 3 = 1$$
$$X2 = 2$$

Finally, this process of back-substitution can repeat to solve for X1. In this case, both the values of X2 and X3 are substituted into equation 1. Solving this equation lets you know that X1 was equal to 1.

As you can see, this process can be quite tedious and time-consuming for a large set of equations/unknowns. However, VB easily can automate this technique by reading all of the variable coefficients and equation solutions (i.e., 6 for equation 1) into a 2-D matrix (array). For example, consider that each equation from the example is in the form AX1 + BX2 + CX3 = #. Table 5-2 illustrates how the 2-D mathematical matrix would look.

Table 5-2. Two-Dimensional Matrix

A	B	C	#
1	1	1	6
2	1	3	13
1	5	2	17

VB code could then easily manipulate these matrix elements to get the same results as your hand-calculated solution.

Gaussian Elimination with VB

Now that you understand Gaussian elimination, you can code a VB application to solve the system of equations shown previously. First, start with a new VB .NET project form, and add a single command button to the form, as shown in Figure 5-3. This interface is much simpler than the previous interfaces because it doesn't support any direct user data entry. This doesn't mean that direct user data entry is impossible for mathematical matrices, however.

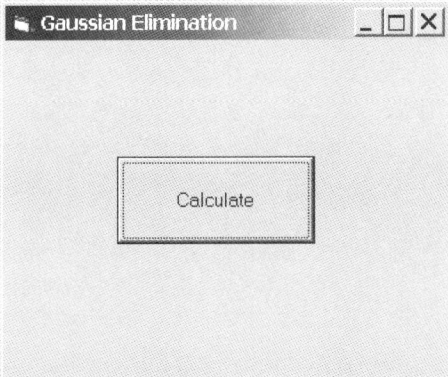

Figure 5-3. The GUI to the Gaussian elimination application

As the book progresses, techniques will demonstrate the entry of mathematical matrices and other data sets into a spreadsheet-like interface. These techniques involve elements of VB programming not yet covered and involve a control not yet discussed: the MSFlexGrid control. The scientific and engineering use of this control, however, can be quite useful. Thus, later in the book a whole chapter is devoted to using this control to develop powerful spreadsheet interfaces for your applications.

> **NOTE** *The MSFlexGrid control is a subset of the capabilities found in VideoSoft's VSFlexGrid control. VideoSoft recently merged with APEX software and is now under the company name Component One. Their latest spreadsheet control is in the Component One FlexGrid for .NET.*

It's also worth mentioning that you often can use Excel spreadsheets as your interface, and with VBA (Visual Basic for Applications) programming, execute similar calculations. The current version of VBA behaves much like VB 6.0, but future releases of Microsoft Office will use VSA (Visual Studio for Applications). For now, though, return to this chapter's focal point of loops and arrays, and add the following code to the command button's Click event:

```
Dim N, M, I, J, K As Integer
Dim A(4, 5) As Double
N = 3
M = 4
A(1, 1) = 1
A(1, 2) = 1
A(1, 3) = 1
A(1, 4) = 6
A(2, 1) = 2
A(2, 2) = 1
A(2, 3) = 3
A(2, 4) = 13
A(3, 1) = 1
A(3, 2) = 5
A(3, 3) = 2
A(3, 4) = 17
```

The Gaussian Elimination
```
For K = 1 To N
    For J = (K + 1) To M
        For I = (K + 1) To N
            A(I, J) = A(I, J) - ((A(I, K) * A(K, J)) / A(K, K))
        Next I
    Next J
Next K
```

Back-Substitution

```
Dim x(4) As Double
Dim Y(4) As Double
If A(N, N) = 0 Then
    x(N) = 0
Else
    x(N) = A(N, M) / A(N, N)
End If
For I = (N - 1) To 1 Step -1
    For J = I + 1 To N
        Y(I) = Y(I) + A(I, J) * x(J)
    Next J
    x(I) = (A(I, M) - Y(I)) / A(I, I)
Next I
MsgBox ("X1= " & x(1) & ": X2= " & x(2) _
    & ": X3= " & x(3))
```

Now that you've entered all of the required code, look at how the code performs the Gaussian elimination routine.

First, define the variables required to perform the routine, and set the variable N equal to the number of matrix rows and M equal to the column number. You may have noticed that all of the declared arrays are one element larger than necessary, and the 0 element is ignored. This is done solely to make the elimination code easier to follow because it simplifies the use of the counter variables. Once you fully understand the routine, you may want to try recoding it without this feature.

Following this, define each element in the matrix array (A) by modifying the index numbers that correspond to the different matrix rows and columns (i.e., A(Row #, Column #)). For a challenge, try putting your own interface on the routine by using 12 text boxes to read this same data into the matrix array. You can place these 12 text boxes on the form at design time, but this can be a little tedious and cumbersome. It's better to use an elegant VB feature called a *dynamic control array,* which allows a large number of similar controls to be treated as a logical group. You need to draw only one text box at design time. The rest of the text boxes can be created and positioned dynamically at runtime.

Once all of the data is read into the array, you can manipulate it using nested loops. For this particular routine, the elimination part involves three nested loops. If you follow these loops through, you'll notice that these loops sequentially eliminate the variables X1 and X2 in the required equations, until a triangular matrix remains. The bottom row of this matrix corresponds to the equation that contains the single unknown.

Now that the routine's elimination part is complete, the back-substitution can begin. This process involves two additional 1-D arrays, x and Y. Array x holds the final "unknown" solutions and array Y stores the contributions to the equation solution of the solved for variables.

1. The back-substitution solves for the unknown variable (X3) present in the bottom row of the triangular matrix.

2. Another nested loop structure is initiated.

3. On the first pass, this structure takes the second to last equation of the matrix, and computes X3's contribution to the overall equation solution. This value is then subtracted from the equation solution, and the value of X2 is solved for.

4. The next pass determines and subtracts the contributions of both X2 and X3. X1 is then solved for.

5. Once all of the answers are calculated, the results are displayed in a message box (see Figure 5-4). The unknown values in this message box match exactly the hand-calculated solution worked out earlier.

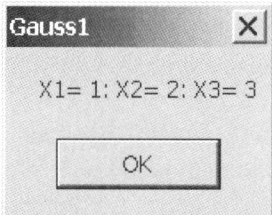

Figure 5-4. The results of our Gaussian elimination

Indeterminate Loops (Do...Loops)

The For...Next loops just discussed are often referred to as *determinate loops*; they loop through their routine a predetermined number of times. VB, however, supports another useful class of loops called *indeterminate loops*. These loops will repeat their action until either a certain condition is met or a certain condition is no longer met. As you'll see, indeterminate loops are extremely useful in coding routines that perform different types of mathematical iterations.

The Do...Until Loop

The first type of loop is the most commonly used indeterminate loop in scientific programming, the Do...Until loop. This loop will execute its action until a predetermined condition is met. For mathematical programs, this predetermined condition is most often some type of convergence criterion or level of accuracy, but any Boolean (True/False) expression can be used. This loop has the following syntax:

```
Do
    This Action
Loop Until This Condition
```

or

```
Do Until This Condition
    This Action
Loop
```

The only difference between these two structures is when the conditional test is encountered. In the first structure, the action executes at least once. In the second structure, the action executes zero or more times, depending on the condition's result. Thus, when coding your applications, consider where this condition belongs in the program logic. You must ask yourself if you need the condition to be checked before the action is executed, or after the action has already executed.

X-Intercept Calculator

Now that you've seen the basic syntax of the Do...Until loop, look at an example program to get a better understanding of its operation. You are probably aware that calculating the Y-intercept of a function is quite easy, yet determining the X-intercept for a nonlinear function can be quite difficult. However, using Do...Until loops, you can code an iterative mathematical routine to determine the X-intercept of most functions.

This technique works by asking the program user to specify the estimated range where the function crosses the X-axis. Plotting out the function can yield a good estimation, although reading the intercept off a graph won't generate the level of accuracy this technique provides. For your purposes, call the minimum range value X1 and the maximum range value X3 (see Figure 5-5). The general slope trend of the function, positive or negative, is determined within that range, and the range midpoint value, X2, also is calculated.

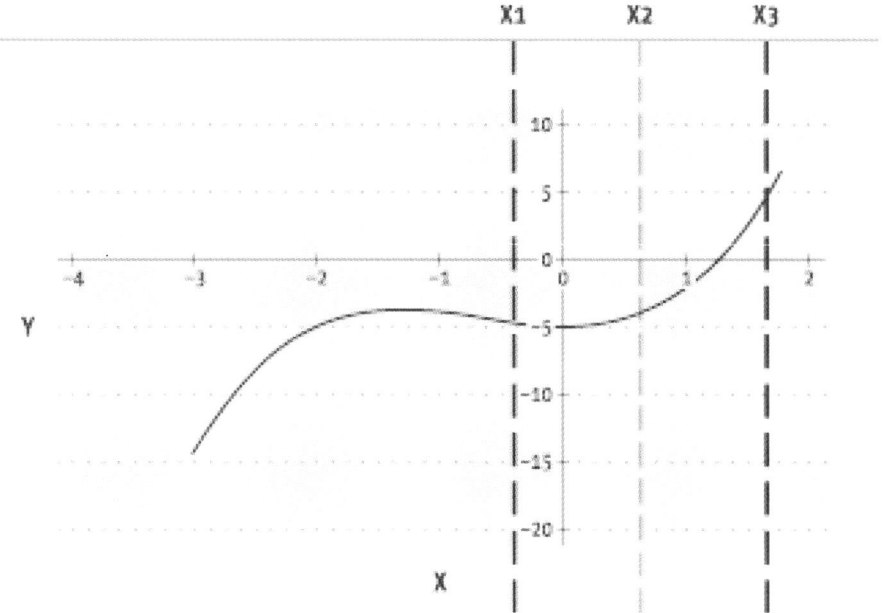

Figure 5-5. Sample range defined by X1 and X3

Next, the value of the function at point X2 is determined. Based on the value of the slope and the value of the function (Y) at X2, there are the following possibilities.

- If Y is positive and X2 is positive, then X2 becomes the new value of X3, and a new value of X2 is determined.

- If both values are negative, X2 also becomes the value of X3 and a new X2 is calculated.

- If one value is positive and the other value negative, then X2 becomes the new value of X1 and a new X2 is calculated.

This process will repeat, narrowing down the range of possible values, until the value of Y(X2) <= 0.0 (to the specified accuracy).

Now that you understand how this technique works, you can write your application. First, take a new project form and add seven text boxes named Text1, Text2, and so on up to Text7, and a command button, as shown in Figure 5-6.

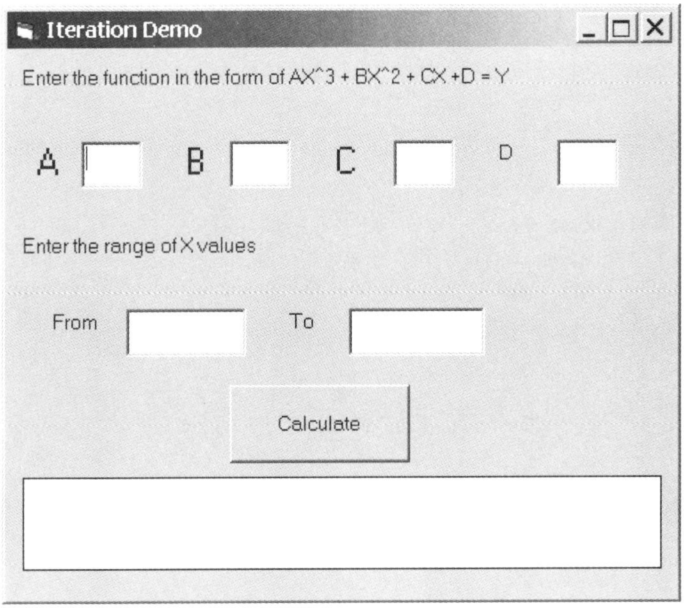

Figure 5-6. GUI for our intercept calculator

Now, add the following code to the command button's Click event:

```
Dim A, B, C, D As Single
Dim X1, X2, X3 As Double
Dim Y, Slope, Y1, Y3 As Double
Dim Count As Integer
A = CSng(Text1.Text)
B = CSng(Text2.Text)
C = CSng(Text3.Text)
D = CSng(Text4.Text)
X1 = CSng(Text5.Text)
X3 = CSng(Text6.Text)
Y1 = (A * (X1 ^ 3)) + (B * (X1 ^ 2)) + (C * X1) + D
Y3 = (A * (X3 ^ 3)) + (B * (X3 ^ 2)) + (C * X3) + D
Slope = (Y3 - Y1) / (X3 - X1)
If Slope > 0 Then
    Do
        Count = Count + 1
        X2 = ((X1 + X3) / 2)
        Y = (A * (X2 ^ 3)) + (B * (X2 ^ 2)) + (C * X2) + D
        If Y < 0 Then
            X1 = X2
```

```
            ElseIf Y > 0 Then
                X3 = X2
            Else
                X2 = X2
            End If
        Loop Until Math.Round(Y * 1000000000) = 0 Or Count = 100
        'VB 6.0 does not _ require_ the Round function
        'to be prefixed with Math.
    ElseIf Slope < 0 Then
        Do
            Count = Count + 1
            X2 = ((X1 + X3) / 2)
            Y = (A * (X2 ^ 3)) + (B * (X2 ^ 2)) + (C * X2) + D
            If Y > 0 Then
                X1 = X2
            ElseIf Y < 0 Then
                X3 = X2
            Else
                X2 = X2
            End If
        Loop Until Math.Round(Y * 1000000000) = 0 Or Count = 100
    End If
    If Count < 100 Then
        Text7.Text = "The function crosses the X axis at X= " & X2
    ElseIf Count = 100 Then
        Text7.Text = "The answer is not in the specified range"
    ElseIf Slope = 0 Then
        Text7.Text = "Modify Range"
    End If
```

As you can see, the program allows you to enter in any function that is a cubic or lower, but this program easily could expand to include even higher order equations. Remember, however, to fill in zero as the coefficient of any element missing from the equation (i.e., any of the coefficients A, B, C, or D). Next, the application calculates the function's general slope within that range. The range narrowing action isn't exactly the same for positive and negative sloping functions, so a conditional statement designates which Do...Until loop to use for the proper range-narrowing routine. In both cases, the routine repeats until $Y < 1 * 10^{-9}$. The word Round, used in this statement, simply rounds off the value of Y * 1000000000 to its nearest integer value. The value of X2 that results in this terminal Y value is then outputted.

You may have noticed that a second method terminates the loop if the value of Count reaches 100. This is because this routine normally converges on the right answer in far fewer than 100 iterations. So, if 100 iterations don't reach an answer, the answer likely doesn't lie in the specified range. If no answer is in the specified range, this loop may keep repeating in an endless cycle. It's good practice to avoid such situations, such as by providing an alternate termination mechanism.

Now that you understand the code and its function, test it out by entering the function –5X + 10 (see Figure 5-7).

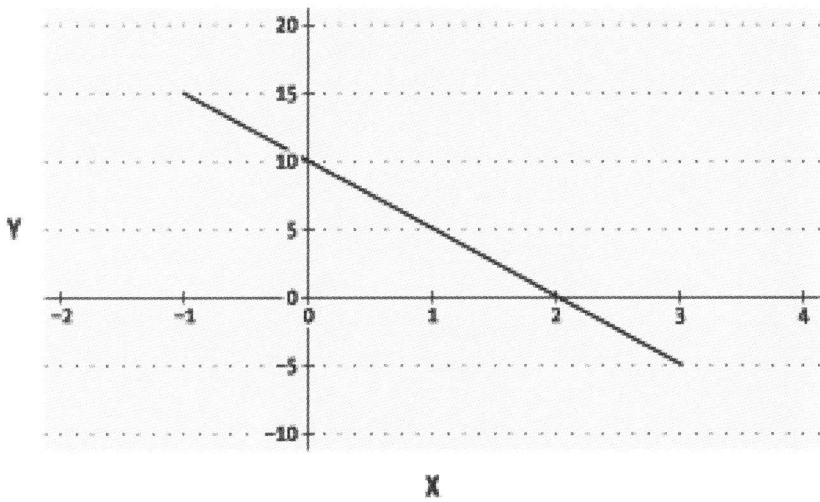

Figure 5-7. The function –5X + 10

This function type is linear, so it can easily show that X-intercept is at X = 2. When the program runs this function, it finds that the iteration calculates the intercept to be at X = 1.99999999997 or X = 2, for all practical purposes (see Figure 5-8).

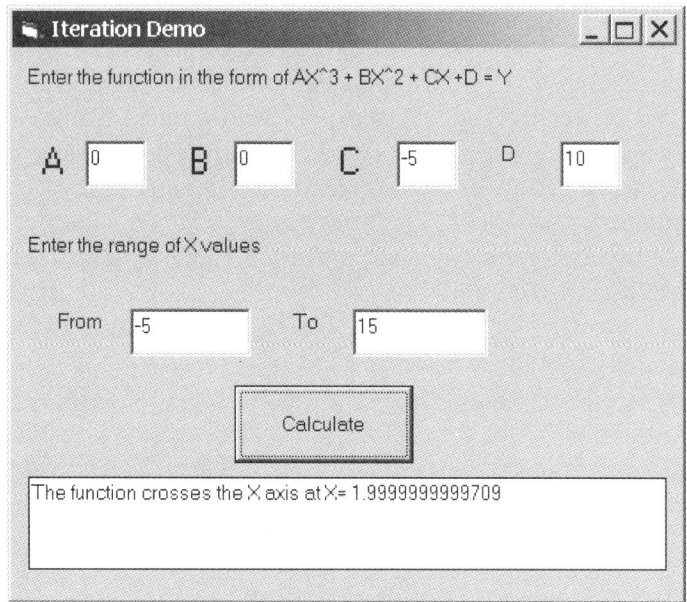

Figure 5-8. The results of our X-intercept calcultor for –5X + 10

Consider the more complex function of $X^3 + 2X^2 - 5$ (see Figure 5-9).

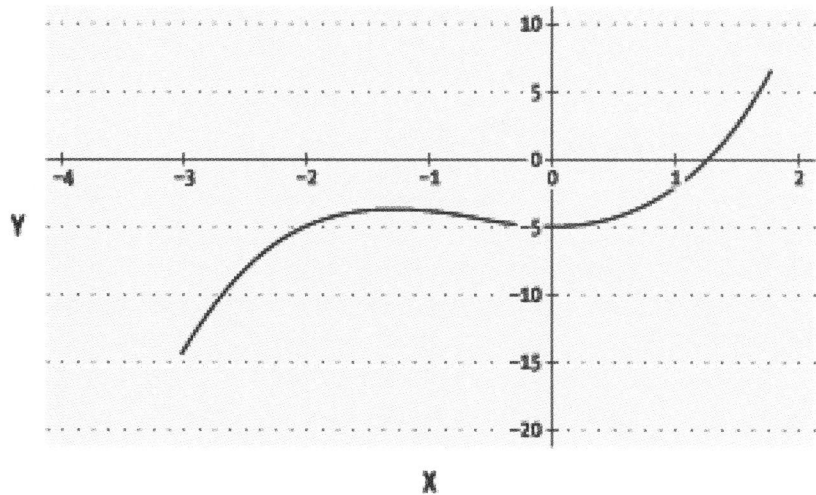

Figure 5-9. The function $X^3 + 2X^2 - 5$

The plot of the function shows that the intercept is at approximately 1.24, and in fact your iterative technique finds the intercept to be at 1.2418965 (see Figure 5-10).

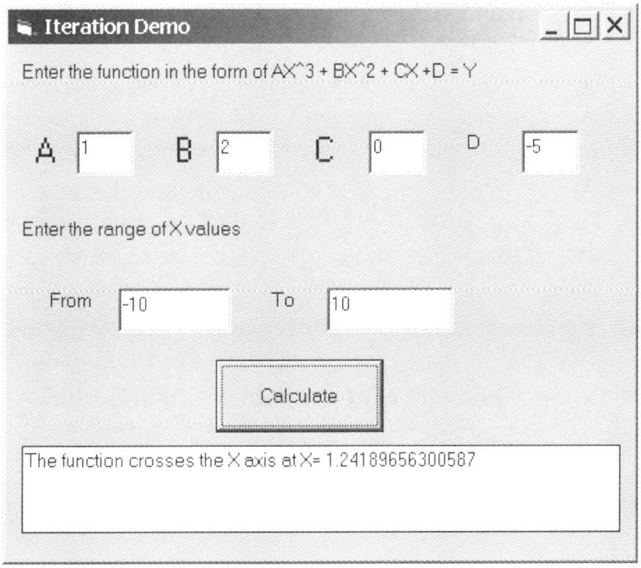

Figure 5-10. The results for X³ + 2X² –5

You can see that this technique applies to a variety of different functions. However, keep in mind that this technique can't solve all function occurrences. For example, if the function crosses the X-axis multiple times, make sure the range only includes one intercept at a time (this is why first plotting the function is a good idea). Also, this technique won't be able to handle parabolas where the minimum or maximum is at Y = 0. The function must have a portion below the X-axis and a portion above the axis.

The Do...While Loop

This loop structure is almost identical to the Do...Until loop, except that the loop doesn't repeat until a certain condition comes into existence, but as long as a certain condition exists. Even the syntax of the Do...While loop is almost identical:

```
Do
     This Action
Loop While This Condition
```

or

```
Do While This Condition
     This Action
Loop
```

In fact, you might have noticed that Loop...While X > 2 has exactly the same effect as Loop...Until X <= 2. This means that you can use these loops interchangeably. However, you should use the loop structure that corresponds closest to the logic of the problem in order to avoid confusion and to keep things as simple and straightforward as possible.

Nested Loops Revisited

Just as you are able to code nested For...Next loops, so too are you able to code nested Do loops, as well as nested loops that combine Do...loops and For...Next loops. In fact, you can use nested loops that combine both structures to code iterative techniques that deal with arrays or mathematical matrices. For example, 2-D temperature distributions are often calculated by performing a Gauss-Siedel iteration on a mathematical matrix.

The Gauss-Siedel Iteration

For simple geometries, analytical techniques can calculate exact temperature distributions. However, these simple geometries rarely exist in real-world situations, and thus numerical techniques such as finite difference analysis are often employed. Unlike analytical techniques, finite difference techniques only allow for the calculation of temperature at discrete points. These points are selected by dividing a 2-D surface into regions, and setting the centermost point of a region as the reference point, or nodal point. The collection of all of these points on the surface is referred to as a *nodal network* or *nodal grid*. Each reference point of unknown temperature can then be defined by an energy balance equation. Therefore, if you have N unknown nodal points, you should end up with N equations. Each equation can be written as

$$a_{i1}T_1 + a_{i2}T_2 + \cdots + a_{iN}T_N = C_i$$

where the values of *a* are known coefficients that relate the unknown temperatures (*T*s) to the value of *C*, a known temperature. The temperature *T*s are present at the nodal points.

You can enter these coefficients of these nodal finite difference equations into an *N* x *N* array along with the values of *C* in another array of length *N*. An educated estimate of the temperature at each point *T* can help speed the iteration process. Enter these matrix elements in a diagonally dominant manner, which is required to perform a Gauss-Siedel iteration. This iteration solves for each unknown temperature (T) by employing the equation

$$T_i^{(k)} = \frac{C_i}{a_{ii}} - \sum_{j=1}^{i-1} \frac{a_{ij}}{a_{ii}} T_j^{(k)} - \sum_{j=i+1}^{N} \frac{a_{ij}}{a_{ii}} T_j^{(k-1)}$$

where i can be any value from 1 to N and k is the iteration number. The initial temperature values employed in the iteration are based on the educated guesses. This iterative technique repeats and refines its calculated values until every value meets the following convergence criterion:

$$\left| T_i^{(k)} - T_i^{(k-1)} \right| \le \varepsilon$$

You can manipulate the value of ε to ensure that the model performs all calculations to the desired level of accuracy.

At this point in time, you won't code a full application of this example, but you'll examine the code for the Gauss-Siedel iteration itself. This routine can be coded as

```
Do Until Conv = True
Conv = True
For I = 1 To N
    S1 = 0
    S2 = 0
    T1(I) = (C(I) / a(I, I))
    If I - 1 > 0 Then
        For J = 1 To I - 1
            S1 = S1 + (a(I, J) / a(I, I)) * T2(J)
        Next J
        T1(I) = T1(I) - S1
    End If
    If I + 1 <= N Then
        For K = I + 1 To N
            S2 = S2 + (a(I, K) / a(I, I)) * T2(K)
        Next K
        T1(I) = T1(I) - S2
    End If
    If T1(I) - T2(I) > E Then
        Conv = False
    End If
    T2(I) = T1(I)
Next I
Loop
```

In this code, the array a stores the N x N matrix, while the array C stores the different C values. The T2 array starts off holding the guessed temperature values, while the T1 array stores all of the calculated temperature values. Looking carefully at the code, you'll see that the Do loop repeats until all of the past and present iteration's temperature values are less than or equal to the convergence criterion E. The For...Next loops nested inside the Do...Until loop manipulate the various arrays so that the needed calculations are performed. Look back to the formula for the iteration and try to match up the code with the different elements of the equation. Try to familiarize yourself as much as possible with this routine; in the chapter on programming spreadsheets you'll revisit this routine and code a full application with a powerful and dynamic spreadsheet interface.

CHAPTER 6
Built-in Functions

WHILE YOU'VE MADE SOME LIMITED USE of functions throughout this book's various sample applications, functions haven't yet been formally discussed. Functions are a simple concept in that they're segments of code that perform a specific action or task. More specifically, functions perform an action, such as a mathematical calculation, that results in a single value being returned. This ability to return a single value sets functions apart from other types of procedures and subroutines, which can perform any set of tasks, including calculations, but don't explicitly return a value.

For example, you used several different functions to convert data entered into a text box (i.e., a string) into one of the various numerical data types (i.e., the function returned a single numerical value). You even used the Round function, which rounds numbers off to their nearest integer value in your X-intercept program. These built-in functions are generally commonly used tasks that come with the VB development environment. Many of these routines don't have to be custom coded each time, but can instead be called up with a keyword and the proper syntax.

This chapter provides an overview of the most relevant scientific programming functions. However, you should get acquainted with the help system to look up function uses and properties, because this chapter won't cover every possible function that comes with VB. For example, certain readers may be interested in many different specialized financial functions that are outside the scientific scope of this book.

Searching for functions with the help system is easy (see Figure 6-1).

1. Go to the Help menu and select the Search option. You'll see a search screen pop up in the right corner of your screen.

2. Enter your search query and set the filter to Visual Basic, so that you don't also get a listing of C++, C#, Platform SDK, or other topics.

3. When you're finished, click the Search button. You'll see a list of topics appear at the bottom of your screen. VB functions are listed alphabetically and by category, including Math Functions and Type Conversion Functions.

4. Choose the option that fits your needs. A list of the suitable functions in that category will appear on your screen. Select the name of the function that interests you, and a screen describing that particular function will appear. If you know the name of the function you're interested in you can also search for it by name and save yourself a few steps.

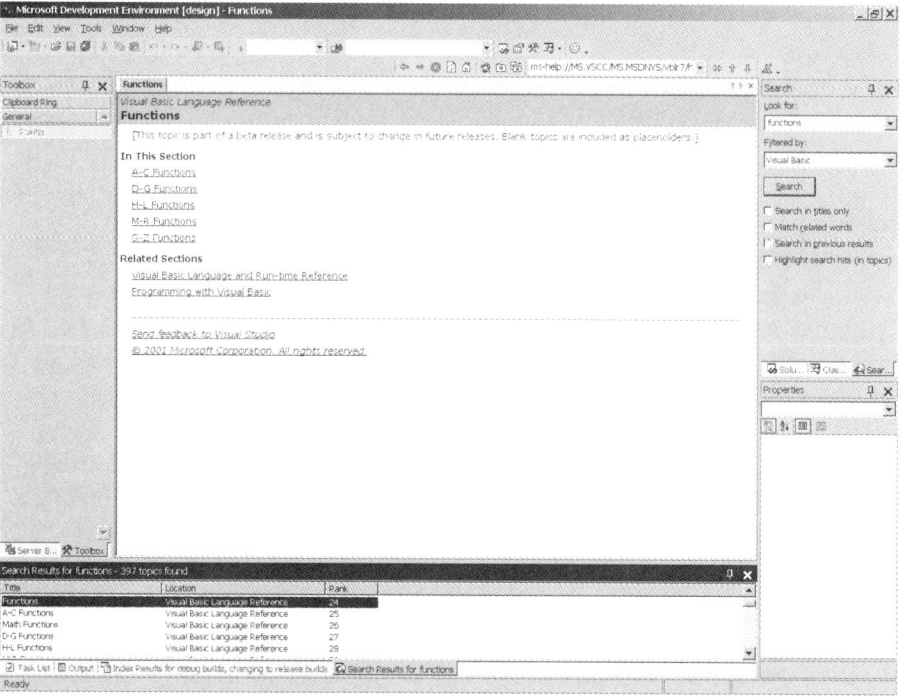

Figure 6-1. Accessing VS .NET help

Conversion Functions

You already used several of these functions in some of this book's example programs, so this chapter will cover them first. Their purpose is quite simple: They convert data of one type into data of another type. Their functionality is laid out in the System.ComponentModel namespace.

The CByte Function

The System.ComponentModel.ByteConverter class defines this function. It converts any integer value between 0 and 255 into a value of the Byte data type. A noninteger value is rounded to its nearest corresponding integer value. The function also accepts a string expression that evaluates to a value between 0 and 255.

The CChar Function

Defined by the System.ComponentModel.CharConverter class, this function converts any integer value between 0 and 65535 into its corresponding Unicode character. When the function is used in conjunction with a string instead of an integer value, only the first character of that string is converted to the Char data type.

The CDate Function

The System.ComponentModel.DateTimeConverter class defines this function. It converts any date found between January 1, 100 and December 31, 9999 into the Date data type. The date, however, must be in a format that VB recognizes as a valid date expression. VB recognizes almost all commonly used date notations as a valid format, but check your notation with the VB help section. The Regional Settings (in the Control Panel) of your computer determine the order of day, month, and year.

The CDbl Function

The System.ComponentModel.DoubleConverter class defines the CDbl function, which is among the most useful for scientific and engineering. It converts any numerical value or string expression that can evaluate to a number into a value of the Double data type. Bear in mind that, though unlikely, the value being converted can't exceed the Double values range that this data type holds.

The CDec Function

The System.ComponentModel.DecimalConverter class defines the Cdex function. Like the CDbl function, this function converts values into values of the Decimal data type; as with CDbl, you should make sure that the value being converted is within the acceptable range of values.

The CInt Function

The System.ComponentModel.Int32Converter class defines this function. Although similar to the CDbl and CDec functions, the CInt function only converts numeric values or string expressions that evaluate to a number into values of the integer data type. If the value to be converted isn't an integer, the value will round off to the nearest integer value. As with the CDbl function, remember that the value being converted can't exceed the limits set by the Integer data type.

The CLng Function

Defined by the System.ComponentModel.Int64Converter class, the CLng function works exactly the same as the CInt function, except that the value is converted into the Long data type. Noninteger values are rounded, and values can't exceed those set forth by the Long data type.

The CSng Function

The CSng function works just like the CDbl function, except that the values are converted into the Single data type. The System.ComponentModel.SingleConverter class defines this function. As with the other numeric data types, the value to be converted can't exceed the acceptable range provided by the Single data type.

The CStr Function

The System.ComponentModel.StringConverter class defines the CStr function, which changes a Boolean or numeric value, or a Date expression into a string. For example, if CStr changed the integer 12345 into a string equal to "12345," the value wouldn't be able to be manipulated mathematically. If you performed this function on a Boolean value, you'd end up with a string containing either the word "True" or "False."

Function Syntax

All of the preceding conversion functions use a similar syntax that has the general form of `Conversion Function (Expression)`. To illustrate this syntax, take a look at some examples.

```
Dim A as Integer
Text1.Text = "123" 'a string
A = CInt(Text1.Text)
```

If you execute this code, you find that A now equals the integer value 123. That is, 123 can now be manipulated mathematically, instead of as a string. You used this method in some of your previous examples to read in numeric information from text boxes.

These conversion functions, however, also can convert data between data types, and they aren't limited to accessing information from controls. For example, consider the following code:

```
Dim A as Integer
Dim B As String
Dim C As Single
Dim D As Boolean
A = 12345
C = CSng(A)
D = True
B = CStr(D)
```

If you execute this code, you find that C is a single-precision floating point equal to 12345.00, and not an integer value. You also find that B contains a string of letters that spell the word "True."

If you convert a real number value (i.e., Single, Double, etc.) back to an integer value, you find that VB rounds it off to the closest integer value. For example, if you convert the 54.2 into a Short, you end up with the integer 54. When doing these types of conversions, make sure that the variable you're converting doesn't exceed the variable's limits; otherwise, it will cause an error when the program runs. To illustrate, execute the following lines of code:

```
Dim A as Double
Dim B As Byte
A = 545.7786
B = CByte(A)
```

As you can see, VB can't handle this type of conversion because Byte variables are limited to values between 0 and 255. Thus, try at all costs to avoid converting from a larger to a smaller ranged data type (e.g., Long to Short) as you may exceed the smaller variable's range and induce program errors (see Figure 6-2).

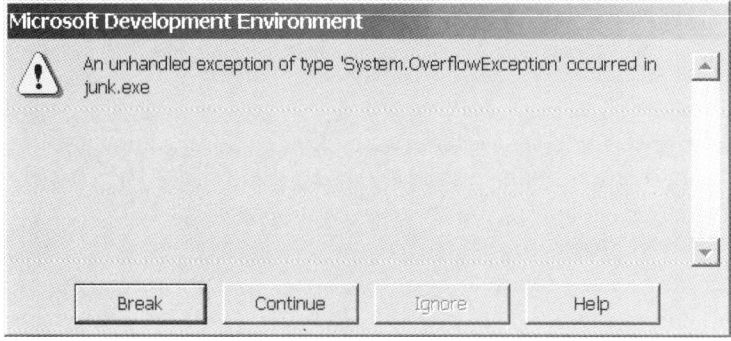

Figure 6-2. The error message you receive if you try to convert 545.7786 into a Byte variable

CBool Function and Syntax

The System.ComponentModel.BooleanConverter class defines the CBool function; as you'd expect, it converts values into the Boolean data type. It does this in two ways. First, it converts the integer 0 into a value of False and the integer 1 into a value of True. Second, it can return the value of a relational expression. It accomplishes these as follows:

```
Dim A, B as Boolean
Dim C, D as Short
C = 1
D = 0
A = CBool(C) 'A is True
B = CBool(C = D) 'B is False
```

This ability to convert a relational expression into a data value makes CBool slightly different from the other conversion functions. Just keep in mind that the expression must be able to be evaluated and, as with the other conversion functions, don't try to convert a non-Boolean value into the Boolean data type.

String Functions

String functions may not seem like the most scientifically relevant functions, but they can be quite useful, especially to biologists. With the surge of molecular biology and the wealth of biological data being generated, bioinformatics is a rapidly growing field. This bioinformatics data largely consists of DNA and protein sequences that can be treated as strings of characters. For example, the nucleotides adenine, guanine, thiamine, and cytosine compose DNA sequences. The letters A, T, C, and G represent these nucleotides, respectively. Thus, strings of the letters A, T, C, and G can represent DNA sequences. These strings make it possible to analyze DNA and protein sequence data. This section introduces this concept, but you can find more complete coverage in the upcoming chapter on bioinformatics. However, strings are also useful outside of biology; you can combine many of the following functions to create text-searching algorithms, as well as other types of alphanumeric data manipulation.

The Len Function

Simplest of all of the string functions, the Len function solely determines a given string's length. While this seems a meaningless task, it's actually one of the most widely used string functions. As a programmer, you won't always be given a string's exact number of characters, but you'll often need to perform some type of analysis that involves iterating through every character in the string, such as finding the compositions of each nucleotide in a DNA sequence. Understating or overstating the loops will likely generate incorrect results. Thus, it's important to keep the Len function in mind.

The Len function's syntax is extremely simple; it's illustrated in the following example that determines the number of nucleotides in a DNA sequence. To start off on this sample application, add a rich text box to a form. You'll use a rich text box instead of the standard text box because you, as programmer, have no idea how long the sequence/string might actually be. Next, add a label, a command button, and a normal text box named Text1 to the form as well (see Figure 6-3).

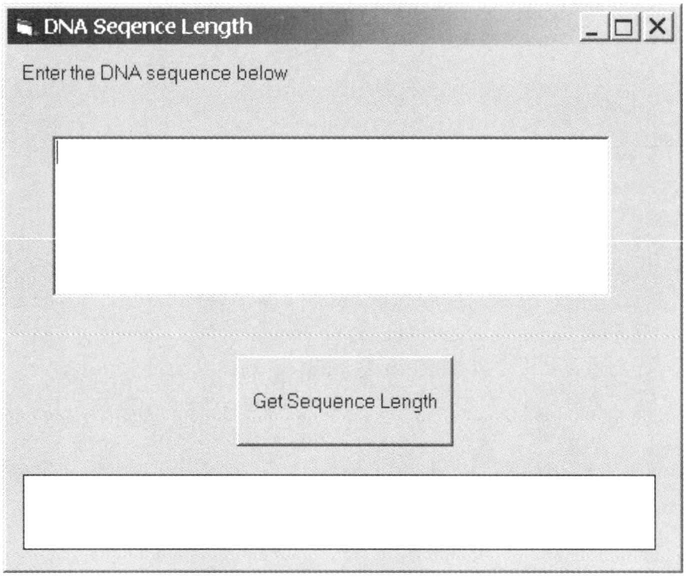

Figure 6-3. The sequence length program's interface

Now, add the following code to the command button's Click event:

```
Dim NucNum As Long
Dim Sequence As String
Sequence = RichTextBox1.Text
NucNum = Len(Sequence)
Text1.Text = "The DNA sequence contains " & NucNum & " nucleotides"
```

If you run this application, you see that the string is first read into the string variable Sequence. The Len function then determines the length of the string stored in Sequence. The numeric value, which corresponds to that length, is stored in NucNum. Last, the number of nucleotides is outputted to the text box (see Figure 6-4).

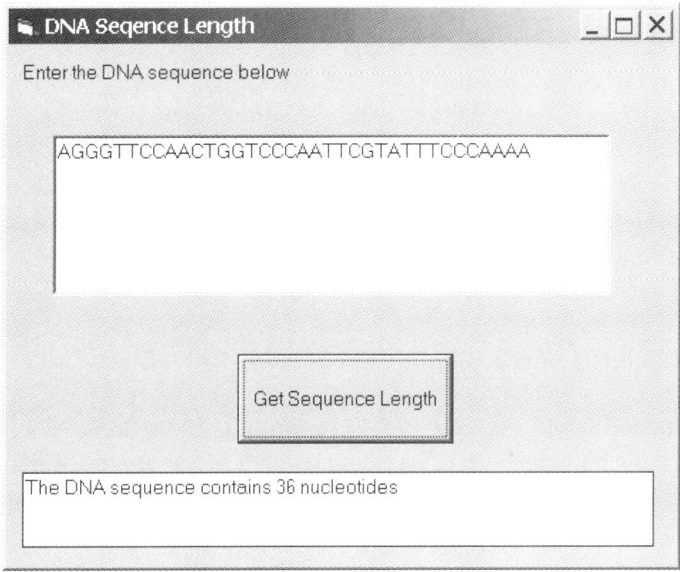

Figure 6-4. The number of nucleotides in our sequence

The Left and Right Functions

These functions share similar functions and syntaxes; they access character sequences from the beginning and the end of strings. The Left function collects the characters in the beginning of a string, while the Right function accesses the characters at the end of a string. Their syntax is as follows:

```
Left(String Name, Length)
Right(String Name, Length)
```

where Length specifies the number of characters that you seek to access. For example, to find out the first three and last three nucleotides in your Sequence string in VB 6.0, you'd code the following:

```
FirstThree = Left(Sequence, 3)
LastThree = Right(Sequence, 3)
```

In VB .NET, the seemingly benign-looking code simply wouldn't compile due to namespace considerations. The preceding string functions need to be "qualified" by the Microsoft.VisualBasic namespace. Also, the Left and Right functions happen to be members of the String class, which is part of the Microsoft.VisualBasic namespace. The following VB .NET code is the equivalent of the previous VB 6.0 code:

```
FirstThree = Microsoft.VisualBasic.Strings.Left(Sequence, 3)
LastThree = Microsoft.VisualBasic.Strings.Right(Sequence, 3)
```

These two functions aren't used extremely often, however, because most programmers turn to the more flexible and versatile Mid function, which the next section covers. The Mid function, however, doesn't suffer from namespace conflicts and can be used directly without the lengthy prefix that was necessary for the Left and Right functions.

The Mid Function

The Mid function works similarly to the Left and Right functions because it can access and pull characters out of an existing string. However, the Mid function is much more versatile; it can access characters anywhere in the string, not just at the beginning and the end. The Mid function has the following syntax:

```
Mid(String Name, Starting Character #, length)
```

Thus, if you have the DNA sequence ATTTACCGATTG stored in the variable Sequence and you want to access the second set of three nucleotides (i.e., a codon), you use the following code:

```
Codon2 = Mid(Sequence, 4, 3)
```

Executing this line of code yields the nucleotide sequence TAC, which is exactly what you were seeking.

Protein Molecular Weight Determination

The Mid function is very important to many bioinformatics routines, so take a deeper look now at the function by coding a sample application. This application reads in a sequence of amino acids in their single-letter representations and determines the protein's molecular weight. Lay out the form as you did for the DNA sequence length routine, only this time add the following code to the command button's Click event:

```
Dim Sequence As String
Dim MW, MW2 As Double
Dim I As Integer
Dim S As String
Sequence = RichTextBox1.Text
```

```
MW = 0
For I = 1 To Len(Sequence)
      S = Mid(Sequence, I, 1)
If  S = "G" Then
        MW = MW + 57
      ElseIf  S = "A" Then
              MW = MW + 71.1
    ElseIf  S = "V" Then
              MW = MW + 99.1
      ElseIf  S= "L" Then
              MW = MW + 113.2
      ElseIf  S = "I" Then
              MW = MW + 113.2
      ElseIf  S = "M" Then
              MW = MW + 131.2
      ElseIf  S = "P" Then
              MW = MW + 97.1
       ElseIf  S = "F" Then
              MW = MW + 147.2
    ElseIf  S = "W" Then
              MW = MW + 186.2
    ElseIf  S = "S" Then
              MW = MW + 87.1
      ElseIf  S = "T" Then
              MW = MW + 101.1
      ElseIf  S = "N" Then
              MW = MW + 114.1
      ElseIf  S = "Q" Then
              MW = MW + 128.1
      ElseIf  S = "Y" Then
              MW = MW + 163.2
      ElseIf  S = "C" Then
              MW = MW + 103.1
      ElseIf  S = "K" Then
              MW = MW + 128.2
      ElseIf  S = "R" Then
              MW = MW + 156.2
      ElseIf  S = "H" Then
              MW = MW + 137.1
      ElseIf  S = "D" Then
              MW = MW + 115.1
```

```
        ElseIf  S = "E" Then
                MW = MW + 129.1
        Else
                MsgBox ("is Not a valid entry!")
        End If
Next I
MW2 = (MW / 1000)
Text1.Text = "The Molecular Weight of the Protein is " & MW & " Daltons or " _
& MW2 & " KiloDaltons."
```

If you execute the routine you see that it uses a For . . . Next loop in conjunction with the Mid function to travel through the string's entire length and to examine each character one at a time. The Block If . . . Then statements evaluate each character and add the correct molecular weight to the total weight, based on the amino acid that the character represents. Finally, the results are outputted in a text box (see Figure 6-5).

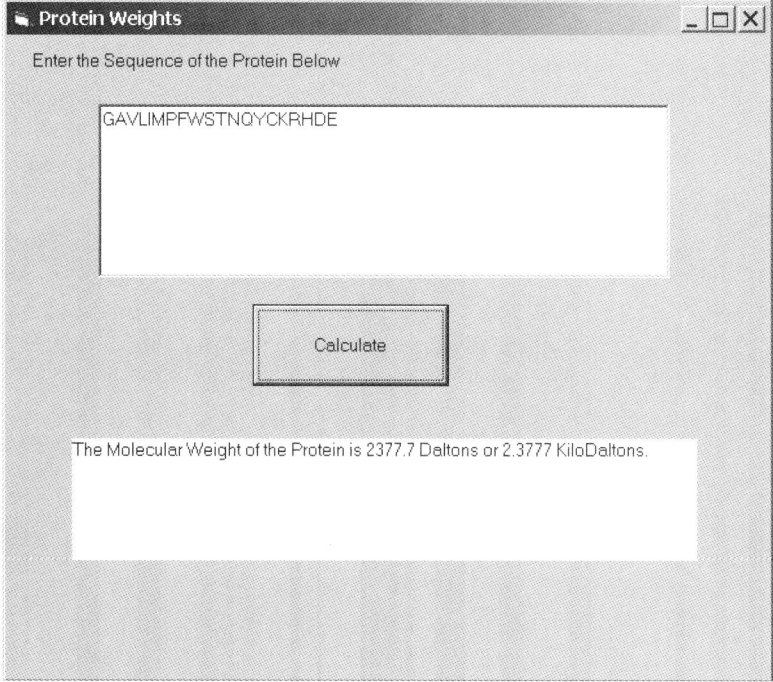

Figure 6-5. The amino acid sequence's resulting molecular weight

The LCase and UCase Functions

The LCase and UCase functions are quite simple in terms of syntax and function. They simply convert all of a string's characters into either lowercase (LCase) or uppercase (UCase) letters. For example, it's wise in the preceding routine to use the UCase function to convert all of the amino acid sequence's characters into capitals (the normal accepted way), just in case the user accidentally entered in his sequence in lowercase letters. This prevents the program from behaving improperly. To use the Ucase function, simply place the following line of code after the sequence is read in, but before the loop begins:

```
Sequence = UCase(Sequence)
```

Now the code works equally well with both lowercase and uppercase input because all lowercase input is converted to uppercase.

The StrComp Function

You can use the StrComp function in place of relational operators to compare two strings. It has the following syntax:

```
X = StrComp(String1, String2, Criteria)
```

where `Criteria` can be either vbTextCompare for a non-case-sensitive comparison or vbBinaryCompare to perform a case-sensitive comparison. This function returns a value of –1 if `String1` is less than `String2`, a value of 0 if the strings are equal, and a value of 1 if `String1` is greater than `String2`. In VB .NET, the criteria can be either TextCompare or BinaryCompare (the "vb" prefix is dropped). The function's behavior remains the same.

The Like Operator

The Like operator acts somewhat like the StrComp function. Both allow for comparisons between strings. Because of this, it's very tempting to think of Like as a function, but it is, in fact, a comparison operator. The major difference is that the Like operator allows for fuzzy comparisons. That is, wildcard characters can find matches that are similar but not necessarily exact to the original search string. For example, a ? can represent any single character, while a # can be any single digit. An * can represent zero or more characters of any kind, or a list of acceptable characters can be placed in brackets (i.e, [ ]). When using brackets, a hyphen can account for an ascending range of characters. Thus, [1,2,3,4,5] would equal [1-5].

> **NOTE**   *To better define an operator, consider some of the simpler ones*
> *Chapter 4 discussed, such as the arithmetic and logical operators. Unlike*
> *a function, which returns a value based on information passed into oper-*
> *ators, operators don't directly return data values. Instead, they form*
> *components of expressions in order to make the expression evaluatable.*
> *In this case, the expression is either evaluatable to like or not like.*

Examine the syntax and functionality a little deeper by considering the following situation. You have three strings—String1 equals ABCDEFG, String2
equals ABC?, and String3 equals ABC*. Now, consider the following lines of VB
6.0 code:

```
If String1 Like String2 Then
    Print "String1 Like String2"
Else
    Print "String1 Not Like String2"
End If
If String1 Like String3 Then
    Print "String1 Like String3"
Else
    Print "String1 Not Like String3"
End If
```

The equivalent VB .NET code is

```
If String1 Like String2 Then
    Debug.WriteLine("String1 Like String2")
Else
    Debug.WriteLine("String1 Not Like String2")
End If
If String1 Like String3 Then
    Debug.WriteLine("String1 Like String3")
Else
    Debug.WriteLine("String1 Not Like String3")
End If
```

If you run this code you're presented with the output "String1 Not Like
String2" and "String1 Like String3" because the ? wildcard in String2 only equals
one character, but the * wildcard in String3 can be any number of characters. The
Like operator and its wildcards are often combined with string parsing routines
to create powerful fuzzy search routines.

The InStr and InStrRev Functions

You'll often find that you're interested in a certain character or sequence of characters that may or may not be in a string. These functions search through a specified string and determine if the sought-after character sequence is a substring. In other words, they'll let you know if the character sequence is "in the string." These two functions differ in that InStr searches from left to right and InStrRev searches from right to left. If these functions find the sought-after character sequence, they return the sequence's starting position. If the sequence isn't located they return a value of 0. The syntax of the InStr and InStrRev functions are as follows:

```
InStr(Start Position, Search String, Sequence to Find, Criteria)
InStrRev(Search String, Sequence to Find, Start Position, Criteria)
```

Start Position specifies the character number where you wish to begin your search, while Search String specifies the string to be searched. Sequence to Find is the character sequence you're seeking, and Criteria allows you to choose between vbTextCompare and vbBinaryCompare (TextCompare and BinaryCompare in VB .NET).

The following example demonstrates the InStr function, which will search an mRNA sequence for the start codon AUG and return the position it starts at. Though not of great use by itself, the routine can help provide a building block for more useful routines, such as a translation program. The upcoming chapter on bioinformatics demonstrates this routine. To begin your example, however, set up the same form as you did for the nucleotide count and protein molecular weight routines. Next, add the following code to the command button's Click event:

```
Dim Sequence As String
Dim Start As Integer
Sequence = RichTextBox1.Text
Sequence = UCase(Sequence)
Start = InStr(1, Sequence, "AUG")
If Start > 0 Then
Text1.Text = "The start codon begins at nucleotide #\ " & Start
Else
    Text1.Text = "The start codon not found! "
End If
```

If you run this code, you see that the function searches through the string and picks out the first AUG that is encountered (see Figure 6-6). To continue searching for other AUG sequences, you'd employ a second InStr statement that had Start + 3 as the start position.

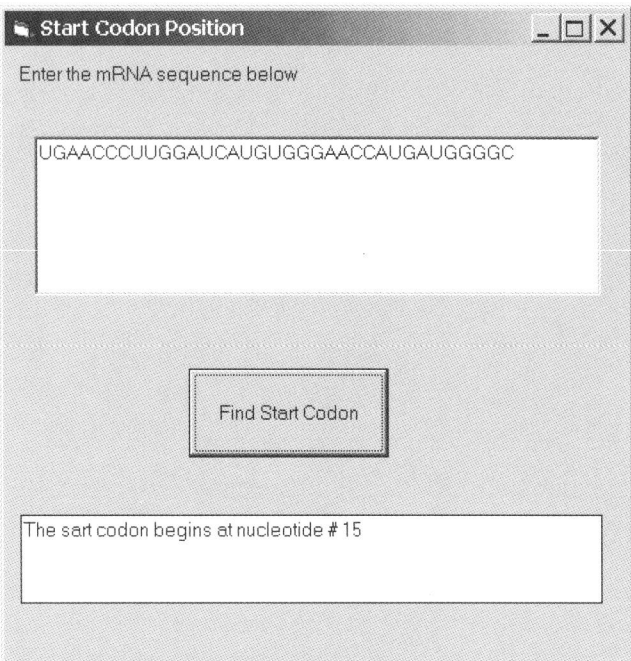

Figure 6-6. Finding the start codon of our mRNA sequence

The Replace Function

This function works much like the InStr function; it seeks out occurrences of a certain substring (sequence) within a string. The main difference is that, as the name implies, the Replace function removes the substring and replaces it with another specified substring. The syntax of this function is as follows:

```
Replace(String1, Search Substring, Replacement Substring, Start Position, _
 #\ Times, Criteria)
```

where String1 is the string to be searched. Search Substring is the sequence you're looking for and Replacement Substring is the character sequence you seek to replace the Search Substring with. Start Position specifies the character number where you want to begin your search. The # Times parameter is important if multiple instances of the Search Substring are within the main string; it dictates how many times the Search Substring is replaced. For example, if # Times was set at 2, the first two instances of the Search Substring are replaced. If no parameter is specified for # Times, all instances of the Search Substring after Start Position are replaced.

The Split Function

This function lets you split a single string into an array of smaller strings based on the occurrences of some type of separation unit (a delimiter), such as a space or a comma. The syntax for this function in VB 6.0 is as follows:

```
Function Split(Expression As String, [Delimiter], [Limit As Long = -1], _
 [Compare As VbCompareMethod = vbBinaryCompare])
```

In VB .NET the function prototype is

```
Function Split(ByVal Expression As String, Optional ByVal Delimiter As _
String = " ", Optional ByVal Limit As Integer = -1, Optional ByVal Compare As _
CompareMethod = CompareMethod.Binary) As String()
```

The Join Function

This function is the opposite of the Split function in that it takes an array of strings and allows you to combine them into one large string. The function lets you place a delimiter between each string you are joining together. The syntax for this function is as follows:

```
Join(ArrayofStrings(), Delimiter)
```

The function returns a string created by joining a number of substrings contained in an array.

The LTrim, RTrim, and Trim Functions

These are simple formatting functions that can remove blank spaces from the ends of strings. The LTrim functions remove spaces at the beginning of the string, the RTrim function removes spaces at the end of the string, and the Trim function removes spaces at the beginning and the end. The syntax of these functions is as follows:

```
LTrim(String)
RTrim(String)
Trim (String)
```

Mathematical Functions

If you're in the physical sciences and engineering disciplines, you'll find many of these functions indispensable. They allow for the easy execution of many basic mathematical procedures that often form the building blocks of powerful mathematical routines. They also allow you to take square roots or absolute values, or to determine many trigonometric parameters. As a scientific programmer, you must familiarize yourself with these functions. In VB .NET, most of the mathematical functions are now part of the System.Math library. Because of this, you must import the System.Math library before using the following statement at the beginning of the code:

```
Imports System.Math
```

If the statement isn't included in the code and you still want to access the math functions in the System.Math library, the function name must be prefixed with System.Math prefix. For example, `System.Math.Abs(x)`.

The Abs Function

This function's purpose is quite straightforward; its sole purpose is to take the absolute value of any number. You also can use the Abs function on a mathematical expression, in which case the Abs function returns the absolute value of the expression resultant value. The Abs function is part of the System.Math library in VB .NET.

The Atn Function

The VB 6.0 Atn function deals with arctangents. You can obtain arctangents in VB .NET with the Atan function, which is part of the System.Math library. The Atn function takes the ratio of two sides of a right triangle and returns the corresponding angle in radians. To convert this radian measure to degrees, you must multiply the radian value by 180/pi. Keep in mind that the arctangent is different from the cotangent, which is equal to 1/tangent.

The ACos Function

This function is new to the VB .NET System.Math library. It reads in the provided cosine value and returns the angle whose cosine is equivalent to that value. As with the Atan function, the returned value is in radians, and you must convert it to degrees manually.

The ASin Function

This function is new to VB .NET System.Math library as well. It reads in the provided sine value and returns the angle whose sine is equivalent to that value. As with the previous two functions, the results are returned in radians.

The Cos Function

This function takes the cosine of an angle, as you'd expect. The only important thing to remember is to enter the angle in radians and not degrees. To convert degrees to radians, simply multiply the degree value by pi/180. The Cos function is part of the System.Math library in VB .NET.

The Cosh Function

This function is new to the System.Math library of VB .NET. It returns the hyperbolic cosine of the provided angle (radians).

The Exp Function

This function raises the value e to the specified power (i.e., the number in parentheses). The value of e equals approximately 2.718282. Keep in mind that raising e to a power greater than 709.782712893 results in an error. The Exp function is part of the System.Math library in VB .NET.

The Fix and Int Functions

For positive numbers, Int and Fix function exactly the same. They remove a number's fractional (decimal) portion and return the resulting integer value. However, when dealing with negative numbers, Fix returns a negative number greater than or equal to the number (i.e., –6.3 to –6), while Int returns a negative number less than or equal to the number (i.e., –6.3 to –7).

The Log Function

The Log function gives a number's natural logarithm, or the logarithm to the base e. To determine the logarithm of any number x to some other base n, simply apply the following formula:

$$\ln_n(x) = \frac{\ln(x)}{\ln(n)}$$

Thus, to use base 10 logarithms you simply use the code

```
Log10 = Log(X) / Log(10)
```

The Log function is part of the System.Math library in VB .NET.

The Pow function

This function is new to the System.Math library of VB .NET. It can raise a specified number to a specified power. For example, to raise 3 to the 8th power, you'd use

```
Pow(3, 8)
```

The Sgn Function

The Sgn function determines the sign of a given value. If the number is positive, the Sgn function returns a value of 1; if the number is negative the function returns a value of –1. If the number supplied is 0, the function returns a value of 0. VB .NET renames this function "Sign," which is part of the System.Math library.

The Sin Function

The Sin function determines a given angle's sine. As with the Cos function, remember to convert your degrees to radians before applying this function. The Sin function is part of the System.Math library in VB .NET.

The Sinh Function

This function is new to the System.Math library of VB .NET, and returns the hyperbolic sine of the specified angle (radians).

The Sqr Function

The Sqr function takes the square root of any given number. The number supplied must be greater than or equal to zero, however, as this function is not equipped to deal with imaginary roots. VB .NET renames this function "Sqrt," which is part of the System.Math library.

The Tan Function

The Tan function determines a given angle's tangent. Remember, though, to input the angle in radians and not degrees. The Tan function is part of the System.Math library in VB .NET.

The Tanh Function

This function is new to the VB .NET System.Math library. It returns the hyperbolic tangent of the radian angle specified.

The Ceiling and Floor Functions

These functions are new to the System.Math library of VB .NET. They somewhat resemble the Round function, except that they allow you to dictate whether or not to always round up or round down. The Ceiling function always returns the smallest whole number larger than the number provided. The Floor function, on the other hand, always returns the largest whole number smaller than the number provided.

Syntax

All of the preceding functions share the same basic syntax. That is, you provide the function name followed in parentheses by the number or expression that the function will evaluate. Thus, to take the sine of X and raise e to the Y power, you employ the following lines of code:

```
A = Sin(X) ' A = System.Math.Sin(X) in VB .NET
B = Exp(Y) 'B = System.Math.Exp(Y) in VB .NET
```

This syntax is quite straightforward and should be easy to remember because it follows the normal f(x) format used in mathematics. Now, examine one of these functions in action by calculating the standard deviation of a data set.

> **NOTE** *If you already imported the System.Math namespace, you don't need to prefix your math functions with System.Math.*

Standard Deviation Determination

Standard deviations are a commonly used statistical parameter to determine variability of observed data. Calculate a standard deviation by applying the following formula:

$$s.d. = \sqrt{\frac{\sum (x_i - \bar{x})^2}{n-1}}$$

where x_i is one of the data points, $\bar{x}$ is the mean and n is the number of data points.

To begin developing your application, you'll add a text box named Text1, a list box named List1, and a command button to your form (see Figure 6-7).

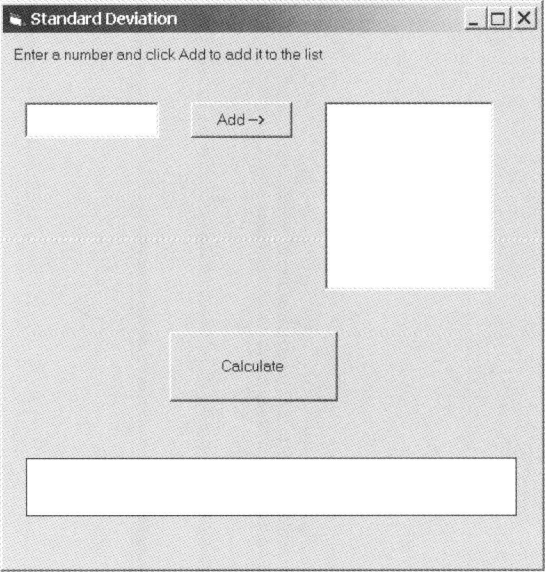

Figure 6-7. The standard deviation program's user interface

This enables you to enter a number into the text box, click the command button, and send the data point to the list box for storage. This process can repeat until all relevant values are added to the list box. In VB 6.0, you accomplish this by adding the following code to the command button's Click event:

```
Dim Num As String
Num = Text1.Text
List1.AddItem Num
Text1.Text = ""
Text1.SetFocus
```

In VB .NET the code will be as follows:

```
Dim Num As String
    Num = Text1.Text
    List1.Items.Add(Num)
    Text1.Text = ""
    Text1.Focus()
```

Next, add a second command button to initiate the actual calculation, and a text box named Text2 to output results into. In VB 6.0, you then add the following code to the command button's Click event:

```
Dim NumList() As Single
Dim Mean, SD As Single
Dim N As Integer
Dim I As Integer
Dim J As Integer
Mean = 0
SD = 0
N = List1.ListCount
ReDim NumList(N - 1) As Single
For I = 0 To (N - 1)
NumList(I) = CSng(List1.List(I))
Mean = Mean + NumList(I)
Next I
Mean = Mean / N
For J = 0 To (N - 1)
NumList(J) = (NumList(J) - Mean) ^ 2
SD = SD + NumList(J)
Next J
SD = Sqr(SD / (N - 1))
Text2.Text = "The mean is " & Mean & " and the standard deviation is " & SD
```

In VB .NET the code will be as follows:

```
Dim NumList() As Double
Dim Mean, SD As Double
Dim N As Integer
Dim I As Integer
Dim J As Integer
Mean = 0
SD = 0
N = List1.Items.Count
ReDim NumList(N)
For I = 0 To (N - 1)
    NumList(I) = CDbl(List1.Items(I))
    Mean = Mean + NumList(I)
Next I
Mean = Mean / N
For J = 0 To (N - 1)
    NumList(J) = (NumList(J) - Mean) ^ 2
    SD = SD + NumList(J)
Next J
SD = System.Math.Sqrt(SD / (N - 1))
Text2.Text = "The mean is " & Mean & " and the standard deviation is " &
SD
```

Now, you'll execute the code and examine what it does. First, declare the variables and determine the number of entries in the list box by using the ListCount property (Items.Count in VB .NET). Next, dynamically resize the array (NumList) to hold the exact number of list box entries. Remember that arrays start at zero, so you want the array to go from 0 to N-1 and not from 0 to N. Next, use a For . . . Next loop to read the list box values into the array and Sum up all of the values. The summation's result is then divided by N to determine the data set's actual mean. A second For . . . Next loop subtracts the mean from every element in the data set and squares the resultant values. These resultant values are summed up and temporarily stored in the variable SD. Finally, SD is divided by N-1, and the Sqr function determines the square root. This yields the actual standard deviation for the data set, which is outputted in the text box (see Figure 6-8).

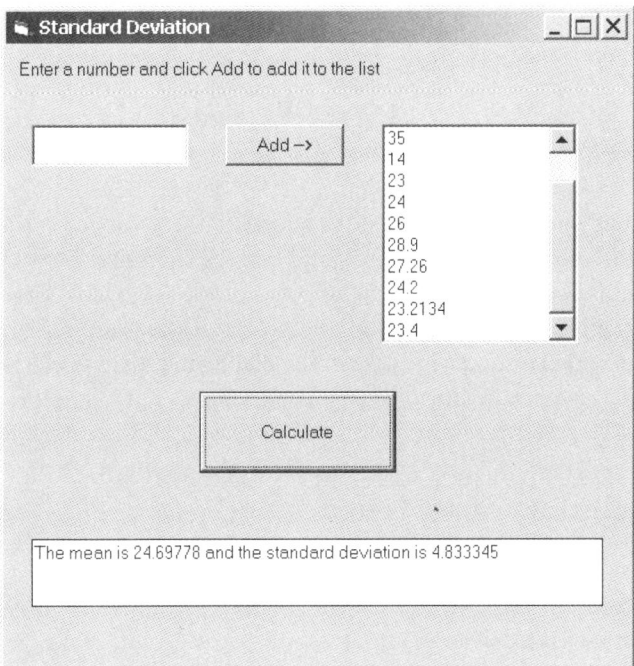

Figure 6-8. The results of the standard deviation program

The Round Function

This function is simple in operation, but its syntax is slightly different from the other numerical functions. It allows you to round off numbers, but you also can specify the decimal place where you want the rounding off to occur. This is a great feature because it eliminates scaling a number up by some factor of 10, rounding off to the nearest integer, and scaling the number back down. This function has the following syntax:

```
Round(X, #\ Decimal Places)
```

where X is the number to be rounded and # Decimal Places is the number of places after the decimal point that you want to obtain. If you choose not to specify a number of decimal places and instead use Round(X), X will round off to the nearest integer. In VB .NET the Round function is part of the System.Math library and has four "overloaded" variations, as shown in the following function prototypes:

```
Round(ByVal d As Double) As Double
Round(ByVal d As Double, ByVal digits As Integer) As Double
```

```
Round(ByVal d As Decimal) As Decimal
Round(ByVal d As Decimal, ByVal decimals As Integer) As Decimal
```

Deriving Math Functions

Remember that you don't always need to access these functions in the form of X = Function(Number); they can be part of a larger expression. For example, you could obtain the secant of an angle by using the code Sec = 1 / Cos(X). You even could employ more than one function in the same expression. Thus, to calculate the arccosine, which until recently wasn't available as a ready-to-use function, you could use the following formula in VB 6.0:

```
ArcCos = Atn(-X / Sqr(-X * X +1)) + 2 * Atn(1)
```

In VB .NET the formula would be:

```
ArcCos = System.Math.Atan(-X / System.Math.Sqrt(-X * X +1)) + _
2 * System.Math.Atan(1)
```

Note the change in names of the math functions in VB .NET and the need to prefix the function name with System.Math. Feel free to employ these basic functions as building blocks to derive even more powerful mathematical functions and routines. The next chapter describes this in greater detail when you learn to code your own custom functions and procedures. For now, you might be interested in checking out the Derived Math Functions listing found in VB's help section—it demonstrates how the basic functions just covered can create a number of functions.

The Rnd Function

The Rnd function is quite useful in applications that require the simulation of random events. The Rnd function accesses the VB random number generator; each time the random number generator is accessed, a number between 0 and 1 is generated. This number generation follows no set pattern, and thus the numbers are considered to be random. To demonstrate, you'll code a really simple routine that prints out a list of ten random numbers. In VB 6.0, add the following code to a blank form's Click event:

```
Dim I As Integer
Form1.Cls
For I = 1 To 10
Print Rnd
Next I
```

The VB 6.0 code prints the numbers directly to the form, which you can't do in VB .NET. To do this in VB .NET, use the following code to output the random numbers to the Output window found in the bottom of your IDE. This code is added to the Click event as well.

```
Dim I As Integer
For I = 1 To 10
  System.Console.WriteLine(Rnd())
Next I
```

If you run the application, you see that each click on the form returns a completely different list of numbers that have no connection to each other (see Figure 6-9).

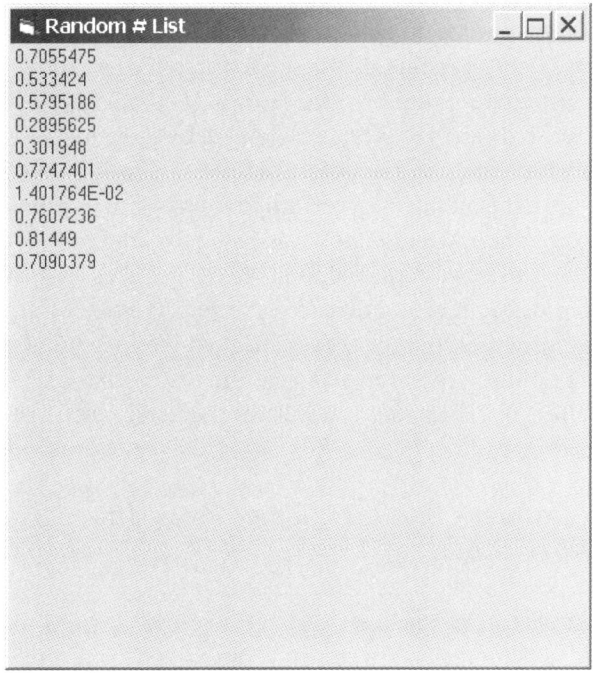

Figure 6-9. A listing of random numbers

However, restart the application and write down the ten numbers you get after activating the Click event. Now close the application and restart it again. If you run the application, you notice that you get the same ten numbers. This is because an application written in this manner (i.e., the Rnd function alone) isn't truly random, but only pseudorandom. That is, the Rnd function behaves similarly to the books of random number tables that statisticians often use. The numbers inside the book are completely random, but you wouldn't get random values if you always started in the same place in the book. This is, in effect, what VB does. You can get around this, though. Go back to the original routine and type the word `Randomize` at the beginning of the routine. You'll notice that each time the application runs, you get a different set of numbers. This is because the Randomize word reseeds the random number generator. That is, it makes VB choose a different starting point based on the exact time of the system clock.

Another benefit of the Rnd function is that you can seed the random number generator with the value of your choice. This can be accomplished with the following syntax:

```
Rnd(numeric seed)
```

where `numeric seed` is any number less than or equal to zero. If you use a positive number, the function still works, but it just generates the next random number in the sequence, the same as if no seed was supplied. Negative numbers are useful, however, because they will generate the same number every time. If zero is supplied, then the last random number generated is generated again. This makes both negative numbers and zeros highly useful debugging tools.

All in all, the Rnd function can be useful for small-scale simulations. Large-scale simulations that generate a large number of random numbers are better suited to a custom random generator because the pseudorandom nature of the intrinsic Rnd function may produce unreliable results. This is especially true, because not even reseeding guarantees truly random results. One flaw of many random number generators is that they often can't produce numbers that correspond to the endpoints of their range. This is the case with the VB random number generator; you'll find that you will never actually get 0 or 1.

Using the Random Number Generator in a Simple Probabilistic Model

Let's create a simple model based on the laws of probability to simulate tossing a coin in the air 1,000 times. You're going to count the numbers of heads and tails over 1,000 throws. As you'd expect, if your simple model is accurate you should receive approximately 500 each of heads and tails. Begin by adding two text boxes and a command button to your WinForm. Next, add the following code to the command button's Click event:

```
Private Sub Button1_Click(ByVal sender As System.Object, ByVal e As _
System.EventArgs)  Handles Button1.Click
        Randomize()
        Dim NumHeads, NumTails As Short
        Dim I As Short
        Dim RandNum As Double
        NumHeads = 0
        NumTails = 0
        For I = 1 To 1000
            RandNum = Rnd()
            If RandNum < 0.5 Then
                NumHeads = NumHeads + 1
            ElseIf RandNum > 0.5 Then
                NumTails = NumTails + 1
            Else
                RandNum = Rnd()
                If RandNum < 0.5 Then
                    NumHeads = NumHeads + 1
                ElseIf RandNum > 0.5 Then
                    NumTails = NumTails + 1
                End If
            End If
        Next
        TextBox1.Text = NumHeads
        TextBox2.Text = NumTails
End Sub
```

As you can see, you generate a random number during each loop's pass, and you use an If . . . Then construct to determine if the random number is equivalent to a head or to a tail. If it is less than 0.5, it's a head. If it's greater then 0.5, it's a tail. In the rare case that it's exactly 0.5 and can't be distinguished as a head or a tail, you generate a new random number and make the comparison again. If you run the model, you see that you get approximately the same number of heads and tails (see Figure 6-10).

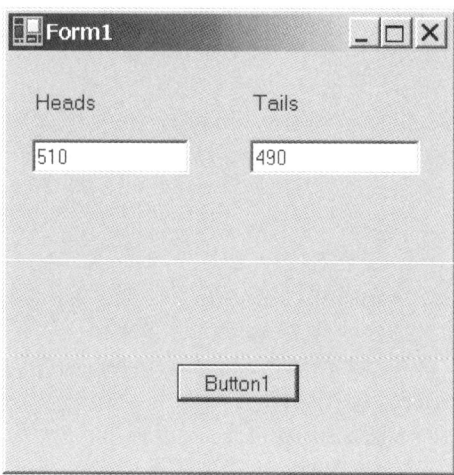

Figure 6-10. A distribution of heads and tails obtained from our simulation

If you increase the number of iterations, the results probably would improve even more. However, if you decrease the number of iterations, the results would worsen. Even in computer simulations, a larger sample size is always better than a smaller one.

Also keep in mind that with probabilistic simulations, if you need a number outside of the range 0 to 1, you can always scale the number by a multiple, or add or subtract a value to or from the random number. For example, to get numbers in the range of 12 to 14, multiply the random number by 2 and add 12 to that value. If you need both negative and positive random numbers, one nice trick is to generate two random numbers. One number serves as the actual random number, while the second decides negative or positive in the same way as you decided heads or tails in the coin toss example.

UCalc Fast Math Parser

UCalc is a commercial third-party application and not part of VB or VB .NET, but every scientific and engineering programmer should seriously check it out. This software lets you define mathematical equations at runtime, instead of predefining it in the code. It's very useful for coding many different scientific and financial applications. For example, say you need to code some type of custom spreadsheet application, and you want users to be able to enter formulas into cells. To get these formulas to work, you'd need some type of mathematical parsing routine to break down the formula and make some mathematical sense of it. This is exactly what UCalc does. UCalc also works rapidly, and can handle over

1,000 mathematical expressions in under 1 second. Its other great benefit is that it comes with an extensive library of algebraic, trigonometric, and statistical functions, which are always useful. For more information visit the Web site at `http://www.UCalc.com`.

MatrixVB

For any scientist or engineer who routinely deals with a large number of mathematical matrices, MATLAB's MatrixVB is another great VB add-in. MatrixVB is a COM library that contains a wealth of matrix manipulation functions for performing powerful matrix-based computations with just a simple function call. Some functions include methods of taking determinants, finding polynomial roots, Fourier transforms, and forming Eigenvectors. This product is definitely worth checking out because many of its preprogrammed (and battle tested!) functions will save you a lot of time and headaches trying to code your own custom functions that perform similar operations. For more information, go to `http://www.mathworks.com`.

As you can see from the preceding functions, many functions included with VB are highly useful tools for the scientific programmer because they cover many routine mathematical tasks. However, in many instances you'll want to accomplish more than just taking the sine of an angle. It'd be great if you could code your own functions to handle these advanced tasks. In fact, this is possible, as you'll see in the next chapter on coding your own custom functions and procedures.

Writing Your Own Functions and Procedures

Up to this point in the book, everything you've coded has ended up in one single listing of code within the same event procedure. This is fine for small programs like the examples presented so far, but coding large-scale applications in this manner is extremely tedious and arduous. This is especially true if you need to reuse the same calculation repeatedly, since you'd need to keep rewriting the same code. Luckily, VB, like other programming languages, lets you code your own functions and procedures, and incorporate them into your projects.

It's highly advisable to program your applications this way; it simplifies development by letting you break up a large task into a series of smaller ones. It also prevents repetitive coding and makes errors easier to locate and address. Another great benefit to coding custom functions and procedures is that you can develop your own specialized library of routines, which you can cut and paste into any VB project.

Custom Functions

As you saw in the last chapter, a function is a routine that's designed to read in certain parameters and return a specific value. You also saw that VB contains a number of highly useful functions, yet these intrinsic functions don't even come close to approaching every type of function a scientific programmer needs. For example, consider the Log function. This function can calculate natural logs, which is very important, but can't handle logarithms to any other base. Unfortunately, not all logarithms are always natural logarithms. Therefore, it's useful to code your own function that calculates the log of a number to any base N. In fact, the following example does just that, presented here to show you the typical structure of a function:

```
Public Function LogN(X, N As Double) As Double
    LogN = Log(X) / Log(N)
End Function
```

The VB .NET equivalent of the preceding code would be

```
Public Function LogN(ByVal X as Double, ByVal N As Double) As Double
    LogN = System.Math.Log(X) / System.Math.Log(N)
End Function
```

As you can see, this function contains the same formula derived in the last chapter to convert natural logarithms into logarithms of base N. This function's first line, the *function header*, is responsible for declaring how the function is accessed and what information it returns. The first term, Public Function, is known as the *access specifier* and controls what code can access the specific function. Code can access Public Functions anywhere in the program even if the code resides on a different form. Only variables that reside on the same form as the actual function code can access Private Functions. The next item you'll encounter as you read across the header is the *function name*, which in this case is LogN. It's a good idea to give all of your functions logical names to easily identify them. Following the function name, you'll come across a set of parentheses that contains one or more variables, known as *parameters*. They control what information and what type of information the function receives from the program. In this case, the function receives the number it is to take, the logarithm of (X) and the base for the logarithm (N). After the parentheses you'll see the term As Double. This is referred to as the *return type* and controls what type of information the function returns to the code.

After the header comes the function's body, which, in this case, is your code to calculate the logarithm of X to the base N. This body, however, can be much more complex, as you'll see in some upcoming functions. In fact, the bodies of functions can come complete with their own variable declarations and can even call other functions. Thus, you may even want to view functions almost as subprograms. Finally, the statement End Function declares that the function code has come to an end. Now that you've been exposed to the structure of a function, you can gain a better understanding of exactly how they work by coding a simple program that uses your LogN function.

You'll write a program that calculates the pH of a solution, in which a strong acid (i.e., a dissociation constant of 1) was diluted in water (assumed to be pH 7). You'll approach this problem by taking the concentration of the acid stock and multiplying it by the amount of acid you are going to add. Then, you'll divide this value by the total volume of the solution, which will equal the water volume plus the acid volume. That will yield the concentration of H^+ within the final solution. You'll then calculate the pH based on the formula

$$pH = -\log_{10}\left[H^+\right]$$

In order to set this application up, first add four text boxes named TextBox1, TextBox2, TextBox3, TextBox4 and one command button to your form, as demonstrated in Figure 7-1. Now, add the following code to your command button's Click event.

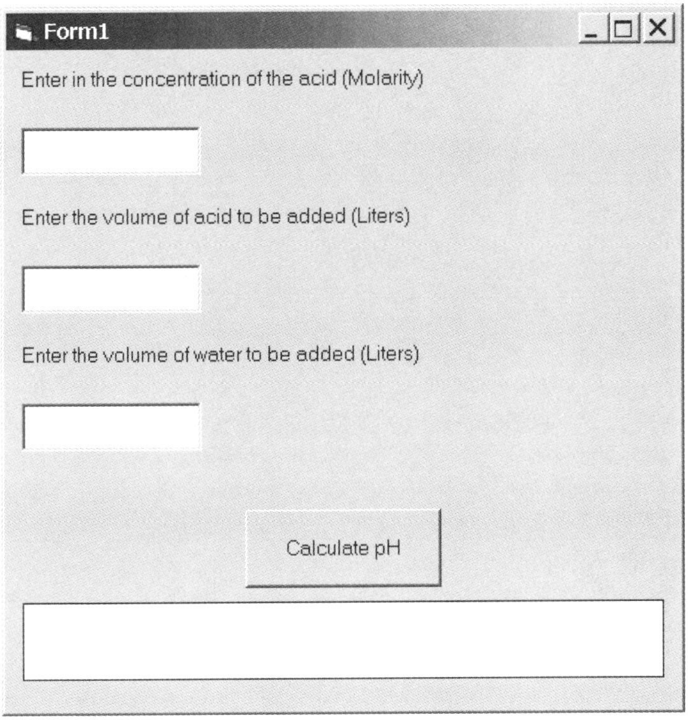

Figure 7-1. Your pH program's interface

```
Dim M, AV, WV, HC, pH As  Double
'M = Acid Concentration
'AV = Acid Volume, WV = Water Volume
'HC = H+ Concentration
M = CDbl(TextBox1.Text)
AV = CDbl(TextBox2.Text)
WV = CDbl(TextBox3.Text)
HC = (M * AV) / (AV + WV)
pH = -LogN(HC, 10)
TextBox4.Text = "The pH is " & pH
```

Also, remember to add the code to your LogN function to that form's code window. Otherwise, the application will try to call a function that doesn't exist, and the program won't run properly.

Now that the application is set up, run the application and examine how it works. Your application should resemble Figure 7-2.

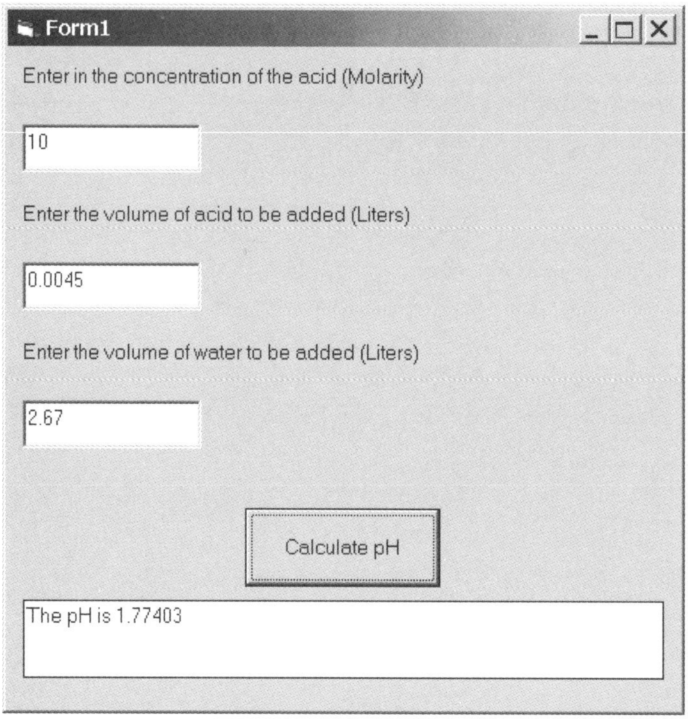

Figure 7-2. Viewing results in your pH program

As you can see, the first step is to read in the data, which is used to calculate the H$^+$ concentration, HC. Next, this value of HC is fed into the LogN function along with the base for the logarithm. HC's value is set equal to the function's value of X, and the base 10 is set equal to the function's value of N, and then the function calculation proceeds. Thus, keep in mind that the order you list the function parameters is important. For example, if you instead wrote LogN(10, HC), you'd incorrectly calculate the logarithm of 10 to the base HC. It's good practice to clearly annotate your functions to ensure that you keep all of your variable parameters straight.

NOTE *In VB .NET, the new Log10 function can calculate base 10 logs. However, this chapter will use the example custom function for illustrative purposes. The Log10 function didn't exist in past versions of VB.*

This simple example provides some insights into coding and using custom functions in VB, so you now can build on these basic concepts. You'll code some more complex functions and applications with some real scientific and engineering relevance. First off, you'll examine how to approximate integrating a function by making use of the trapezoidal rule.

The Trapezoidal Rule

Many scientific and engineering computations require integrating a function, yet this is often difficult or impossible to do with purely analytical techniques. Thus, scientists and engineers often turn to computer-based numerical techniques to approximate these integrations for them. The trapezoidal rule evaluates integrals by using trapezoids to approximate the area under a curve. It may not always be easy to determine the area under a curve, but determining the trapezoid's area is quite simple. Thus, consider the simple function $y = \sqrt{45x}$ in Figure 7-3.

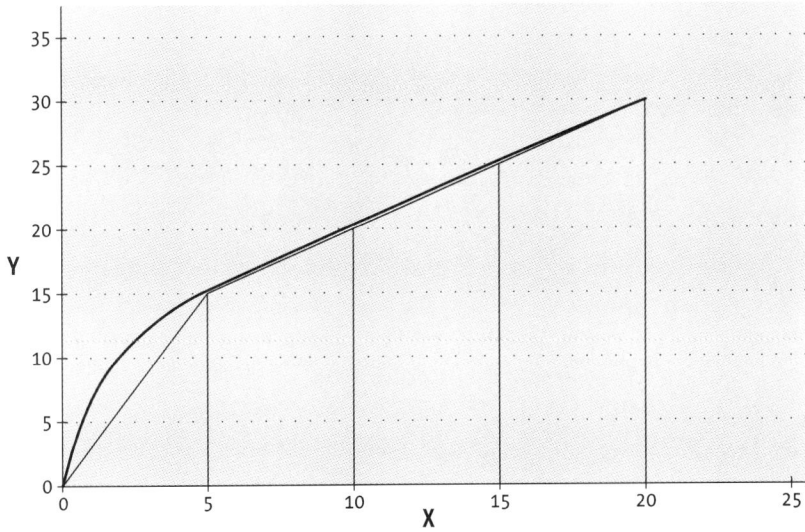

Figure 7-3. Using trapezoids to find the area under a curve

As you can see, dividing the region under the curve into four trapezoids yields a fairly good estimate of the area under the curve, especially where the slope isn't as steep. However, in the initial steep-sloped region, the trapezoid that approximates this area probably isn't accurate enough. You can easily rectify this by increasing the number of trapezoids to approximate the region under the curve. Thus, using a large number of trapezoids is desirable because it enhances the approximation's accuracy.

Now that you are familiar with this approximation method, you can examine the mathematics behind calculating the trapezoid's area in the following formula:

$$A = \Delta x \left(\frac{y_0 + y_n}{2} + \sum_{i=1}^{n-1} y_i \right)$$

where Δx is the size of the trapezoidal increments, y_o is the function's value at the initial point, y_n is the function's value at the final point, and y_i is function's value at the intermediate points. This formula evaluates the trapezoids' area using the normal geometrical formula A= $\frac{1}{2}$ (base1 +base2) * height. In this case, the bases are the different values of y and Δx is the height. The reason only y_0 and y_n are divided by 2 is that every other value of y is used twice, since it forms bases in two adjacent trapezoids.

Now that you know how the mathematical formulations are employed in approximation, you can begin to code a VB routine that evaluates the integral of $y = \sqrt{45x}$, between $x = 0$ and $x = 20$. You'll do this by writing two custom-written functions: One evaluates $y = \sqrt{45x}$ and a second uses the trapezoidal rule to solve for the area under the curve between $x = 0$ and $x = 20$. First, add two text boxes and a button to your form and use the following code:

```
Private Sub button1_Click(ByVal eventSender As System.Object, ByVal eventArgs As _
System.EventArgs) Handles button1.Click
    Dim LB As Double
    Dim UB As Double 'upper and lower bounds
    Dim Interval As Short 'number of intervals
    Dim Answer As Double
    LB = 0
    UB = 20
    Interval = CShort(TextBox1.Text)
    Answer = Trap(LB, UB, Interval)
    TextBox2.Text = CStr(Answer)
End Sub
Private Function F(ByVal X As Double) As Double
    F = System.Math.Sqrt(45 * X)
End Function
Private Function Trap(ByVal LB As Double, ByVal UB As Double, ByVal Interval As _
  Short) As Double
    Dim Y As Double
    Dim I As Integer
    Dim Sum As Double
```

```
    Dim X As Double
    Dim DeltaX As Double
    DeltaX = (UB - LB) / Interval
    X = LB
    Sum = 0
    For I = 1 To Interval - 1
        X = X + DeltaX
        Y = F(X)
        Sum = Sum + Y
    Next I
    Trap = DeltaX * ((F(LB) + F(UB)) / 2 + Sum)
End Function
```

Once the coding is complete, execute the routine and examine how it works. First off, the form's Click event defines the upper and lower bounds, or the values the function will integrate between. In this case, you integrate from 0 to 20. Next, read a user-defined variable from TextBox1 to define the number of intervals that you want to dissect the function into (i.e., the number of trapezoids). Call upon the trapezoidal rule function and pass the boundaries and number of intervals to it as parameters.

> **NOTE** *See if you can take advantage of setting the Interval variable by trying a range of values. If you plot the number of intervals versus the area, you'll notice that after a certain point the calculated area no longer changes and plateaus on the graph. In this region, the approximation can be considered accurate.*

Now that you are inside the Trap function, notice that you declare five variables, X, Y, DeltaX, I, and Sum. These variables are considered local to the function. That is, only code found within this particular function can view the values stored in these variables. These variables wouldn't be accessible to any other code in the same project, even if it is found on the same form. To get more universally modifiable and accessible variables you must use public and private variables, as discussed in Chapter 4.

After the variable declarations, the routine's mathematical essence begins. First off, Delta X is calculated by dividing the distance between the upper and lower bounds by the number of trapezoids desired. Next, the initial value of X is set equal to the lower bound. You then enter a loop structure that solves the portion of the formula that follows the summation sign ($\sum_{i=1}^{n-1} y_i$). It does this by calling on the function F that lets you evaluate $y = \sqrt{45x}$ at different values of x.

Thus, as you can see it's possible to call on other functions (even custom functions) while inside a function. After the loop is completed, the resultant value is stored in Sum. The Sum's value is used with the F(LB), F(UB), and DeltaX to complete the approximation of the area under the curve. This value then returns to the Click event procedure where it's stored in the variable Answer. Finally, the value of Answer is outputted into TextBox2 (see Figure 7-4).

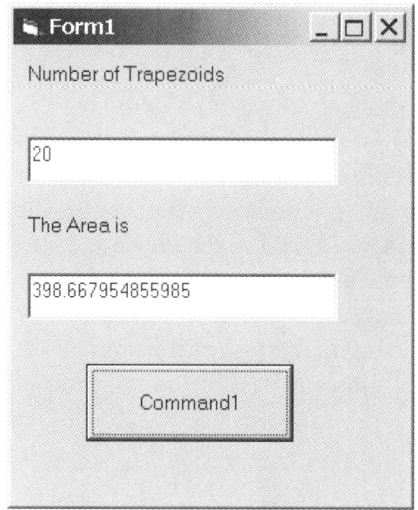

Figure 7-4. The results of your trapezoidal rule program

Custom Procedures

You can imagine, most likely, that functions like the trapezoidal rule function are crucial components of any scientific program. They allow you to use complex mathematical expressions repeatedly without recoding the equation. This not only speeds up the actual coding process, but also makes error locating much easier and programming debugging much faster. In fact, almost any large application you code probably makes numerous uses of functions.

> **NOTE** *For more information on debugging your functions and procedures, see Chapter 11.*

Functions aren't as all-encompassing as you'd like, however, because they return only a single value. Thus, another type of subroutine exists, a *procedure*. A procedure is almost like a miniprogram in that it isn't limited to just returning a single value. In fact, procedures can carry out a series of actions or can execute to modify multiple values. By this point in the book, you should be somewhat familiar with procedures; you've been using them all along. One of VB's main types of procedures are the *event procedures*, which initiate when a control is clicked (Click event) or when a control receives the focus (GotFocus event). This chapter, though, doesn't concentrate on VB's intrinsic event procedures, but rather on coding your own custom procedures.

Resizing a Control

To begin to examine custom procedures, consider a simple example. You'll place a command button on a form and add code that enlarges the command button every time it's clicked (see Figure 7-5).

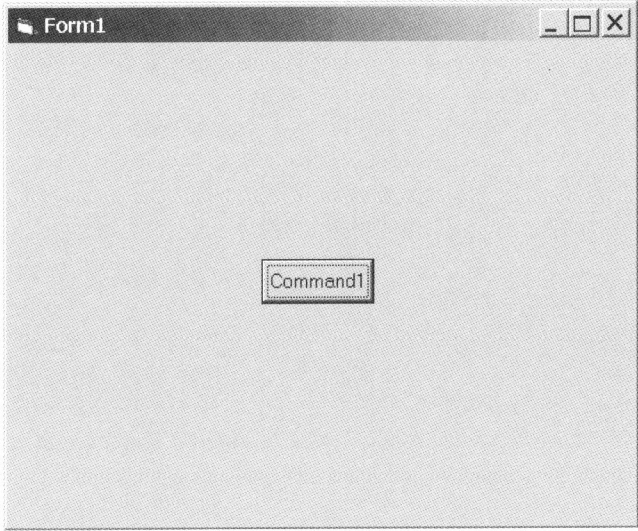

Figure 7-5. The initial sized command button on your form

However, you'll accomplish this by calling the MakeBigger procedure every time the Click event is initiated. Thus, add the following code to the application:

```
Private Sub MakeBigger()
    With Button1
        .Top = .Top - 25
        .Left = .Left - 25
        .Height = .Height + 50
        .Width = .Width + 50
    End With
End Sub
```

```
Private Sub button1_Click(ByVal eventSender As System.Object, ByVal eventArgs As _
System.EventArgs) Handles button1.Click
     MakeBigger
End Sub
```

As you can see, every time the Click event is invoked the MakeBigger procedure is called. This procedure modifies all of the command button's dimensions, as shown in Figure 7-6, but unlike a function, returns any value to the Click event procedure. Also, notice that this particular procedure is argumentless and has empty parentheses in its declaration section. While modifying a control's dimensions may seem pretty useless, a similar routine is essential to the techniques Chapter 9 uses for programming your own spreadsheets. For now, take a look at some of the mathematical uses of procedures.

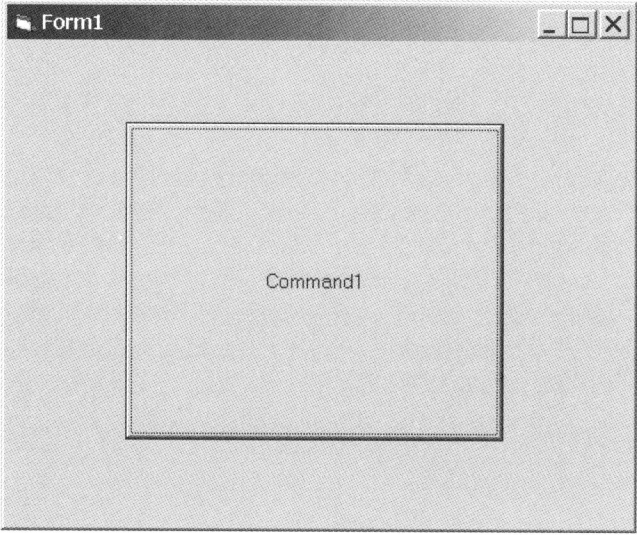

Figure 7-6. The increased size of your command button

Transposing a Matrix

Procedures are great tools for manipulating values stored in arrays, such as vectors and matrices. The functions' ability to only return a single value somewhat limits their usefulness for modifying every element in an array. Thus, procedures are required. For example, consider the idea that you need to transpose matrices. A matrix transposition occurs when an n X m matrix rotates to form an m X n matrix. In this case you want to transpose the matrix

```
2 -5  4
6  3 -1
```

into the new matrix

```
 2  6
-5  3
 4 -1
```

In VB 6.0, begin with a blank form, and declare the following two Private variables:

```
Private A() As Single
Private A2() As Single
```

In VB .NET, the declarations are

```
Private A( , ) As Single
Private A2( , ) As Single
```

In VB 6.0, add the following code to the command button's Click event:

```
Dim n As Integer
Dim m As Integer
n = 2
m = 3
ReDim A(1 To n, 1 To m)
A(1, 1) = 2
A(1, 2) = -5
A(1, 3) = 4
A(2, 1) = 6
A(2, 2) = 3
A(2, 3) = -1
Call Transpose(n, m)
Print A2(1, 1) & "  " & A2(1, 2)
Print A2(2, 1) & "  " & A2(2, 2)
Print A2(3, 1) & "  " & A2(3, 2)
```

This VB 6.0 code prints the numbers directly to the form, which VB .NET can't do. Thus, VB .NET uses the following code to transform the matrix and output it to the Output window found in the bottom of your IDE. This code will be added to a Click event as well.

```
Dim n As Integer
Dim m As Integer
n = 2
m = 3
ReDim A(n+1, m+1)
A(1, 1) = 2
A(1, 2) = -5
A(1, 3) = 4
A(2, 1) = 6
A(2, 2) = 3
A(2, 3) = -1
Call Transpose(n, m)
System.Console.WriteLine(A2(1, 1) & "   " & A2(1, 2))
System.Console.WriteLine(A2(2, 1) & "   " & A2(2, 2))
System.Console.WriteLine(A2(3, 1) & "   " & A2(3, 2))
```

You noticed, most likely, that the arrays A and A2 were declared as dynamic arrays. This illustrates how the transposition routine could be used with any sized 2-D array. In fact, test it out by changing the size of n and m and observing how the transposition is changed. Next, notice you enter the original matrix values into their proper locations in the array. The Transpose procedure is called on to transpose array A and store the result in array A2. Then, the values of A2 print out on the form. Please note, however, that the Call statement that calls the transpose procedure is optional. Instead, you may call the procedure simply by stating the function name (as with the MakeBigger procedure); but make sure to omit the parentheses around the argument parameters. For example, you could have instead coded

```
Transpose n, m
```

Your approach here is stylistic, but you should be familiar with both because other programmers may not have the same stylistic preferences as you.

Let's return to the main focus though, and examine the code for the Transpose procedure.

```
Private Sub Transpose(ByVal n As Integer, ByVal m As Integer)
Dim I As Integer
Dim J As Integer
ReDim A2(1 To m, 1 To n) ' VB 6.0 code
' In VB .NET change the above statement to ReDim A2(m+1, n+1)
For I = 1 To n
    For J = 1 To m
        A2(J, I) = A(I, J)
    Next J
Next I
End Sub
```

As you can see, the procedure's first step is to redimension array A2 to the appropriate m X n size. A set of nested For . . . Next loops performs the actual transposition, which copies the I, J allocation of array A into the J, I allocation of array A2. Keep in mind that both arrays are Private variables and are thus usable by both the Click event and the Transpose procedure. That's why it's unnecessary to pass information from either array into the Transpose procedure as a parameter (see Figure 7-7).

Figure 7-7. The transposed matrix

Passing Arrays and Array Elements into Procedures and Functions

You'll often work with arrays and will want to pass either a single element from that array or an entire array into your procedure. The syntax for this is quite simple and not much different from anything you've already seen. However, to eliminate any confusion, this section briefly demonstrates the required syntaxes.

To pass a single element of an array into a procedure, place the array name along with the index of the element in the procedure call. For example, to pass element 3 of array A into procedure Example you'd use code similar to the following:

```
Private Sub Example(ByVal SingleElement As Integer)
'Code
End Sub


Dim A(10) As Integer
Example(A(3))
```

However, to pass in a whole array, the syntax is a little different. First, you wouldn't specify any element numbers or ranges in the call statement; you'd just specify the name of the array to be passed. Next, the procedure's header differs slightly because wherever the array is being passed you'd need to place parentheses immediately after the variable name. Thus, to pass in all of array A you use the following code:

```
Private Sub Example(ByVal ArrayA() As Integer)
'Code
End Sub


Dim A(10) As Integer
Example(A)
```

> **NOTE** *Just as with regular variables, arrays must match the data type of the procedural array it's being passed into.*

Passing By Reference and By Value

Visual Basic 6.0 and the other previous versions of VB pass argument (variable) information into functions and procedures in a way called *by reference*. That is, the actual value isn't passed into the argument parameters, but rather the memory location that stores that particular value. This means that if the procedure in some way modifies the value, the value remains modified even after the procedure completes its execution.

VB .NET doesn't take this approach for passing argument values. Instead, VB .NET uses *by value* passing of information. This means that the variable value's memory location isn't passed to the procedure, but rather just the variable value itself. The procedure can modify the value all it wants without affecting the variable anywhere besides that very procedure. In other words, once the value is passed into the procedure, it's treated the same as a variable that is local to that procedure. Anyone with past scientific programming experience should recognize by value passing because the commonly used scientific programming language FORTRAN also uses it.

VB .NET and VB 6.0 offer ways to change by value and by reference defaults, however. For example, to pass VB 6.0 variables by value, place an extra set of parentheses around the variable to be passed by value. This works as follows:

```
Func X, (Y)
```

```
Call Func (X, (Y))
```

In both cases, the value of X is passed by reference because it's the default, but the value of Y is passed by value. You also can do this in the actual function/procedure header by using the ByVal keyword. For example, you could code the Func functions header as follows:

```
Private Function Func (X As Integer, ByVal Y as Integer)
```

With this type of argument in the function's argument list, Y is always passed in by value, whether or not extra parentheses were used. This method is more similar to VB .NET's method to pass values by reference instead of the default by value. The only difference is that the ByRef keyword is utilized in place of the ByVal keyword.

After reading this, you're probably wondering which method of passing variables is the better method. This is somewhat of a stylistic preference, but I personally prefer to pass variables by value. I find it prevents the variable's value from being accidentally modified because variables passed by value are treated as being local to that procedure.

Functions and Procedure with Optional Arguments

Oftentimes functions and procedures you code might benefit from having some extra information passed to them, yet this information isn't really essential for the routine to work. This is when optional arguments come in handy. They let you pass extra nonessential information into a function or a procedure. In other words, the procedure works regardless of the information. In fact, looking back at the procedure call for a MsgBox you'll notice that you can add special optional arguments to give the message box special characteristics.

Optional arguments also have their uses in scientific programming, such as with different kinds of iterative techniques. Most iterative techniques process until two consecutive answers converge to within the limits of a set convergence criterion. However, if the answers begin to diverge, the routine could run forever. Thus, an optional argument that specifies the maximum number of iterations is a good idea. This maximum number isn't essential for the routine to work, but it does provide a great safety feature. For example, the chapter on loop structures demonstrated how to find the x intercept of a curve using the bisection method. In this routine, the Count variable counted the number of iterations. If this variable reached 100, the iteration stopped.

Optional arguments are declared last in the argument list and use the Optional keyword. If optional arguments are used, all subsequent arguments in the argument list must also be optional and declared using the Optional keyword. Also, optional parameters must always specify a default value. Thus, the header for a function with optional arguments might look as follows:

```
Private Function Func (X as Integer, Y As Integer, Optional Z As Integer = 0) _
As Integer
```

The caller can call the preceding function with either two or three arguments. The function determines whether or not the third argument was passed by using the IsMissing function if the optional argument was declared as variant. In VB .NET, the IsMissing function is dropped in favor of the IsNothing function because Object is the default data type instead of variant. Also, VB .NET compels you to initialize an optional argument to a default value. Please see MSDN for Visual Studio .NET 7.0 documentation for more details.

You now should have a good understanding of functions and procedures. This chapter's example code was kept to simple routines so that you easily could learn about custom functions and procedures, instead of being bogged down with complex mathematical calculations. Make sure you understand thoroughly the workings of custom functions and procedures, however, because this book, like any real-world scientific application, will make extensive use of custom functions and procedures. It's well worth spending the time to master these simple examples before moving on to the book's more advanced chapters. You might want to also try coding some of the simple, but useful, examples listed here:

- **A function that takes the nth root of a given value:** VB only provides a function that enables you to take square roots. For cube roots or higher powers, you need to code your own function that can read in both the value of n and the value whose root you desire.

- **Function(s) that calculate the volumes of different shapes:** Creating libraries of small, useful functions like these is a great way of reducing coding time and avoiding grammatical errors in larger projects, since you'll find it easier to test the accuracy of a single function than to individually test every occurrence of length X width X height, etc.

- **A procedure that takes in an array containing XYZ coordinates and orders those coordinates:** Sorting data sets is often an important part of programming and data analysis. There are a variety of ways you could choose to do this, depending on your need. For example, do you want to go from lowest to highest, or highest to lowest, etc.?

- **For a more advanced challenge, code functions and/or procedures that take the dot products and cross products of two vectors.** You can code a routine to work with a specific size vector, or you can try to make it work with any size vector for even more of a challenge. Either way, these functions will be quite useful to those in the physical and engineering disciplines.

CHAPTER 8

Getting Data from External Sources

As you probably know, even with the greatest interface, some data sets are just too large to manually enter all of the values required or to output all of the results to the screen. This is where file handling comes in handy. This chapter covers sequential access files, and reading and writing data to and from files. These abilities are very useful in developing scientific applications because they make manipulating files and large volumes of data in larger routines more feasible. Also, file handling archives and stores data generated by your application's different runs, which is an essential aspect to any scientific discipline. In addition to file handling, you'll look at the MSComm control, which gives VB programs a way to communicate with devices connected by a RS232 port. You'll be able to write your own data acquisition software with this control.

Common Data File Types in Science

Sequential text files are the most common types of files that you will be dealing with as a scientific programmer, and therefore they are the focus of this chapter. These files consist of alphanumeric text that is written in a set order, such as you would do with a word processor. The most commonly associated extension for files of this type is .txt; however, in science a variety of other extensions are often used to distinguish the content or the format of the information in the file. For example, Protein Data Bank files are sequential text files that contain information pertaining to the structure of biomolecules. These files have the extension .PDB and in order to use the information in them properly, you need to be aware of the PDB standards (available at http://www.rcsb.org). Thus, before manipulating data files it is imperative that you make yourself aware of the format of the data within the file. A good way of doing this is to consult the documentation of the program that generated the file or check to see if it is an internationally standardized specification.

File Commands

The file commands covered here are valid in both VB 6.0 and VB .NET because they are incorporated in the Microsoft.VisualBasic namespace. But keep in mind that in VB .NET many of these commands have newer counterparts found in the System.IO namespace.

> **TIP** *As you become a more advanced programmer, you will discover that much of this functionality can also be obtained by using more sophisticated Windows Application Programming Interfaces, or API. Although the use of API is beyond the introductory scope of this book, a great place to learn more about API is* Dan Appleman's Win32 API Puzzle Book and Tutorial for Visual Basic Programmers *(also by Apress).*

The ChDrive Command

This command works pretty much as you would expect: It changes the current logged drive. For example, let's say you wanted your program to work with a floppy disk in drive A rather than the default C drive. In VB 6.0, to change the logged drive from C to A you could use the following line of code:

```
ChDrive "A:\"
```

In VB .NET, you'd use

```
ChDrive("A:\")
```

In other words, to take advantage of this command, you call the command and place a string containing the drive letter of the drive that you wish to become the logged drive inside the quotation marks, in VB 6.0, or the parentheses, in VB .NET.

The ChDir Command

This command is very similar to the ChDrive command, only it changes the default directory and not the logged drive. The syntax of this command is similar as well, except that you use a string containing the path to the new directory instead of just a string containing a new drive letter.

The CurDir Command

This command returns an object type or variant type (depending on whether you are using VB .NET or VB 6.0) that contains the current drive's path. In VB 6.0, the following code easily implements this command and gathers the current path information:

```
Current =  CurDir
```

In VB .NET, the code would be

```
Current = CurDir()
```

If you execute this code, you'd see that the current path is stored in the variable Current. You can gather more than just the full path, however, by combining this command with the Left function as follows:

```
Current = Left(CurDir, 2) 'VB6 code
```

or

```
Current = Strings.Left(CurDir, 2) 'VB.NET code
```

Notice that Current now contains the current drive letter, such as C:.

The MkDir Command

The MkDir command creates a new directory. There are two basic ways to implement this command. If you simply type the line of code

```
MkDir "Name" 'VB6 Code
```

or

```
MkDir("Name") 'VB.NET Code
```

you'll end up with a new directory, Name, inside your current default directory. However, sometimes you don't want to create a directory inside the current default directory. You can simply specify the full or absolute path of the new directory as follows:

```
MkDir "C:\MyDocuments\Name"  'VB6 code
```

or

```
MkDir("C:\MyDocuments\Name") 'VB.NET code
```

If you execute this command, you'd create a new directory called Name within MyDocuments in drive C.

The RmDir Command

This command is the opposite of the MkDir command. The RmDir command removes an existing directory rather than creating a new one. Just like the MkDir command, you can give just a directory name (relative path), in which case the directory is removed from the current directory, or you can specify the full or absolute path to the directory of interest. When using this command, make sure the directory you are removing actually exists, or else you'll generate errors.

The Name Command

This command has two purposes. First, you can change a filename within a directory by using code similar to the following:

```
Name "FileName" As "NewFileName" 'VB6 Code
```

in which case you'd change the file FileName into a file called NewFileName. Second, this command can also move a file from one directory to another directory. For example,

```
Name "FileName" As "C:\MyDocuments\FileName" 'VB6 Code
```

moves the file FileName from the current directory into the directory MyDocuments in drive C. Remember that you can specify a path to the file you want to move or rename, and that you can simultaneously move and rename a file.

In VB .NET the Name command isn't available in the same form as in VB 6.0, but is available as Rename command as follows:

```
Rename("FileName" , "NewFileName")
```

The Kill Command

Caveat emptor! This command blows away files, and there's no "undo," so please only use it with great care. For example, to delete the file called FileName from MyDocuments, you'd use

```
Kill "C:\MyDocuments\FileName" 'VB6 Code
```

or

```
Kill("C:\MyDocuments\FileName") 'VB.NET Code
```

You also can use this command more broadly, however, such as by deleting files specified by wildcard characters. Say you want to delete all your current directory's files. You'd easily accomplish this with the code

```
Kill "*.*"'VB6 Code
```

or

```
Kill("*.*")'VB.NET code
```

Don't take the preceding line of code lightly, however—every file in the directory will be wiped out. Always make sure the directory contains no important files before executing such a command.

File-Handling Functions

These functions carry out several common Windows-based file-handling tasks, and are common to both VB 6.0 and VB .NET. Keep in mind that none of these functions interpret wildcard characters as wildcards. For a brief description of the different wildcard characters and what they represent, refer to Table 8-1.

Table 8-1. The Various VB Wildcard Characters

WILDCARD CHARACTER	FUNCTION
?	Any character
#	Any digit (numeric)
*	0 or more characters
[list]	Any character from list
[!list]	Any character not in list

The FileCopy Function

The FileCopy function accomplishes just what its name suggests. It copies a file from the specified source path to the designated output path, using the syntax

```
FileCopy(SourcePath, CopyToPath)
```

In other words, you must first tell the function the original file's location and then specify where you want the copied file to be placed.

The FileDateTime Function

This function returns the date and time a file was last changed, which is useful for determining when a file was either created (if it's a new file) or last modified. In science, it's often useful to include the date and times of the respective input files (along with the filenames) within your output, in order to keep track of exactly what data sets were used. To use this function, simply follow the syntax

```
FileDateTime(FilePath)
```

The GetAttr Function

This function's name is an abbreviation for Get Attributes, which is exactly what this function does. The function returns an integer value that can be correlated with the file's. File attributes somewhat control how files are handled and are summed up in Table 8-2.

Table 8-2. File Attributes

ATTRIBUTE	VALUE
Normal	0
ReadOnly	1
Hidden	2
System	4
Volume	8
Directory	16
Archive	32

Looking carefully at the values column, notice how the values of one or more attributes can't add up to equal the values of one or more other attributes. In the following line of code

```
A = GetAttr(FilePath)
```

you find that the value of A equals 3 if the file specified by FilePath is a hidden, read-only file. Thus, the GetAttr function returns the integer value equivalent to the sum of all of the component attribute values.

The SetAttr Function

This function enables you to change the attributes of files. For example, your application may generate important data that you don't want to chance getting corrupted, so after writing data to the file you mark it as a read-only file to prevent further changes. Accomplish this using the following code

```
SetAttr "C:\Name",vbReadOnly 'VB6 Code
```

or

```
SetAttr("C:\Name", IO.FileSystemAttributes.ReadOnly) 'VB.NET code
```

This particular line of code takes the file Name in the root directory of C and sets the attributes as ReadOnly.

> **NOTE** *Once you declare a file read only, your applications will no longer have permission to write additional content to that file.*

Basic Sequential File Handling

Sequential files are the simplest file type because they only hold normal text, such as Notepad or other word processor text, saved with the .txt option. The functionality of these files is somewhat limited; it's difficult to make internal changes to them, and text can only be added easily to the end of a file. In other words, you must process all sequential file information in sequence, from start to finish. On the upside, sequential files are also the easiest to work with, and are commonly used in scientific programming. Many scientific applications generate large volumes of data that follow a time series, a coordinate system, or set order that produces values in a sequential data set. The data acquisition software of thermocouples, voltmeters, flow meters, and various other monitoring devices often generates these data sets. The following section looks at VB 6.0 file handling, which closely resembles the different versions of BASIC file handling. After learning the basics of manipulating files, you'll explore VB .NET's more powerful and flexible methods.

VB 6.0 Sequential File Handling

As mentioned, VB 6.0 file handling is largely based on file handling in past versions of BASIC; most lines of code use file identifiers, instead of repeatedly using filenames. You'll get into more specifics about file identifiers shortly, but keep in mind that they numerically represent the open file you are dealing with. Thus, rather than constantly typing out C:\MyDocuments\FileName to read/write data, you'd simply refer to the file as #1, #17, #108, etc. File identifiers aren't unique to VB or BASIC; they're employed in many traditional top-down design programming languages, like FORTRAN.

Opening Files

Before you can take any action (read or write), you must open the file and set up a conduit with the file, so that the application can access the file. You do this in VB 6.0 with the Open command. For example, to access data found in a file called "File1" in the root directory of drive C, you'd open the file using the code

```
Open "C:\File1" For Input As #1
```

As you can see, the open statement, not only opens the data file, but also specifies the application's type of access to the data file. In this case, Input specifies the access, so that data can be read from the file but not written to the file. To write data to the file, you'd specify Output, which would allow your application write access to the file. The Open command is also essential in that it establishes the file identifier for the data file as well (i.e., As #1). In VB 6.0, the file identifier must be an integer value between 1 and 511.

Reading Data from a File

After you open the file, one of the most important functions in file handling is to gather the required information. This is generally accomplished by using an array in conjunction with a loop structure, and then using the Input command in the syntax

```
Input #1, A(I)
```

This command reads the next available file element into the first position of array A. With sequential file handling, it's important to keep in mind this idea of the next available element. When you first open the file, the next available element is the file's first piece of data, which, in the usual scientific case, is some form of number. Thus, the Input command's first execution reads in this value from the beginning of the file. After this element is read in, the file (file pointer to be specific) moves past this first value and on to the sequence's next element, which is the next value, if any, on the same line as the previous value. If no other pieces of data are on the same line as the previous element, then the file reads the elements on the next line. Thus, VB reads sequential files the same as you would: It starts on the top line on the left side and proceeds to read from left to right. When that line is complete, VB moves down one line to read from left to right again.

This idea is especially important when you are working with multidimensional arrays. If you structure your loops wrong and thereby execute your Input commands in the wrong order, the wrong data points will likely be in the wrong dimension. When reading in data, keep in mind that you don't want to read past the end of the file (EOF) because this leads to execution errors (you'll visit this topic again later in the chapter).

Also, it's possible to read multiple elements using just one Input statement. For example, to read the next three available elements into the array elements A(1), A(2), and A(3), you'd execute the following line of code:

```
Input #1, A(1), A(2), A(3)
```

This is often a great way to read in 2-D arrays that don't contain too many elements in the column direction, such as a listing of XYZ coordinates.

Writing Data to a File

You now know how to read data from a file, but this only covers half of file handling. You also need to record generated data; that is, to write data to a file as well. You can write data to a file using the Print command:

```
Print #1, "A(1)= ", A(1)
```

This line of code first prints the string "A(1)= " and then prints the value contained in position 1 of array A to the file specified by the identifier #1. Because the two elements use the same Print command, they are written to the same line of the file. If you instead use two Print commands as follows

```
Print #1, "A(1)= "
Print #1, A(1)
```

you'd find that "A(1)= " is on the line above the actual value of A(1). Thus, remember that each Print command writes to the next line of the file.

Closing Files

Once you're done reading data from files and writing data to files, it's good to close all open files and free up any system resources these read/write conduits were using. The Close command accomplishes this.

```
Close #1
```

In other words, you'd only invoke the command and enter the file's identifier that you want to close. Once a file is closed, its association with that particular file identifier ends. Thus, after executing the preceding statement you could associate a new file with #1.

A Simple Example

Now that you've learned a little about reading and writing to files, take some time to code a simple example. You'll read in data from the file Infile.txt (see Figure 8-1) and add 1 to every value read in. Then, you'll output the results to the file Outfile.txt. Start a new VB 6.0 project and add the following code to the form's Click event:

```
Dim A(1 To 10) As DoubleDim I as Integer
Open "C:\Infile.txt" For Input As #1
Open "C:\Outfile.txt" For Output As #2
For I = 1 To 10
     Input #1,A(I)
     A(I)=A(I)+1
     Print #2,A(I)
Next I
Close #1
Close #2
```

If you execute this code, you'd see that both files are first opened. The data contained in Infile.txt is read in and stored in array A (see Figure 8-1).

Figure 8-1. The contents of Infile.txt

Next, 1 is added to each element in the array and all of the elements are outputted to Outfile.txt (see Figure 8-2).

Figure 8-2. The contents of Outfile.txt

The routine then ends by closing both files and freeing up the system resources used by the open files.

File Handling with VB 6.0 Compatibility Functions in VB .NET

VB .NET still offers all of the functionality just discussed. However, the syntax is greatly changed, so you'll look at using these file commands under VB .NET.

Opening Files with the VB 6.0 Compatibility Functions

Everything discussed in the preceding section for opening up data files still holds true with VB .NET's equivalent command, FileOpen. For example, you still use file identifiers and specify your program's type of access. Thus, the functionality between the two lines of code is the same, but the syntax is drastically different. If you recall, in VB 6.0 you open up a file with a line of code like the following:

```
Open "C:\File" For Input As #1
```

In VB .NET, this same piece of code is instead

```
FileOpen(1, "C:\File", OpenMode.Input)
```

As you can see, VB .NET drops the use of the # sign before the identifier and moves the identifier specification up to the front, rather than leaving it for last. Also, instead of For Input or For Output, you specify the type of OpenMode. OpenMode can be specified three ways:

- If you want read access to a file, set OpenMode to Input.

- If you need write access to a file, use OpenMode.Output.

- If your application needs read/write access to the file, specify InputOutput.

Reading Data with the VB 6.0 Compatibility Functions

Just as the syntax changed with opening files, so too did it change for reading files. You now read from files with a line of code similar to the following:

```
Input(1, A(I))
```

The syntax change here isn't as drastic, however; the only real difference is that the # sign is dropped from the file identifier and parentheses are added. For this particular line of code, you'd find that the next available element of file 1 is stored in the Ith element of array A.

Writing Data to Files with the VB 6.0 Compatibility Functions

The Print function is similar in structure to the Input function, and is accessed with a line of code similar to the following:

```
Print(1, "A(I)= ", A(I))
```

This line of code prints "A(I)= " and the value of A(I) on the same line of the file. However, unlike VB 6.0, different calls to the Print functions won't result in data being written to different lines. In VB .NET a separate Sub known as PrintLine prints data to different lines.

Closing Files with the VB 6.0 Compatibility Functions

The VB 6.0 Close command is renamed FileClose, and can be used in two ways. First, assume you have several files open. To close the open files identified by 1, 3, and 7, you use the following line of code:

```
FileClose(1,3,7)
```

Thus, to close select files you specify the file identifiers within the Close command. However, a new feature of the .NET Close command is that if you don't specify any file identifiers, you can close all open files. Thus, the line of code

```
FileClose()
```

closes every file that is open.

An Example of VB 6.0 Compatible File Handling

To illustrate this type of VB .NET file handling, you'll look at a simple but useful example from computational chemistry. Many theoretical chemistry computations entail information about the van der Waals surface of a molecule, since this surface encloses about 95 percent of the electron density and has been shown to dictate what types of intermolecular reactions can occur. This surface has been empirically defined as the region where the electron density is 0.002 electrons/bohr^3. Furthermore, chemical software packages, which generate electron density data, often do so by drawing a cube around the molecule of interest. The software then steps through this cube at evenly distributed XYZ spacings and determines each point's density. Thus, for the surface geometry, you must read through the file of data points and select those points that correspond to a density of approximately 0.002.

For this problem, assume that the data file contains the Cartesian coordinates and a cube density of 1,000 points. On each file line, you'll first find the X coordinate, followed by the Y and Z coordinates. Finally, you'll find the value of the electron density. You're going to write a routine that reads through this file and selects all of the point data that corresponds to a density of 0.002±d, where d is a tolerance factor used to establish a range of acceptable values. Start a new VB project and add the following code to the form's Click event:

```
Dim A(1000, 4) As Double
Dim I, J As Short
Dim d As Double
d = 0.0002
FileOpen(1, "Infile.txt", OpenMode.Input)
FileOpen(2, "Outfile.txt", OpenMode.Output)
For I = 0 To 999
  For J = 0 To 3
    Input(1, A(I, J))
  Next J
Next I
For I =  0 To 999
  If A(I, 3) > 0.002 - d And A(I, 3) < 0.002 + d Then
    PrintLine(2, A(I, 0), A(I, 1), A(I, 2), A(I, 3))
  End If
Next I
FileClose()
```

First, you declare the necessary variables and then open the data file (Infile.txt). In addition to the data file, you open an output file (Outfile.txt) to which you'll write the data that corresponds to the surface points with a density of 0.002±d. Next, a loop structure reads in all of the required data into an array. Another loop then searches through the array's density values. If the search successfully finds a density value within the acceptable range, then the point information is written to the output file. Finally, you invoke the Close command to close both open files.

Some Other Useful VB 6.0/VB 6.0 Compatibility File Functions

In this section, you'll look at a few other file-handling functions that may be handy in your work. VB 6.0 and the VB 6.0 Compatibility library both contain these functions.

The LOF Function

The LOF function, short for Length Of File, returns the size of an open file in bytes. You can invoke this function easily with the syntax

```
LOF(1)
```

where any file identifier could replace 1. Just keep in mind that this function won't return a number that corresponds to the number of alphanumeric characters. It also considers spaces and carriage returns as characters and includes them in the count.

The FreeFile Function

As you can imagine, a large project with numerous files and multiple developers makes it hard to keep track of what file identifiers are currently in use. This is where the FreeFile function comes in. When called, it returns the next available file identifier. This works as follows:

```
Dim fid As Integer
fid = FreeFile()
FileOpen(fid, "C:\File", OpenMode.Input)
```

This example also illustrates a good point: You should always store the value returned by FreeFile in a variable and never use

```
FileOpen(FreeFile(), "C:\File", OpenMode.Input)
```

The rationale behind this is if you then read the file using FreeFile as the identifier again, you won't read the file you opened and instead will generate an error. The value returned by the second FreeFile call won't be the same as the first because the first value is already in use.

The EOF Function

As the chapter mentioned earlier, a file's length and number of pieces of information aren't always known. This lack of information makes it difficult to use a deterministic loop structure, such as those in the previous examples. However, you can combine an indeterminate loop (Do...Until Loop) with the EOF function to handle such situations. EOF, short for End Of File, tests to see if the file has reached its end. When combined with a Do...Until Loop as follows

```
Do Until EOF(1)
   Input(1, A(I))
Loop
```

you're able to read data until you reach the end of the file. Also remember to keep the loop test (i.e., Until EOF) at the top, since this prevents errors if you open a file that exists but contains no data.

New VB .NET File-Handling Methods

In addition to supporting file-handling methods found in past versions of VB, VB .NET contains a dramatically different approach to Input/Output (I/O) operations. This new approach involves the System.IO namespace, which provides a generic layer of access to different I/O operations. These I/O operations extend beyond basic data files and provide tools for dealing with other I/O operations, such as network data transfers. This chapter sticks to basic file-handling techniques, which are most in line with this book's introductory nature. The basic file-handling skills you learn, however, will provide a basis for other types of I/O operations that you may one day encounter.

The System.IO Namespace

As mentioned in the previous section, the System.IO namespace provides the generic functionality that all types of I/O operations require. Within this namespace, the Stream class is a very crucial component of the .NET way of dealing with I/O operations. It allows you to view I/O operations as streams of bytes. Depending on how these data streams are managed, the code can either read data from an input source or write it to an output source. Thus this class provides the functionality necessary to read and write one or more bytes of data. In your specific case, you'll treat your files' data as a FileStream object.

Within the System.IO namespace a TextReader class enables specialized objects to access stream data. Of these specialized objects you'll usually interact with the StreamReader object. The StreamReader object provides all of the required tools for reading data from sequential files, like those this chapter covered. In addition, you can write to sequential file using the StreamWriter object. When working with binary files (not a traditional VB strongpoint) you can use the BinaryReader object. This object is important because it allows you to read binary data directly into data types. For example, values can be read in as Boolean variables, Strings, Shorts, Longs, Singles, Doubles, or any other numeric data type. Likewise, just as a specialized BinaryReader can read in these types of values, a BinaryWriter lets you write these types of data in binary values.

Using System.IO Based File Handling

These techniques are very different from the other types of file handling you've seen, so it's probably best to start off with some example code. You'll code a simple routine that reads in four numbers from a file, sums them up, and writes the answer to the same file. You'll accomplish this by adding the following code to the form's Click event:

```
' Remember to Include the line
'Imports System.IO
'at the beginning of the code module to Import the System.IO namespace
Dim A(4), Sum As Double
Dim I As Short
Dim fs As New FileStream("C:\test.txt", FileMode.Open, FileAccess.Read)
Dim br As New StreamReader(fs)
Sum = 0
br.BaseStream.Seek(0, SeekOrigin.Begin)
For I = 0 To 3
    A(I) = br.ReadLine()
    Sum = Sum + A(I)
Next I
br.Close()
fs.close()
Dim fs2 As New FileStream("C:\test.txt", FileMode.Open, FileAccess.Write)
Dim bw As New StreamWriter(fs2)
bw.BaseStream.Seek(0, SeekOrigin.End)
bw.Write(ControlChars.CrLf & "Sum= " & Sum)
bw.Close()
fs2.Close()
```

As you can see, the file stream is declared using a Dim statement, just as with a variable. Within this declaration you specify the FileStream's and FileMode's path. FileMode specifies how the operating system opens the file specified in the path. You can use several possible methods to open a file, with the first option being FileMode.Append. Append opens the file and then positions the pointer at the end of the file, so any necessary additions can be made. Next, the Create option creates a new file if no file already exists in the specified path. This option also overwrites any existing file in the specified path and leaves an empty file in its place. CreateNew, however, can create a new file, but won't overwrite any existing files. Open, as you saw in the previous code, can open an existing file. OpenorCreate can open an existing file, but also can create a new file if the file in the specified path doesn't exist. In addition to the mode, however, you must specify the declaration's FileAccess. FileAccess controls how the application interacts with files; you can specify whether the application has Read, Write, or ReadWrite access.

In addition to the FileStream declaration you must declare the StreamReader by chaining into the FileStream fs. Use this StreamReader to access the information contained within the file. In this particular case, the StreamReader invokes the ReadLine method, which reads all of the characters from a line in the file. After reading in the characters and summing them, close the StreamReader and initial file stream in that order. Then open up a second file stream and declare a StreamWriter. This StreamWriter writes the sum to the file (see Figure 8-3). Finally, close the StreamWriter and the second file stream.

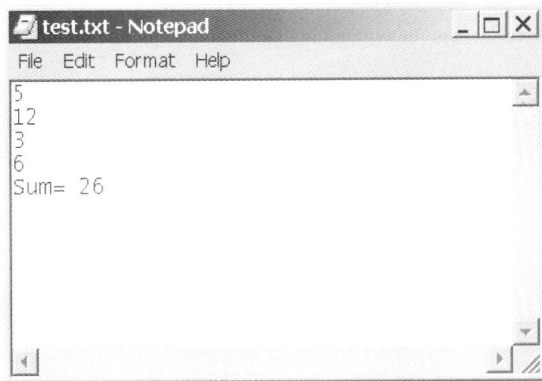

Figure 8-3. A sample output file

The MSComm Control

The MSComm control (AxMSComm in VB .NET) is an ActiveX control that can handle RS232 communications, a common serial data transmission method in scientific research labs. This protocol allows you to both send information to and receive information from your laboratory instruments. You'll examine this control and some of the basics of VB RS232 communication by first exploring the MSComm control's properties.

The MSComm Control Properties

Before exploring the MSComm control, however, you must add it to your toolbox because it isn't in the toolbox by default. Right-click the toolbox and select the Customize ToolBox option from the resultant pop-up menu. Then, add the control to your toolbox using the dialog box that appears.

The CommEvent Property

This property holds one of 17 constant values that defines the last communication event or error, such as data being sent or received. Changing the CommEvent value will initiate the OnComm event. This property's constant values are members of the CommEventConstants or OnCommConstants. The CommEventConstants and OnCommConstants are enums and are members of the MSCommLib Namespace. Some common constants are listed here:

- **comEvSend:** Indicates that the last communication event to occur was the completion of a data send

- **comEvReceive:** Indicates that the last event to occur was the complete reception of a data transmission

- **comEvEOF:** Indicates that an end of file character was received

- **comEventRxOver:** Indicates that the receive buffer has overflowed (i.e., more data was added to it than it was sized to handle)

- **comEventRxParity:** Indicates that a parity error occurred during reception

- **comEventTxFull:** Indicates that the transmit buffer is full and no more data can be stored in it

The remaining 11 constants are comEvCD, comEvCTS, comEvDSR, comEvRing, comEventBreak, comEventCDTO, comEventCTSTO, comEventDSRTO, comEventDCB, comEventFrame, and comEventOverrun. You're urged to look up the meaning of these advanced constants in the online help. It's essential to understand these constants for writing sophisticated serial port applications.

The CommPort Property

This property gets or sets the number of the communications port currently in use. The default setting is 1. To check your machine's available communications ports, open the Control Panel and click the System icon. Once the System Properties window appears, select the Hardware tab and click Device Manager. Within the Device Manager you'll find a listing of all communications ports.

The Handshaking Property

The term *handshaking* describes different techniques that can control the flow of information through an RS232 connection. The default is no handshaking or comNone. The comXonXoff setting employs a software-based handshaking protocol, while comRTS is a hardware-based handshaking protocol. ComRTSXonXoff employs both hardware- and software-based techniques.

The InBufferCount Property

This property stores the number of characters currently in the receive buffer. The property isn't available at design time.

The InBufferSize Property

This property sets or returns the receive buffer's size in bytes.

The Input Property

This property removes data from the receive buffer. To do this, the property must be assigned to a variable. Data can be input as either a string or as binary data. Once a variable is assigned the value of the Input property, the property is cleared, allowing more data to transmit. This property isn't available at design time.

The InputMode Property

As mentioned previously, data can be received as either a string or as binary data. This property determines how your received data will be read in. For text strings, you set the property equal to comInputModeText and for binary you set the property equal to comInputModeBinary.

The OutBufferSize Property

This property controls the transmit (send) buffer's size. The default unit is bytes.

The Output Property

This property puts data into the transmit buffer in order to facilitate its transfer. Data can be sent as either a string or as binary data. To begin a data transmission, simply set this property equal to the data to be sent.

The PortOpen Property

This property opens or closes the RS232 port to communications.

The RThreshold Property

This property sets the number of characters that can be received before the CommEvent property's value is changed. Changing the value of this property will trigger an OnComm Event.

The Settings Property

This property sets the baud rate (data transfer rate), parity, data bits, and stop bits. It is defined using a comma-delimited string, and the default is 9600,n,8,1.

The SThreshold Property

This property establishes the number of characters that can remain unsent from the transmit buffer before the CommEvent property's value is changed. In other words, if the value is set to 5 and four or fewer characters remain, the CommEvent changes to indicate that the data was sent.

The MSComm Control OnComm Event

This is MSComm control's sole event, and it launches when the CommEvent property's value is changed. For data acquisition projects, this control's most common use in science and engineering, you're mostly interested in when the event launches as a result of the CommEvent property becoming equal to comEvReceive, indicating that your instrument's data was just received.

Using the OnComm Event

The data acquisition code is specific to your device's type and make, so the following example is more general. You'll set up the basic backbone required for a data acquisition project, but you won't proceed beyond this into any system-specific code.

Data acquisition initially starts with the data collection device sending data to the computer, via the RS232 connection. The Receive buffer collects that data until the RThreshold is reached and the CommEvent property is set equal to comEvReceive. At this point, the OnComm Event is triggered and you'd add the following code to it:

```
Private Sub AxMSComm1_OnComm(ByVal sender As System.Object, ByVal e As _
System.EventArgs) Handles AxMSComm1.OnComm
    If AxMSComm1.CommEvent = MsCommLib.OnCommConstants.comEvReceive Then
        'Use Input property to read data from buffer and process
    End If
End Sub
```

Once the OnComm event is triggered, you'd isolate why it was triggered and take the appropriate action. Obviously, you'd want to handle errors, data sends, and data reception differently. You can use If . . . Then statements or Select Case statements to distinguish between the CommEvents as shown previously. You could then add your device-specific code to these clauses in order to properly handle your incoming and outgoing data.

You can create especially robust applications using the techniques this chapter presents if you combine them with the techniques that Chapters 9 and 10 illustrate, which show you how to visualize your data in spreadsheet and graphical formats.

Programming Your Own Spreadsheets

IN THIS CHAPTER, YOU'LL LEARN how to code the spreadsheet-type interfaces that are common to so many scientific applications. These interfaces are extremely useful when dealing with matrix math or other scenarios that require a large amount of data. To develop such an advanced interface, this chapter introduces a new control along with some user events you haven't yet encountered. The examples require you to use almost everything you've seen so far, so make sure that you have the basics covered.

The MSFlexGrid Control

The MSFlexGrid control, when it's displayed on a form, appears like any spreadsheet grid. It consists of a number of intersecting rows and columns, and the points where the rows and columns intersect are known as *cells*. If you add such a control to your form and click Run, you'll see that it behaves almost like a spreadsheet program's worksheet. For example, you can move between cells with the arrow keys and mouse. The only real difference between this control and an actual spreadsheet is that you can't enter (type) data directly into a grid cell. Thus, this chapter will concentrate on coding a way to allow direct user data entry. But first, take some time to examine the important properties and events associated with this control. The MSFlexGrid control isn't a part of the standard VB toolbox. In VB 6.0, you must go to the Project menu and select the Components option. You then select the MSFlexGrid control from the Components list. In VB .NET you have to go to the Tools menu and select the Customize Toolbox option. You next select the MSFlexGrid control from the COM controls list. The control icon then appears in the toolbox, where you can drag and drop it onto a form as with any other control.

MSFlexGrid Properties

The following sections outline the properties for the MSFlexGrid control.

The AllowBigSelection Property

This property determines whether or not a whole row or column will be selected if the user clicks a row or column header. If it's set to the default of True, such whole row/column selections are allowed. If the property is set to False, only single cell selections are allowed.

The AllowUserResizing Property

This property works pretty much as you'd expect from its name. Its settings determine if neither rows nor columns can be resized (flexResizeNone) by the user, if just columns can be resized (flexResizeColumns), if just rows can be resized (flexResizeRows), or if both rows and columns can be resized (flexResizeBoth).

The Cols and Rows Properties

These properties are integer values, which determine the grid's number of columns and rows. The default for each property is 2, but you can easily adjust this through code (i.e., MSFlexGrid1.Cols = Number of Columns) or through the Properties window.

The Col and Row Properties

Be careful not to confuse these two properties with the Cols and Rows properties because they have a different function. These properties don't set the number of rows and columns, but rather store the numbers that represent the row and column containing the active cell. Also keep in mind that this property starts counting columns (left to right) and rows (top to bottom) from 0 and not 1. Thus, if the Cols property is set to 5, you'll find that Col property can equal any integer between 0 and 4, depending on which column contains the active cell. Please note that the Col and Row properties are available only at runtime.

The ColWidth and RowHeight Properties

You only can manipulate these properties at runtime. Nevertheless, they can be useful because they let you set a specified row's height as well as a specified column's width. You'll often find yourself needing to do this if default row or column dimensions are too large for the data to be displayed. The height and width is measured in twips.

The ColAlignment Property

This property's value determines whether or not the data displayed in a particular column is centered or justified. Setting it equal to 0 results in left justification while setting it to 1 right justifies the data. If the property is set equal to 2, the information displayed will be centered. This property isn't available at design time (except indirectly through the FormatString property).

The CellLeft, CellWidth, CellTop, and CellHeight Properties

Just like with the control-level Left, Width, Top, and Height properties (now referred to as Location.X, Size.Width, Location.Y, and Size.Height in VB .NET), these properties return the size and position of the current cell in twips. The only difference is that the cell properties refer to the frame that encloses the grid and not the form. These properties aren't available at design time and are read-only at runtime.

The FixedCols and FixedRows Properties

These properties control the grid's number of fixed rows and columns. The fixed rows and columns always appear at the grid's top and left sides (non-scrollable) and in gray instead of white. These types of cells generally provide some type of header for the rows and columns.

The FixedAlignment Property

This property works exactly like the ColAlignment property. The only difference is that it controls the alignment in fixed cells and not normal cells.

The GridLines Property

This property controls whether or not grid lines are within your grid control. The default displays the grid lines, which generally makes it much easier for the end user to distinguish the different cells.

The Sort Property

This property allows you to sort the contents of selected columns according to selected criteria. For example, the user could choose to sort in ascending or descending orders, or not sort the data at all. This property isn't available at design time and is write-only at runtime. When set at the code level, the sorting takes place immediately after the line of code executes.

The Text Property

You're very familiar with the Text property by now, but keep in mind that property stores only the text of the active cell, and not the text in any other cell. Thus, this property continually changes as you switch from cell to cell. Reading the Text property returns the current cell's contents as defined by the Row and Col properties. Writing to the Text property sets the contents of the current cell or selection (a range of cells) depending on the FillStyle property.

MSFlexGrid Events

MSFlexGrid controls respond to many of the events you've already seen, such as the Click and DoubleClick events. However, several useful events are unique to this control, and are covered in this section.

The EnterCell Event

This event occurs when the program user clicks on or keys into a new cell that is different from the cell that is currently selected. The EnterCell event works like the GotFocus event, only it deals with single cells instead of a control.

The LeaveCell Event

This event is the opposite of the EnterCell event: it occurs when the focus is shifted away from the active cell to a new cell. Thus, this event is always triggered just prior to the EnterCell event. You can use this event to validate a cell's contents.

The RowColChange Event

This event is triggered when either the current row or column is changed, which is essentially whenever the user changes cells. It always follows both the LeaveCell and EnterCell events.

MSFlexGrid Methods

The two methods discussed in this section are important to MSFlexGrid controls. These methods allow you to insert or delete rows at specific locations within the grid. However, because these methods involve the syntax of AddItem and RemoveItem, don't confuse them with the ones used in conjunction with list and combo boxes.

The RemoveItem Method

You'll begin with the RemoveItem method because its syntax is slightly simpler than the AddItem method. To invoke the RemoveItem method, you only need the control's name and the row number you want to remove. Remember that the first row begins with zero and not one, however. For example, the code

```
MSFlexGrid1.RemoveItem(5)
```

would remove the sixth row and not the fifth row in the MSFlexGrid named MSFlexGrid1. In VB .NET the default name for MSFlexGrid is AxMSFlexGrid1.

The AddItem Method

This method works like the RemoveItem method; however, you gain the additional ability to specify the contents of cells within the row you're going to add. For example, say that you want to add the values contained in String1 and String2 to cells 1 and 2 of the new row. In VB 6.0, you'd accomplish this with the following code:·

```
Dim Strings As String
Strings = "String1"  & vbTab & "String2"
MSFlexGrid1.AddItem  Strings, 5
```

In VB .NET, you'd use the code:

```
Dim Strings As String
Strings = "String1" & Microsoft.VisualBasic.ControlChars.Tab & "String2"
AxMSFlexGrid1.AddItem(Strings, 5)
```

This code adds the strings found in the Strings variable into the new row you created. If you look closely, a Tab separates the two substrings within Strings. This is
how VB distinguishes the information going to each cell. In essence, the Tab is the
factor that tells VB that one column ended and a new column began. The number
5 that follows the String argument is an optional argument that tells VB to add the
new row in the sixth position.

Entering Text into MSFlexGrid Cells

Now that you're familiar with the different MSFlexGrids events, properties, and
methods, you can apply this knowledge by coding a method of allowing typed-in
text to be entered into the grid cells. As mentioned before, the grid itself doesn't
support direct user data entry, so you must type the text into the text box and set
the Text property of the desired cell equal to the text in the text box. The trick, however, is in integrating this text box with the active grid cells so well that it seems
part of the cell itself. You also need to enable the text box to move around on the
grid in response to the arrow and return keys, as if it were part of the grid itself.

This process requires many different event procedures, as well as a custom
procedure, so begin the process by coding a simple application. This application
calculates a compound's number of moles based on the supplied total number
of moles and mole fraction. You want to perform this calculation on a listing of
different compounds typed into grid cells. To begin this application, add
a MSFlexGrid control named AxMSFlexGrid1 along with three text boxes named
TextBox1, TextBox2, and TextBox3 to the form. TextBox1 is the text box that floats
around the grid cells, while TextBox2 reads in the total number of compounds in
the solution. TextBox3 reads in the solution's total number of moles.

```
After placing your controls on the form, format the MSFlexGrid by adding the
following code to the form's Load event. Private Sub Form1_Load(ByVal
eventSender As System.Object, ByVal eventArgs _
As System.EventArgs) Handles MyBase.Load
TextBox1.Visible = False
TextBox1.Font = AxMSFlexGrid1.Font
With AxMSFlexGrid1
    .Cols = 3
    .Rows = 25
```

```
    Show()
    .Col = 0
    .Row = 0
    .Text = "Name"
    .Col = 1
    .Text = "X"
    .Col = 2
    .Text = "Moles"
    .Row = 1
    .Col = 0
End With
DimTextBox()
End Sub
```

As you can see, this procedure first sets the Visible property of TextBox1 equal to False. In order for the text box to integrate seamlessly with the grid cells, you want the text box to appear only after it's properly formatted. Next, set the text box's font equal to the grid control's font. The Set keyword ensures that the fonts stay in sync even if the MSFlexGrid font is later modified. Next, establish the grid's size by setting the number of rows equal to 25 and the number of columns equal to 3. Then, make the cell present in row zero, column zero the active cell and enter the text "Name" into the cell. Remember, the grid control's Text property stores only the text present in the active cell. Then, move the active cell over and enter "X" and "Moles" in the corresponding cells. These columns store the mole fraction (X) and the calculated number of moles. Finally, move the active cell to the grid's top leftmost cell, excluding the header titles just added. Now that your grid setup is complete, call the custom procedure DimTextBox to properly position TextBox1 in this cell.

This section presents both VB 6.0 and VB .NET versions of this procedure because of their significant differences. The code for the DimTextBox routine in VB 6.0 is as follows:

```
Private Sub DimTextBox()
With AxMSFlexGrid1
        TextBox1.Left = .CellLeft + .Left
        TextBox1.Top = .CellTop + .Top
        TextBox1.Width = .CellWidth
        TextBox1.Height = .CellHeight
        TextBox1.Visible = True
        TextBox1.SetFocus
End With
End Sub
```

Looking closely at this procedure, notice that the text box's Left, Top, Height, and Width properties adjust to correspond to the active cell's equivalent positions. This places a text box of equal size as the cell directly on top of the active cell. In fact, the text box should blend in so well that the program user won't even know it's separate from the grid control. Now that the text box is so well concealed, you can make it visible and set the focus on it. This lets users type in the text box while thinking they are entering data directly into the grid control.

To have the same effect in VB .NET, you must first address some MSFlexGrid compatibility issues. As the chapter on graphics describes, the VB .NET's default graphical display unit is pixels. However, MSFlexGrid's CellLeft, CellWidth, CellTop, and CellHeight properties are all in twips. To get the text box into the correct dimensions, access the TwipsToPixelsX and TwipsToPixelsY conversion functions by selecting Add Reference from the Project menu. Scroll down the list of choices and add the Microsoft Visual Basic .NET Compatibility dll. You should see it appear under the reference heading of the Solution Explorer window. Next, import the previously unavailable Microsoft.VisualBasic.Compatibility.VB6 namespace by adding the following line of code to the declarations section:

```
Imports Microsoft.VisualBasic.Compatibility.VB6
```

> **NOTE** *This compatibility issue exists with the current MSFlexGrid 6.0 control. If a newer version comes out, it may address this incompatibility, and the conversion functions may no longer be required.*

The VB .NET code for the DimTextBox routine is as follows:

```
Private Sub DimTextBox()
        With AxMSFlexGrid1
            TextBox1.Location = New Point(TwipsToPixelsX(.CellLeft) _
+ .Location.X, TwipsToPixelsX(.CellTop) + .Location.Y)
            TextBox1.Size = New Size(TwipsToPixelsY(.CellWidth), _
 TwipsToPixelsY(.CellHeight))
            TextBox1.Visible = True
            TextBox1.Focus()
        End With
    End Sub
```

This code functions the same way as the VB 6.0 procedure, only it makes use of the newer Location X and Y properties as well as the Size property, rather than the older syntax of Left, Top, Height, and Width.

It isn't enough, however, to just call this routine for that starting cell. Instead, you must accomplish this for every cell in the grid when it becomes the active cell. The EnterCell event discussed earlier can address this by offering a way to redimension your text box every time a new cell is entered (i.e., made active). Therefore, proceed by adding the following code:

```
Private Sub AxMSFlexGrid1_EnterCell(ByVal eventSender As System.Object, ByVal _
eventArgs As System.EventArgs) Handles AxMSFlexGrid1.EnterCell
    TextBox1.Text = AxMSFlexGrid1.Text
    DimTextBox()
End Sub
```

As you can see, this code will reposition your text box by calling the DimTextBox procedure every time a new cell is entered. Before calling on this procedure, however, set the text box's text equal to the MSFlexGrid cell's text. This ensures that users can view the text when the text box is placed on top of the grid cell.

Now that you've developed a way to reposition the text box over any active cell, you must get text entered into the text box also entered into the underlying grid cell. You accomplish this by taking advantage of the text box's Change event, so let's add the following code.

```
Private Sub TextBox1_TextChanged(ByVal eventSender As System.Object, ByVal _
eventArgs As System.EventArgs) Handles TextBox1.TextChanged
        AxMSFlexGrid1.Text = TextBox1.Text
End Sub
```

This code sets the text in the active grid cell equal to any text entered into or modified in the text box. Thus, this procedure keeps the text box in sync with its underlying cell.

However, your data entry code isn't complete. You still need to activate the arrow keys so the grid's rows and columns change even when the text box has the focus. To do this, you'll use two text box events not yet discussed, the KeyDown event and the KeyPress event.

The KeyDown Event

This event is used most often with arrow keys and function keys and is invoked when a key is pressed down. Releasing the key invokes a KeyUp event. While these events work with most keys, they can't be used in conjunction with the

Enter key, the Esc key, and the Tab key. For your purposes, you want to use the KeyDown event to activate the arrow keys by utilizing the following code:

```
Private Sub TextBox1_KeyDown(ByVal eventSender As System.Object, ByVal _
eventArgs As System.Windows.Forms.KeyEventArgs) Handles TextBox1.KeyDown
    Dim KeyCode As Short = eventArgs.KeyCode
    Dim Shift As Short = eventArgs.KeyData \ &H10000
    With AxMSFlexGrid1
        Select Case KeyCode
            Case  Keys.Down
                If .Row < .Rows - 1 Then .Row = .Row + 1
            Case Keys.Up
                If .Row > 1 Then .Row = .Row - 1
            Case Keys.Right
                If .Col < .Cols - 1 Then .Col = .Col + 1
            Case Keys.Left
                If .Col > 0 Then .Col = .Col - 1
        End Select
    End With
End Sub
```

First, notice that this event involves Text1 and not the grid control. This is because after you enter a cell, the called-upon DimTextBox routine sets the focus on the text box, and only controls with the focus can respond to key events. This procedure's arguments describe the key that was pressed (KeyCode) and the state of the Shift key. Thus, when a key is pressed, this procedure checks to see if it was an arrow key by comparing the value of KeyCode to VB constants that describe the arrow keys (i.e., vbKeyDown). If an arrow key was pressed, it adjusts the active cell of the flex grid control appropriately. Before it makes an adjustment, however, the active cell's row/column number is compared to the values of the border rows and columns to ensure these values aren't exceeded. This eliminates possible program errors by preventing users from keying off the grid.

The KeyPress Event

Although enabling arrow keys is a great feature, most spreadsheet interfaces also allow you to move down columns by hitting the Enter key. As mentioned earlier, though, the KeyDown event won't work in conjunction with the Enter key. Thus, you must use the alternate KeyPress event as follows:

```
Private Sub TextBox1_KeyPress(ByVal eventSender As System.Object, ByVal _
eventArgs As System.Windows.Forms.KeyPressEventArgs) Handles _
TextBox1.KeyPress
    Dim KeyAscii As Short = Asc(eventArgs.KeyChar)
    With AxMSFlexGrid1
        If KeyAscii = Keys.Return And .Row < .Rows - 1 Then
            .Row = .Row + 1
        End If
    End With
    If KeyAscii = 0 Then
        eventArgs.Handled = True
    End If
End Sub
```

In this procedure, KeyAscii stores the value of the ANSI character that was just typed. Thus, to detect the depression of the Enter key, you examine when the value of KeyAscii equals the ANSI value that the return (Enter) key generates when pressed. When this is the case, the value of the MSFlexGrid.Row property increases by one. As with the KeyDown events, a conditional ensures that users can't key past the grid's boundaries.

The Mole Fraction Calculation

Now that the flex grid is fully set up with the ability to allow user data entry, let's move on to actual mole fraction calculation. A mole fraction (X) simply equals the number of a solution component's moles divided by the total number of moles present within the solution. Thus, if 1 mole of compound A is in a solution that contains ten moles of material, A's mole fraction is equal to 0.1.

In your program the user enters the total number of moles along with the mole fraction of each component and calculates each component's total number of moles. To perform this calculation, add a command button to the form and place the following code in its Click event:

```
Private Sub Button1_Click(ByVal eventSender As System.Object, ByVal eventArgs As _
System.EventArgs) Handles Button1.Click
Dim Num As Integer
Dim I as Integer
Dim TotMoles As Single
Dim Moles As Single
Num = CInt(TextBox2.Text)
TotMoles = CSng(TextBox3.Text)
With AxMSFlexGrid1
For I = 1 To Num
        .Col = 1
        .Row = I
        Moles = CSng(.Text) * TotMoles
        .Col = 2
        .Text = Moles
  Next I
  .Row = 1
  .Col = 0
  DimTextBox()
  End With
End Sub
```

As you can see, this event first reads in the number of components and the total number of moles. It then iterates through the column of the grid that contains the values of X and multiplies these values by the total number of moles. This resulting value, equal to the number of moles of a particular component, is then entered into the "Moles" column.

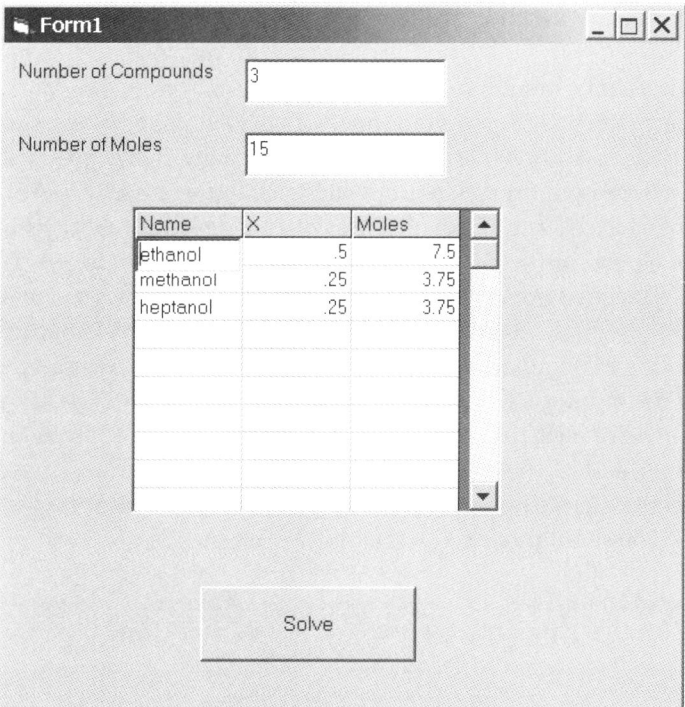

Figure 9-1. A sample output of the Mole Fraction routine

If you think carefully about this routine, one small improvement could make this routine more error-proof. A mole fraction is equal to the number of moles of a certain component divided by the total number of moles. It's impossible to have mole fractions that add up to a value greater than 1. Thus, it would be great to add up the values of X and make sure they are 1 or less before proceeding with the calculation. If they are greater than 1 an error message should alert users of their mistake. A truly well-done program takes as many precautions as possible to ensure the validity of the data generated. By this point, you should be familiar enough with the workings of the MSFlexGrid and the required VB structures. So try adding in this safeguard before moving on to the final section of this chapter.

Working with Excel Data

Microsoft Excel is a commonly used spreadsheet application, thus it is not a rarity to find that data you may want to work with in your application is stored in an Excel workbook (.xls). This is especially true since many data acquisition programs can even output Excel sheets directly. Luckily, there is a way for you to read in data from an Excel workbook and write your changes and additions back to that workbook. You can accomplish this through use of an API called Open Database Connectivity, or ODBC. What this API does is it allows you to link your program to the worksheet data, and through Structured Query Language (SQL) calls access and manipulates the data found in the worksheet. Unfortunately, at the time of this writing, ODBC .NET is not yet a completed project, and thus this book cannot delve further into this topic. ODBC .NET is due out sometime in 2002, however, and can be quite a useful tool because it can also be used for database connectivity as well as spreadsheets. To stay posted on the progress of ODBC .NET you should check with the MSDN Web site.

> **TIP**   *Although not nearly as powerful or flexible, the techniques covered in Chapter 8 allow you to access your Excel data with VB code. All you need to do is save your spreadsheet as a .txt file.*

Getting Your Grids to Dynamically Respond

Now that you understand the basics of coding with MSFlexGrids, you can move past a simple mole fraction calculation and develop a more powerful routine. Think back to Chapter 5, where you looked at an iterative technique called Gauss-Siedel iteration. Engineers often use this technique to calculate 2-D temperature distributions at discrete points along a surface. To use this technique, each point's temperature is described by an energy balance equation and the equation coefficients entered into a matrix. Consecutive iterations perform on the elements of this matrix until the resultant values differ by no more than the set convergence criterion. To make this routine especially powerful, you'll get your grid and program to behave dynamically to handle any size coefficient matrix.

Begin by adding three text boxes named Text1, Text2, and Text3 and an MSFlexGrid named MSFlexGrid1 to your form. Text1 acts as the floating text box, which facilitates data entry into the grid. Text2 allows the user to input the number of nodes (points) and, hence, the number of equations to be entered into your matrix. Last, Text3 allows the application users to specify their required convergence criterion. You'll now add two command buttons named Command1 and Command2 to the form. The first command button (Command1) reformats the grid layout to enable the user to enter the correct number of matrix elements. The second command button initiates the actual iteration once all of the required data is entered.

Now that all of the required elements are on the form, add the code needed to accomplish your goals:

```
Public NumNodes As Short
Public MaxRow As Short

Private Sub Command1_Click(ByVal eventSender As System.Object, ByVal _
eventArgs As System.EventArgs) Handles Command1.Click
    Dim y As Short
    Dim x As Short
    With MSFlexGrid1
        For x = 0 To NumNodes + 3
            For y = 0 To MaxRow + 1
                .Col = x
                .Row = y
                .Text = ""
            Next y
        Next x
        .Row = 0
        NumNodes = CShort(Text2.Text)
        For x = 1 To NumNodes
            .Col = x
            .Text = "ai" & x
        Next x
        .Col = NumNodes + 1
        .Text = "Ci"
        .Col = NumNodes + 2
        .Text = "Estimations"
        .Col = 0
        For x = 1 To NumNodes
            .Row = x
            .Text = CStr(x)
        Next x
        MaxRow = .Row
        .Row = 1
        .Col = 1
    End With
End Sub
```

```
Private Sub Command2_Click(ByVal eventSender As System.Object, ByVal _
eventArgs As System.EventArgs) Handles Command2.Click
    Dim K As Short
    Dim J As Short
    Dim I As Short
    Dim z As Short
    Dim y As Short
    Dim x As Short
    Dim a(,) As Double
    Dim C() As Double
    Dim T1() As Double
    Dim T2() As Double
    Dim T3() As Double
    Dim N As Integer
    N = CShort(Text2.Text)
    ReDim a(N, N)
    ReDim C(N)
    ReDim T1(N)
    ReDim T2(N)
    ReDim T3(N)
    Dim Conv As Boolean
    Dim E As Double 'convergence criterion
    Dim Count As Short
    Dim S1 As Double
    Dim S2 As Double
    E = CDbl(Text3.Text)
    For x = 1 To N
        For y = 1 To N
            MSFlexGrid1.Row = x
            MSFlexGrid1.Col = y
            a(x, y) = CDbl(MSFlexGrid1.Text)
        Next y
    Next x
    For z = 1 To N
        MSFlexGrid1.Col = NumNodes + 1
        MSFlexGrid1.Row = z
        C(z) = CDbl(MSFlexGrid1.Text)
        MSFlexGrid1.Col = NumNodes + 2
        T2(z) = CDbl(MSFlexGrid1.Text)
    Next z
    MSFlexGrid1.Row = NumNodes + 2
    MSFlexGrid1.Col = 0
    MSFlexGrid1.Text = "Iteration"
```

```
        For I = 1 To NumNodes
            MSFlexGrid1.Col = I
            MSFlexGrid1.Text = "T" & I
        Next I
        Count = 1
        Do Until Conv = True
            Conv = True
            MSFlexGrid1.Row = MSFlexGrid1.Row + 1
            MSFlexGrid1.Col = 0
            MSFlexGrid1.Text = CStr(Count)
            For I = 1 To N
                S1 = 0
                S2 = 0
                T1(I) = (C(I) / a(I, I))
                If I - 1 > 0 Then
                    For J = 1 To I - 1
                        S1 = S1 + (a(I, J) / a(I, I)) * T2(J)
                    Next J
                    T1(I) = T1(I) - S1
                End If
                If I + 1 <= N Then
                    For K = I + 1 To N
                        S2 = S2 + (a(I, K) / a(I, I)) * T2(K)
                    Next K
                        T1(I) = T1(I) - S2
                End If
                MSFlexGrid1.Col = MSFlexGrid1.Col + 1
                MSFlexGrid1.Text = (System.Math.Round(T1(I)*10000)/10000)
'The Round Function trims extra decimal places and allows easier viewing in cell
                If T1(I) - T2(I) > E Then
                    Conv = False
                End If
                T3(I) = T2(I)
                T2(I) = T1(I)
            Next I
            Count = Count + 1
        Loop
        MaxRow = MSFlexGrid1.Row
End Sub
```

```
Private Sub Form1_Load(ByVal eventSender As System.Object, ByVal eventArgs As _
System.EventArgs) Handles MyBase.Load
    Text1.Visible = False
    Text1.Font = MSFlexGrid1.Font
    Dim x As Short
    With MSFlexGrid1
        .Cols = 100
        .Rows = 2000
        Show()
        .Col = 0
        .Row = 0
        .Text = "Equation #"
        For x = 1 To 4
            .Col = x
            .Text = "ai" & x
        Next x
        .Col = 5
        .Text = "Ci"
        .Col = 6
        .Text = "Estimations"
        .Col = 0
        For x = 1 To 4
            .Row = x
            .Text = CStr(x)
        Next x
            .Row = 1
            .Col = 1
    End With
    NumNodes = 4
    MaxRow = 4
    DimTextBox()
End Sub

Private Sub DimTextBox()
    With MSFlexGrid1
        Text1.Location = New Point(TwipsToPixelsX(.CellLeft) _
+ .Location.X, TwipsToPixelsX(.CellTop) + .Location.Y)
        Text1.Size = New Size(TwipsToPixelsY(.CellWidth), _
TwipsToPixelsY(.CellHeight))
        Text1.Visible = True
        Text1.Focus()
    End With
End Sub
```

```
Private Sub MSFlexGrid1_EnterCell(ByVal eventSender As System.Object, ByVal _
eventArgs As System.EventArgs) Handles MSFlexGrid1.EnterCell
    Text1.Text = MSFlexGrid1.Text
    DimTextBox()
End Sub
Private Sub Text1_TextChanged(ByVal eventSender As System.Object, ByVal _
eventArgs As System.EventArgs) Handles Text1.TextChanged
    MSFlexGrid1.Text = Text1.Text
End Sub


Private Sub Text1_KeyDown(ByVal eventSender As System.Object, ByVal _
eventArgs As System.Windows.Forms.KeyEventArgs) Handles Text1.KeyDown
    Dim KeyCode As Short = eventArgs.KeyCode
    Dim Shift As Short = eventArgs.KeyData \ &H10000
    With MSFlexGrid1
        Select Case KeyCode
            Case  Keys.Down
                If .Row < .Rows - 1 Then .Row = .Row + 1
            Case Keys.Up
                If .Row > 1 Then .Row = .Row - 1
            Case Keys.Right
                If .Col < .Cols - 1 Then .Col = .Col + 1
            Case Keys.Left
                If .Col > 1 Then .Col = .Col - 1
        End Select
    End With
End Sub

Private Sub Text1_KeyPress(ByVal eventSender As System.Object, ByVal _
eventArgs As System.Windows.Forms.KeyPressEventArgs) Handles _
Text1.KeyPress
    Dim KeyAscii As Short = Asc(eventArgs.KeyChar)
    With MSFlexGrid1
        If KeyAscii = Keys.Return And .Row < .Rows - 1 Then
       .Row = .Row + 1
        End If
    End With
    If KeyAscii = 0 Then
     eventArgs.Handled = True
End If
End Sub
```

Taking a good look at the code, notice that you use the same KeyDown, KeyPress, EnterCell, and Change events as in the previous section, as these events are fairly standard to all applications with this sort of interface. You also use the DimTextBox procedure and the form's Load event to set up the grid's default size. This Load event sets up a grid to hold all of the information needed to perform this iteration on a surface that consists only of four nodes. At the end of the procedure the Load event also stores this number of nodes in the Public variable NumNodes and stores the value of the highest row number that data was entered into in the Public variable MaxRow.

The purposes of these two Public variables is apparent when you look at the Click event for Command1, the reformatting command button. This Click event uses information in these variables to erase all of the grid's information. The procedure then reformats the grid to handle another matrix of the size specified in Text2. As you can see, all of the row and column labels change to correspond to this newly sized grid. Once the grid is established at the correct size, the user enters the correct data and proceeds to clicking Command2. This initiates the Click event of Command2, which contains the code for the Gauss-Siedel iteration discussed in Chapter 5. The procedure reads the matrix information into the required arrays and performs the required iteration. As the procedure iterates, it formats a portion of the grid (below the data entry region) to display the iteration's calculated values. Thus, if the system of equations is a solvable set of equations (as they should be for a real system), you can watch the calculated values converge to within the specified criterion (see Figure 9-2 for an example set). If the equations aren't solvable, the Gauss-Siedel iteration diverges over time and leads to an overflow error. Thus, to challenge yourself, modify the routine so it only runs for X number of iterations and outputs an error message box saying that the results didn't converge in X number of iterations. It can't be stressed enough that good scientific and engineering applications take measures to ensure both the application's stability and the data's integrity.

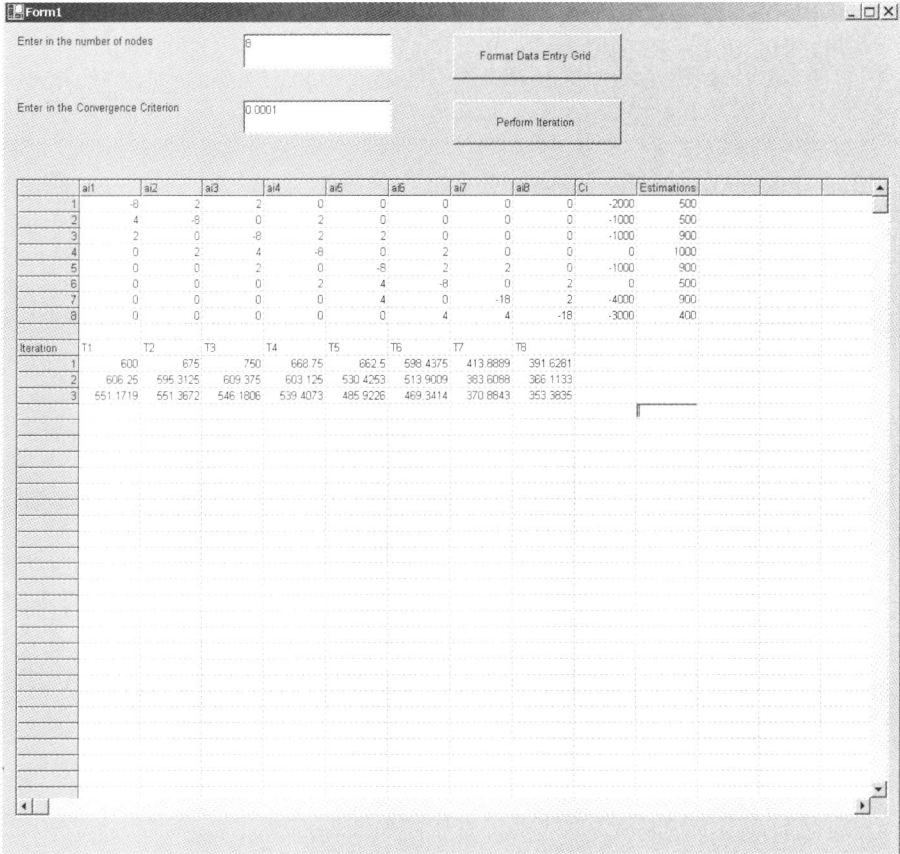

Figure 9-2. A sample Gauss-Siedel iteration

The preceding issue aside, though, this can be a powerful and highly useful iterative technique when used properly. Hopefully, this application also gave you some insights into the types of powerful routines you can develop using spreadsheet type interfaces.

CHAPTER 10

Scientific Graphics

GRAPHICS ARE HIGHLY USEFUL TOOLS for presenting data. Whether for a plot of a mathematical function, a bar graph displaying data, or a schematic diagram, graphics can help researchers support and explain their theories and findings. This chapter explains how to use the Microsoft Chart control to integrate data presentation capabilities within your applications. You'll also look at the new System.Drawing namespace in VB .NET, and explore using it to create a function-plotting program.

The MSChart Control

Readers who have dealt with Microsoft Office Visual Basic for Applications (VBA) might be familiar with the MSChart control; Office developers often use this general-purpose graphing control. With this control, you can create Excel-like charts from your application data and display these charts on a form. You have the flexibility to create a variety of 2-D and 3-D charts, including, but not limited to, bar graphs, pie charts, and line graphs. Additionally, you can control chart and axis labels, as well as axis tick mark increments and a variety of other features. The resultant charts created by this control look similar to Excel, but keep in mind that the MSChart control lacks Excel's level and variety of options. You should remain open to saving your data in a format that you can later import into Excel for charting. However, this control meets most basic graphing needs and provides a highly useful tool for creating independent graphing solutions. You'll begin learning about this useful control by examining its most useful properties.

> **NOTE** *The MSChart control originated as a subset of the Graphics Server control's capabilities, which are discussed in Chapter 3.*

The MSChart control isn't part of the standard VB toolbox. To select it in VB 6.0, go to the Project menu and choose the Components option. Next, select the Microsoft Chart Control from the Controls list. In VB .NET, go to the Tools menu, select the Customize Toolbox option, and then select the Microsoft Chart control from the COM Components list.

The MSChart Control Properties

The following sections describe in more detail the MSChart control properties.

The AllowSelections Property

This property determines whether users can select different chart elements. For example, you can allow users to select chart titles, axis labels, and legend elements when this property is set to True. An upcoming example illustrates how such user selections can dynamically alter selected elements.

The AllowSeriesSelection Property

This property is somewhat similar to the AllowSelections property, except it deals with the actual data presented in the chart and not labels and other elements. When set to True, a user can click a single data point and in the process select the whole data series.

The ChartType Property

Probably one of the most important properties, ChartType dictates what type of chart is created and displayed. Table 10-1 shows you the chart types you can choose from by specifying various VB constants for ChartType.

Table 10-1. The Different Chart Types Available for the MSChart Control

CHART TYPE	VB CONSTANT
3-D Bar Chart	VtChChartType3dBar
2-D Bar Chart	VtChChartType2dBar
3-D Line Graph	VtChChartType3dLine
2-D Line Graph	VtChChartType2dLine
3-D Area Chart	VtChChartType3dArea
2-D Area Chart	VtChChartType2dArea
3-D Step Chart	VtChChartType3dStep
2-D Step Chart	VtChChartType2dStep
3-D Combination Chart	VtChChartType3dCombination
2-D Combination Chart	VtChChartType2dCombination
2-D Pie Chart	VtChChartType2dPie
2-D XY Scatter Plot	VtChChartType2dXY

VB .NET includes a few more constants, like VtChChartType2dPolar and VtChChartType2dRadar.

The Column Property

To use this control effectively, think in terms of populating a spreadsheet grid. In other words, you find each series of data in its own unique column and each point within a series within its own row. The Column property determines which column in this invisible data grid is the active column.

The ColumnCount Property

This property determines the number of data columns within your data grid—that is, how many data series should the control be able to plot.

The ColumnLabel Property

The ColumnLabel property sets the text description associated with the current active data column (the column specified by the column property). For example, if the Column property was set equal to 1, this property could name column 1 as "#1."

The Data Property

As mentioned previously, this control stores data in an invisible data grid where the Column and Row properties specify each data point. The Value property sets this specified data point's value.

The DataSource Property

Although not discussed yet, certain controls like MSFlexGrid controls and the Chart control are data-aware controls. That is, they can be bound to an external data source, such as a database using ActiveX Data Objects (ADO). The data grid is filled with data points specified from the external data source.

The RandomFill Property

This property does just what its name implies. If set to True, it fills your data grid with random data that can then be charted.

The Repaint Property

This property determines whether or not the chart repaints (refreshes) its display after changes are made to it. It's usually a good idea to keep it set to True so that the display always represents the latest data changes.

The Row Property

Just as the Column property sets the active column of the chart's data grid, this control sets the data grid's active row. Together these two properties specify the active data point.

The RowCount Property

This property sets the number of rows in each data grid column. In other words, it gives you control over how many data points are in each series.

The RowLabel Property

This property lets you specify a name for the data grid's current active row.

The ShowLegend Property

As is obvious from the name, this property determines whether or not your chart displays a legend. The Column labels determine the names associated with each series within the legend.

The TitleText Property

Another straightforward property, TitleText simply controls the text displayed as the chart's title.

The MSChart Control Events

Many of this control's events resemble the control events you've already seen, such as Click and DblClick (DoubleClick in VB .NET), but a number of them haven't been encountered. Luckily, these novel events are really the same two events applied to different elements within the chart. In other words, the TitleSelected event operates in the same way as the AxisSelected event, except that the first initiates when the title is selected and the second initiates when the axis is selected.

The Selected Events

As just mentioned, these events initiate when a mouse click selects a certain element of the chart. For example, you could select the MSChart as a whole, a data series, a chart title, an axis, or an axis title. These events provide a great way to let users dynamically change the selected element, as you see in an upcoming example.

Altering Selected Chart Elements

Try coding a brief example that allows you to click a chart's title and enter in
a new title. First, add the MSChart control to your toolbox. Next, add this control
to your form, along with a text box with a visible property set to False. Set the
TitleText property of the MSChart control to some suitable title. For aesthetic
purposes, position the text box over the chart's title. Now add the following code:

```
Private Sub AxMSChart1_TitleSelected(ByVal eventSender As System.Object, ByVal _
eventArgs As AxMSChart20Lib._DMSChartEvents_TitleSelectedEvent) Handles _
AxMSChart1.TitleSelected
    TextBox1.Text = AxMSChart1.Title.Text
    TextBox1.Visible = True
    TextBox1.Focus()
End Sub


Private Sub TextBox1_KeyUp(ByVal sender As Object, ByVal e As _
System.Windows.Forms.KeyEventArgs) Handles TextBox1.KeyUp
        If e.KeyCode = Keys.Enter Then
            AxMSChart1.Title.Text = TextBox1.Text
        End If
End Sub

Private Sub AxMschart1_DblClick(ByVal eventSender As System.Object, ByVal _
eventArgs As System.EventArgs) Handles AxMschart1.DblClick
    TextBox1.Visible = False
End Sub
```

Notice that when the chart title is selected, the first step is to set the text box's
text equal to the title text. You then make the text box visible and set the focus on
the text box. At this point, you're ready to enter the new title into the text box. You
must use the text box's KeyUp event to update the title. Thus, after the text is
changed in the text box and the Enter key is pressed, so too is the text changed in
the Title.Text property of AxMsChart1.

Finally, when you're done with the title change, you can double-click anywhere else on the chart and the textbox will disappear, leaving behind the
changed title (see Figure 10-1).

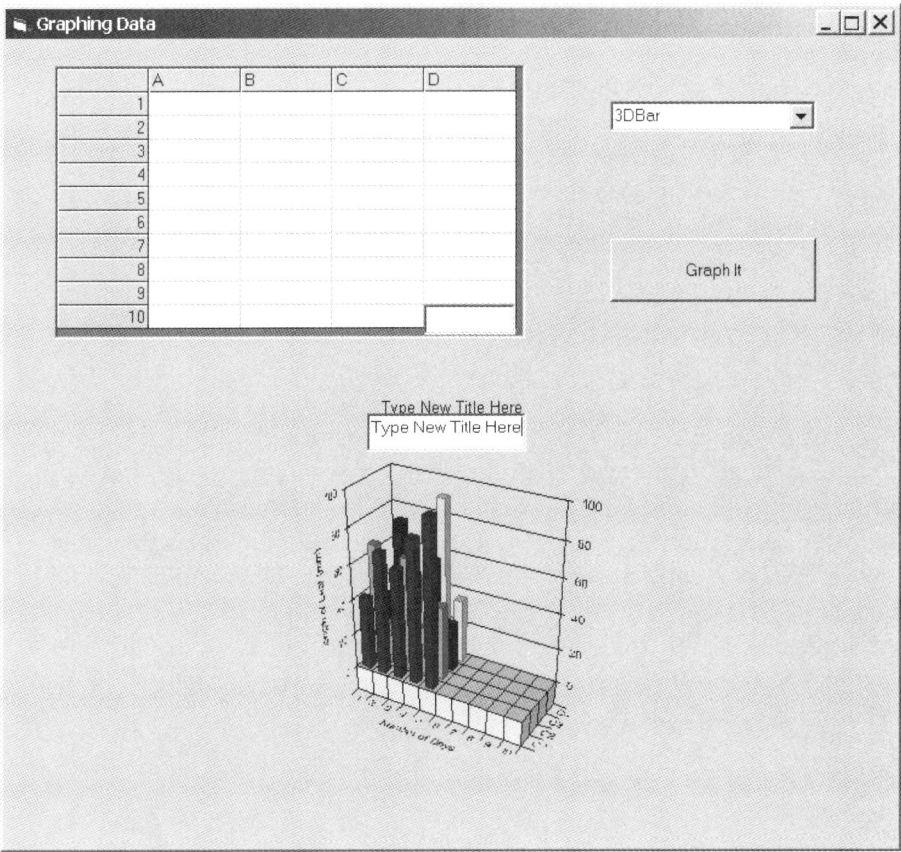

Figure 10-1. Using the TitleSelected event to update the chart's title

The Updated Events

The other set of events specific to the Chart control are the Updated events. Like the Selected events, these events can apply to the chart as a whole or to different elements within the chart. But, looking closer at these events, the only really new concept is the name; they behave much as the Change event found with other controls. In other words, this event initiates when elements or properties are updated or changed.

The Chart Control in Action

Now that you understand the basics of the Chart control, you can use some of this knowledge to code an example. The example situation is as follows. You're part of a botany research group that is studying "newborn" leaf growth. The group's data starts with a baseline measurement of the leaf bud's length. The group measures the leaf's length every day for nine days. Your role is to develop a software application to view the growth curves of four different leaves. You must create a spreadsheet interface for data entry and then plot this spreadsheet's data in both bar and line graphs.

To create this application, add the Chart control and the MSFlexGrid control to your toolbox. Name these controls MSChart1 and MSFlexGrid1, respectively. Next, add a textbox, command button, and combo box named Text1, Command1, and Combo1, respectively. The text box and the MSFlexGrid form the basis of the data entry grid, while the combo box control allows you to select the type of chart you want to present. The command button brings about and updates the Chart control's display. VB .NET has certain MSFlexGrid compatibility issues; it's worth recollecting from Chapter 9 how to properly incorporate MSFlexGrid into a VB .NET application. In particular, remember to add a reference to the Microsoft Visual Basic .NET Compatibility runtime and include the following line of code at the top of the code:

```
Imports Microsoft.VisualBasic.Compatibility.VB6
```

The following listing shows the code of your application:

```
Private Sub Command1_Click(ByVal eventSender As System.Object, ByVal _
eventArgs As System.EventArgs) Handles Command1.Click
    Dim I As Short
    MSChart1.ColumnCount = 4
    MSChart1.RowCount = 10
    With Combo1
        If .Text = "3DBar" Then
            MSChart1.chartType = MSChart20Lib.VtChChartType.VtChChartType3dBar
        ElseIf .Text = "2DBar" Then
            MSChart1.chartType = MSChart20Lib.VtChChartType.VtChChartType2dBar
        ElseIf .Text = "3DLine" Then
            MSChart1.chartType = MSChart20Lib.VtChChartType.VtChChartType3dLine
        ElseIf .Text = "2DLine" Then
            MSChart1.chartType = MSChart20Lib.VtChChartType.VtChChartType2dLine
        End If
    End With
```

```
    For I = 1 To 10
        MSChart1.Row = I
        MSChart1.RowLabel = I
    Next I


PlotData()
        MSChart1.Visible = True
End Sub


Private Sub Form1_Load(ByVal eventSender As System.Object, ByVal eventArgs As _
System.EventArgs) Handles MyBase.Load
    Text1.Visible = False
    MSChart1.Visible = False
    Text1.Font = MSFlexGrid1.Font
    Dim x As Short
    With MSFlexGrid1
            .Cols = 5
            .Rows = 11
            Show()
            .Row = 0
            For x = 1 To 4
                .Col = x
                .Text = Chr(64 + x)
            Next x
            .Col = 0
            For x = 1 To 10
                .Row = x
                .Text = CStr(x)
            Next x
            .Row = 1
            .Col = 1
    End With
    DimTextBox()
    FillCombo()
    ChartLayout()
End Sub
```

```
Private Sub DimTextBox()
    With MSFlexGrid1
        Text1.Location = New Point(TwipsToPixelsX(.CellLeft) _
+ .Location.X, TwipsToPixelsX(.CellTop) + .Location.Y)
        Text1.Size = New Size(TwipsToPixelsY(.CellWidth), _
TwipsToPixelsY(.CellHeight))
        Text1.Visible = True
        Text1.Focus()
    End With
End Sub


Private Sub MSFlexGrid1_EnterCell(ByVal eventSender As System.Object, ByVal _
eventArgs As System.EventArgs) Handles MSFlexGrid1.EnterCell
    Text1.Text = MSFlexGrid1.Text
    DimTextBox()
End Sub


Private Sub Text1_TextChanged(ByVal eventSender As System.Object, ByVal _
eventArgs As System.EventArgs) Handles Text1.TextChanged
    MSFlexGrid1.Text = Text1.Text
End Sub


Private Sub Text1_KeyDown(ByVal eventSender As System.Object, ByVal eventArgs As _
System.Windows.Forms.KeyEventArgs) Handles Text1.KeyDown
    Dim KeyCode As Short = eventArgs.KeyCode
    Dim Shift As Short = eventArgs.KeyData \ &H10000
    With MSFlexGrid1
        Select Case KeyCode
        Case System.Windows.Forms.Keys.Down
            If .Row < .Rows - 1 Then .Row = .Row + 1
        Case System.Windows.Forms.Keys.Up
            If .Row > 1 Then .Row = .Row - 1
        Case System.Windows.Forms.Keys.Right
            If .Col < .Cols - 1 Then .Col = .Col + 1
        Case System.Windows.Forms.Keys.Left
            If .Col > 1 Then .Col = .Col - 1
        End Select
    End With
End Sub
```

```
Private Sub Text1_KeyPress(ByVal eventSender As System.Object, ByVal _
eventArgs As System.Windows.Forms.KeyPressEventArgs) Handles Text1.KeyPress
    Dim KeyAscii As Short = Asc(eventArgs.KeyChar)
    With MSFlexGrid1
        If KeyAscii = System.Windows.Forms.Keys.Return And .Row < .Rows - 1 Then
            .Row = .Row + 1
        End If
    End With
    If KeyAscii = 0 Then
        eventArgs.Handled = True
    End If
End Sub

Private Sub FillCombo()
    Combo1.Text = "3DBar"
    Combo1.Items.Add("3DBar")
    Combo1.Items.Add("2DBar")
    Combo1.Items.Add("3DLine")
    Combo1.Items.Add("2DLine")
End Sub

Private Sub ChartLayout()
    With MSChart1
        .TitleText = "Leaf Growth Curves"
        .Plot.Axis(MSChart20Lib.VtChAxisId.VtChAxisIdX).AxisTitle. _Text = _
"Number of Days"
        .Plot.Axis(MSChart20Lib.VtChAxisId.VtChAxisIdX).ValueScale.Auto = True
        .Plot.Axis(MSChart20Lib.VtChAxisId.VtChAxisIdY).AxisTitle._Text = _
 "Length of Leaf (mm)"
        .Plot.Axis(MSChart20Lib.VtChAxisId.VtChAxisIdY).ValueScale.Auto = True
    End With
End Sub
```

```
Private Sub PlotData()
    Dim I As Short
    Dim J As Short
    With MSChart1
        For J = 1 To 4
            For I = 1 To 10
                MSFlexGrid1.Col = J
                MSFlexGrid1.Row = I
                .Column = J
                .Row = I
                .Data = MSFlexGrid1.Text
            Next I
        Next J
    End With
End Sub
```

As you can see, your first step in the form's Load event is to lay out the grid control. However, towards the end of the Load event you call upon two new procedures that differ from those in Chapter 9. The first subroutine, FillCombo sub, adds the different chart choices to the combo box control by using the AddItem method. Next, the ChartLayout procedure sets the chart title. You also use this procedure to define several axis properties that haven't been discussed.

You can only define these axis properties via code at runtime, not at design time. To define them, you call up the different properties that belong to the Plot subgroup. Next, you use an axis constant such as VtChAxisIdX to define which axis you want to deal with. You also could identify a Z-axis using the constant VtChAxisIDZ or a secondary Y-axis by using VtChAxisIDY2. Once you've identified them, you set the axis title by setting the title property equal to a text string. After defining the titles, however, you call upon ValueScale and set its Auto property equal to True. By doing this you don't have to define your own axis scale; instead, the control picks an appropriate scale based on the data in its data grid. Unless you need a specialized scale, this is usually the best option because it eliminates the possibility of making your chart difficult to read, due to a scale that's too large or too small.

After these procedure calls, the next novel procedure of interest is the command button's Click event. This procedure first examines the user's combo box choice and sets the Chart control's ChartType property accordingly. More importantly, however, the procedure calls the PlotData procedure, which reads and copies the FlexGrid's data into your Chart control's data grid. This data transfer is accomplished by setting the Data property of the chart data cell equal to the corresponding grid cell's contents. Once the data is completely copied, the chart is made visible and users can graphically view any trends in the data (see Figure 10-2).

> **NOTE** *Feel free to adjust the ChartType property to experiment and learn about some of the other charting formats.*

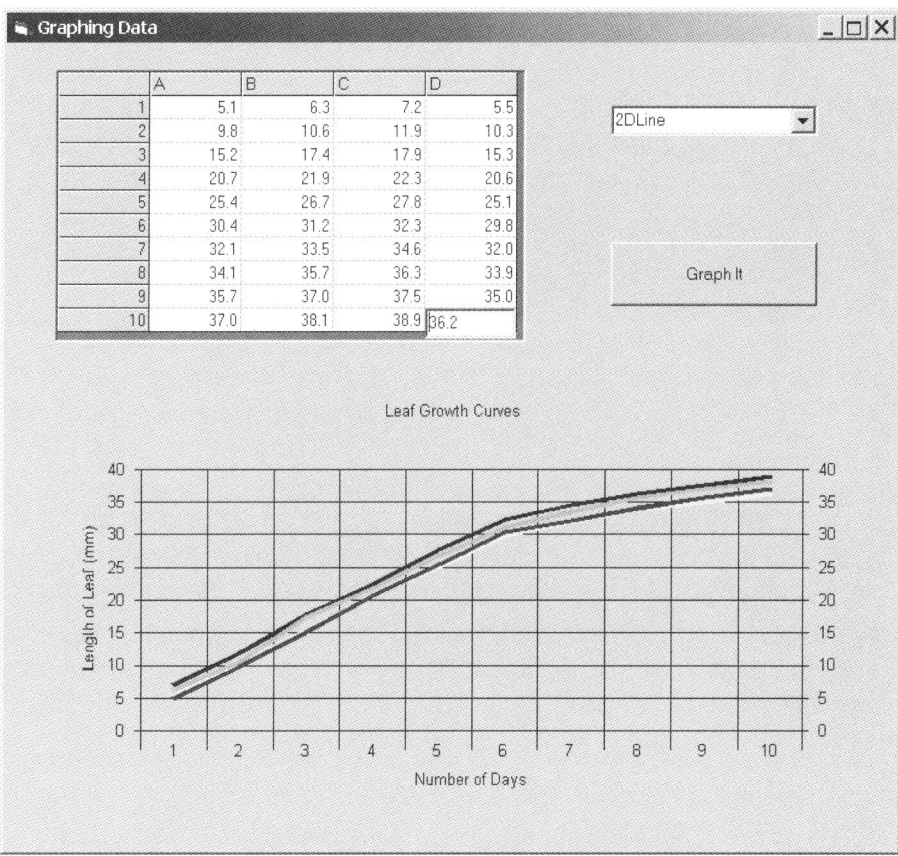

Figure 10-2. The graph of some sample application data

The Flipper CAD Control

Before moving on to the drawing namespace, take a look at a third-party control that interests researchers and developers in more engineering-related disciplines. Many scientific projects often require some form of technical drawing, and you may have thought about incorporating technical drawing into your own software. This ActiveX control, available from ProWorks, greatly simplifies adding CAD capabilities to your applications. The control supports 2-D drawing and allows the creation of a variety of shapes, including lines, rectangles, arcs, ellipses, and polylines. The control also supports more advanced CAD features, such as the ability to group and layer objects. You can save your drawings in the DXF file format, therefore ensuring some compatibility with other CAD applications. As of November 2001, the retail price for the Flipper CAD control is $349. For more information, go to `http://www.proworks.com`.

The System.Drawing Namespace

The System.Drawing namespace is based on the functionality of GDI+, or the Graphics Device Interface. The functions within GDI+, and hence the drawing namespace, enable developers to utilize the Windows graphics library: they can manipulate fonts, draw shapes such as ellipses and rectangles, and use pen- and brush-like effects. Much of this functionality is similar to some of VB 6.0's drawing methods. In fact, .NET retired many of these older drawing methods, and thus you must use the new drawing namespace methods to create these effects. This section covers the various classes that contribute to the drawing namespace; you'll utilize their functionality to plot some mathematical functions.

The System.Drawing.Graphics Class

This discussion covers the System.Drawing.Graphics drawing namespace class most thoroughly because most of its elements create basic graphical displays, such as ellipses, rectangles, and other basic shapes. To demonstrate, add a command button (with its Text property set to "Draw Simple Shapes") to a blank form, as shown in Figure 10-3, and add the following code.

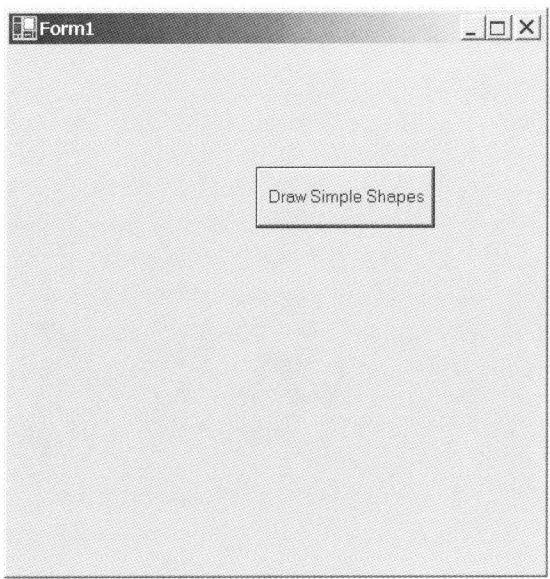

Figure 10-3. The setup of the form you'll draw your graphics on

```
Private Sub Button1_Click(ByVal sender As System.Object, ByVal e As _
System.EventArgs) Handles Button1.Click
        Dim shapes As System.Drawing.Graphics
        shapes = Me.CreateGraphics
        Dim pen1 As New System.Drawing.Pen(System.Drawing.Color.MidnightBlue)
        shapes.DrawRectangle(pen1, 20, 40, 60, 80)
        Dim pen2 As New System.Drawing.Pen(System.Drawing.Color.DarkRed)
        Dim brush1 As System.Drawing.Brush
        brush1 = New SolidBrush(Color.DarkRed)
        shapes.DrawEllipse(pen2, 120, 200, 140, 180)
        shapes.FillEllipse(brush1, 120, 200, 140, 180)
End Sub
```

Now, execute this routine by running your application and clicking the command button. As you can see, a dark blue rectangle and a solid red ellipse appeared on the form when the Click event initiated (see Figure 10-4).

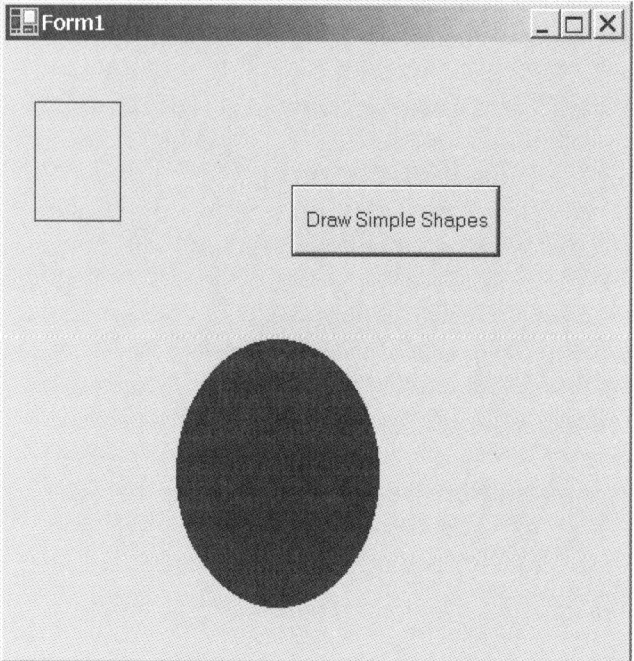

Figure 10-4. The rectangle and ellipse you drew using the Draw methods

If you look closely at the code, the actual invocation of the drawing methods is quite simple. You call upon the DrawEllipse or DrawRectangle method and then specify the desired Pen as well as a set of numerical values. For each method, you specify the numerical values by declaring the X coordinate and the Y coordinate of the top-left corner—that is, you indicate where in relationship to the form's coordinate system the shape will be positioned. Also, remember that the form's top-left corner starts at 0,0. The final two numerical declarations you make when you call upon one of the drawing methods dictate the shape's length (height) and the width.

However, before using these simple methods, you must initialize the graphics' required objects, such as the Graphics object and the different Pens and Brushes. Thus, in the procedure's first two lines of code, you use the form's CreateGraphics method to declare and initialize a graphics object. Next, you declare a new Pen object, because pens are required to create any types of lines that compose your graphics. In this particular example, you create two Pens, Pen1 and Pen2. Pen1 will draw lines of a midnight blue color; while Pen2 produces dark red lines. When you set your Pen's color, you don't have to include the full System.Drawing.Color.[color name] path in the parentheses, but can instead just state Color.[color name]. This example, however, uses the full path to better indicate where the color elements are found. Once these Pens are established you can use them in the drawing methods to draw shape outlines in the specified colors.

However, your basic drawing tools include more than Pens; you also have access to Brush objects. Unlike Pens, Brushes don't draw lines but instead fill in your shape's contents. For example, you use a Brush and a FillEllipse method to generate a dark red ellipse with the filled interior. Like the Pen, you also must specify a color when you declare your Brush. You then utilize the Brush by first drawing the ellipse with Pen2 and the DrawEllipse method. Next, you call upon the FillEllipse method and provide it with the Brush name as well as the Ellipse coordinates. The method then uses the Brush and this information to paint a dark red color inside your ellipse.

In addition to basic shapes, however, this namespace's methods allow you to draw straight lines as well as Bezier curves. As in the past example, the methods are very straightforward to use, but you must first initialize the graphics object as well as a Pen to draw the lines. Take a closer look at these methods; start off with a form containing a single command button with its Text property set to "DrawLines" and add the following code:

```
Private Sub Button1_Click(ByVal sender As System.Object, ByVal e As _
System.EventArgs) Handles Button1.Click
        Dim lines As System.Drawing.Graphics
        lines = Me.CreateGraphics
        Dim pen As New System.Drawing.Pen(Color.Black)
        lines.DrawLine(pen, 25, 225, 225, 25)
        lines.DrawBezier(pen, 25, 225, 46, 167, 79, 46, 54, 233)
End Sub
```

In this particular example, you're first calling upon the DrawLine method, which will draw a diagonal line across the form (see Figure 10-5).

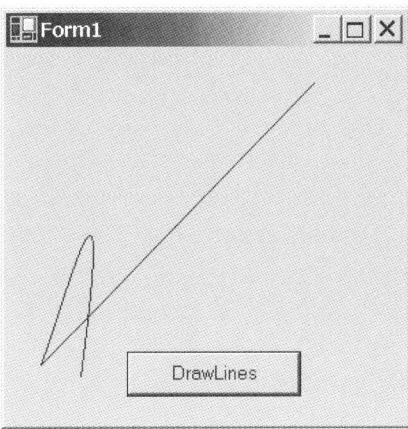

Figure 10-5. The Line and Bezier curve you drew using the Draw methods

As with the previous drawing methods, you must first supply the Pen's name to the method and then provide a listing of coordinates. In this case, the coordinates are of the Single data type that describes the initial point's X coordinate and the initial point's Y coordinate. Finally, the last two parameters describe the endpoint's X coordinate and Y coordinate.

The Bezier method works as the line drawing method just covered. With the DrawBezier method, however, you don't specify two points, but instead specify the coordinates of four points. Thus, each pair of Singles represents an X coordinate and its corresponding Y coordinate. The method then takes this data, and VB draws a curve to connect all of these points in the order specified.

Plotting Mathematical Functions

Now that you've been introduced to the Drawing.Graphics class you'll learn how to utilize this class's DrawCurve method to plot mathematical functions. This method isn't quite as straightforward as the previous drawing methods and encompasses several new elements, such as Point and PointF. However, look at some code first to clearly see how the plotting routine needs to be laid out. You'll begin this example as with the other two, by adding a command button to a blank form. Once the form is set up, you can then add the following code:

```
Private Sub Button1_Click(ByVal sender As System.Object, ByVal e As _
System.EventArgs) Handles Button1.Click
        Dim func As System.Drawing.Graphics
        func = Me.CreateGraphics
        Dim Pen1 As New System.Drawing.Pen(Color.Black)
        func.DrawLine(Pen1, 0, 150, 300, 150)
        func.DrawLine(Pen1, 150, 0, 150, 300)

        Dim y(21) As System.Drawing.PointF
        func1(Y)
        func.DrawCurve(Pen1, y)
    End Sub


    Private Sub func1(ByRef Y() As System.Drawing.PointF)
        Dim X As Integer
        For X = -10 To 10

            Y(X + 10) = New PointF(X + 150, (-1 * X * X) + 150)
        Next X
    End Sub
```

As in the previous examples, you first initialize the graphics objects, and then draw two lines using the DrawLine method. These lines aren't essential for the DrawCurve method, but serve as X and Y axes and make the plot easier to interpret. In this case, the form was 300 by 300, so the lines divide the form into four equal sections.

Once the axes are laid out, you encounter a new statement where you declare the array y as PointF. PointF is a specialized data type that stores point coordinate information. The DrawCurve method requires that point coordinates be passed into the method as either Point or PointF. The difference between them is that Point only holds integer coordinates, while PointF holds floating point values of Single data type.

Now that you've established the array, you pass it into a custom function that sets the array elements equal to the X and Y coordinate values that the function $Y = X^2$ would yield. You're probably wondering why you add 150 to both the X and Y values, and why you are multiplying Y by -1. The answer is that the function should appear in the form's center. Remember, the coordinates 0,0 are found in the form's top-left corner, not in the center. Thus the two additions of 150 work to center the curve, and multiplying Y by -1 inverts the function and makes it appear like a normal plot of $Y = X^2$ (see Figure 10-6).

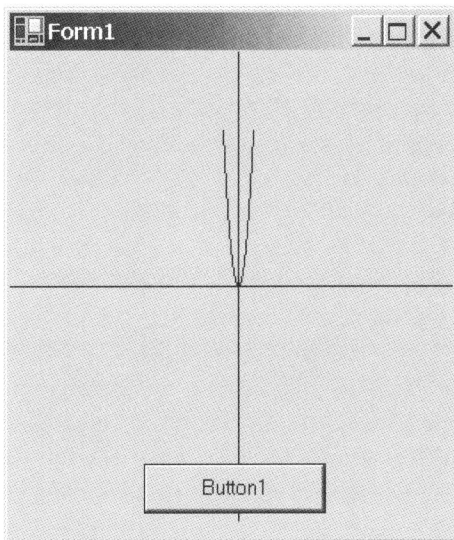

Figure 10-6. The plot of $Y = X^2$

If you don't like the idea of adding 150 to each coordinate, you can simplify this process by looking at your form's Location properties. Under Location, you'll see an X and a Y property set to 0,0 by default. These properties dictate the coordinates of the form's top-left corner. To make 0,0 the center of your 300 by 300 pixel form, you'd simply change the Location coordinates to $-150,-150$.

Other namespaces are found within the main System.Drawing namespace, and the rest of this chapter touches only very briefly on each one's functionality, as they provide more advanced graphics capabilities that go beyond the scope of this introductory graphics chapter.

The System.Drawing.Drawing2D Namespace

The System.Drawing.Drawing2D namespace includes vector rendering. The ability to use vector-based graphics opens the doors to perform gradient fills and other such specialized effects.

The System.Drawing.Text Namespace

The main System.Drawing namespace contains basic font functionality, along with certain more advanced features. For example, some functions within this namespace offer the ability to control line spacing as well as the quality and speed of text rendering.

The System.Drawing.Imaging Namespace

This namespace provides much of the functionality required to work various image formats such as bitmaps, metafiles, JPEGs, GIFs, and Kodak PhotoCD formats. In addition to just reading from and writing to these formats, you can manipulate these images.

The System.Drawing.Design Namespace

This namespace differs from other drawing namespaces in that you don't use it to directly display effects on your form. Instead, it adds the functionality required to enhance and alter design-time drawing of your user interface. For example, you can create custom toolbox items or type-specific value editors.

By now you understand the fundamental techniques to develop graphics in VB. These can be valuable skills in your programming repertoire; graphics can greatly aid in data visualization as well as enhance the user's ability to interpret the data. Keep in mind that graphics also can enhance your GUI by making it more interactive and user friendly.

Debugging and Error Handling

I<small>F YOU'VE TRIED TO WRITE</small> any programs on your own, I'm sure that by this point you've noticed that most programs of length do not work perfectly the first time you run them. In other words, the programs have errors in their code, which are commonly referred to as *bugs*. While, practically speaking, bugs are an unavoidable fact of life, there are several methods you can use to limit the number of bugs in your code and there are certain tools available in VB to help with the debugging process. In this chapter, you'll examine these techniques and tools to help you get your program up and running perfectly with as few corrections as possible.

Making Use of Microsoft's IntelliSense Technology

One of the best defenses against bugs and errors is to prevent them from occurring at all, and in this regard Microsoft's IntelliSense technology is a great tool. The technology works as a sophisticated autocomplete tool that attempts to determine what the possibilities are for completing your current code statement. For example, if you're working with a Boolean variable called "bool" and you begin to type **bool =** you'll find that a dialog box appears with the options True and False. In other words, you're reminded that your variable can only hold True and False values. Likewise, you've probably also noticed IntelliSense technology when you've tried to invoke a method or a property of a control. Once you place the period (.) after the control name, you see a dialog box appear listing all of the possible methods and properties, and you can just pick the appropriate one off of the list. IntelliSense's autocomplete features work when you're declaring namespaces and their component classes as well. By utilizing this technology, you not only save yourself typing time, but you can also avoid grammatical errors in the form of spelling mistakes.

You may have also noticed that IntelliSense technology goes beyond autocompletion—it has a somewhat limited autocorrect capability. This capability most often materializes in the form of letter case correction. In other words, if you declare your variable to be VaR and then type **var** in a code line, IntelliSense autocorrects it back to VaR. The same holds true for control names, function names, and a variety of other objects.

> **NOTE** *IntelliSense technology isn't always perfect, and in some instances, it fails to list all available properties, methods, etc. So be sure to use it frequently as a great guideline, but keep in mind that you shouldn't trust it 100 percent.*

Compile as You Go Technology

Another great error-handling feature of VB .NET is its "compile as you go" capability. If you've ever typed a line of code that contained an error (and who hasn't?), I'm sure you noticed that the questionable part of the expression was underlined, which immediately prompted you to check your code. This is a great advance over earlier compilers, which forced you to compile the whole application before any error checking was performed. These "old-fashioned" compilers would then output a list containing the line numbers that the uncovered errors were associated with. Debugging applications this way took a long time.

Testing for Errors

As you might expect, bugs in your code often lead to errors in your program's output, so one great way to discover if any bugs exist is to actually input some data and examine the output for errors. This is usually a much more complex process than simply running the program a few times with different data sets, however. While such a technique might work for simple programs, it's almost impossible to isolate the source of an error in a program consisting of hundreds or even thousands of lines of code in this way. This is one reason why using functions and procedures in your code is so important. Most scientific programs use a large number of mathematical computations, which you can easily divide up and code as separate functions and/or procedures. It then becomes possible to take each one of these entities on an individual basis and check the calculations it performs, which limits the possible sources of error to the lines of code within that particular procedure rather than to all of the lines of code within the project. Your bug-locating task becomes much simpler, because you're no longer searching for the proverbial needle in the haystack.

Along with this approach, it's still crucial that you use a set of test data that encompasses a broad range of possible procedure input values. A good practice is to include the possible input value extremes, such as zero or a large positive or negative number, in addition to numbers in between. In this way, you can see how your code responds over the range of possible values and not just a small, isolated set of data.

Good testing procedures do more than check mathematical outputs, however—they also help you figure out errors that the program's users might make. For example, back in Chapter 9, you added code to your KeyPress event to prevent program users from keying past the edge of the grid and causing the program to crash. Another common error made by users is typing **one** instead of **1** in a text box that requires a number entry. Because VB can't numerically multiply, divide, add, or subtract "one," this can cause your program to crash or malfunction. Thus, programmers will often generate their own numeric text boxes. The key with such possibility testing is not to discover every source of error before releasing your product; rather, the goal is to discover and eliminate all reasonable sources of error. There will always be somebody who finds some odd, almost unthinkable way of getting the program to malfunction—that's why most software is routinely patched or updated. However, it's your responsibility to ensure that your code is stable and operational for routine use and routine mistakes.

Grammatical Errors

As you test your programs, you'll discover that there are two types of errors possible: grammatical errors and logical errors. *Grammatical errors* are typographical syntax errors—just what you would expect from the use of the word "grammar" in the context of any written language. The most common type of grammatical error is misspelled variables. VB doesn't require that all variables be explicitly declared; that is, VB will let you use a variable without your having previously used a Dim or equivalent statement. For example, you may want to store your calculated value in the declared variable "value1," but if you mistakenly type **valueI** instead of **value1** in your calculation line of code, you'll find that your answer will be stored in valueI and not value1. To make things worse, no error message will result.

There are two good practices you can use to avoid such errors. The first practice is to use logical variable names for each variable. A descriptive variable name will often help prevent you from typing the wrong variable. The second option is also a must for any scientific program. Add the following line of code to the Public declarations section:

```
Option Explicit
```

This code works in the same way as FORTRAN's IMPLICIT NONE command in that it forces you to explicitly declare all of your variables. If any undeclared variables arise, you'll get an error message when you execute the code and VB will go into Break mode. In VB .NET, Option Explicit is "turned on" by default, but in earlier versions of VB you must remember to manually add this line of code.

Just keep in mind, though, that as useful as the Option Explicit command is, it's not foolproof. For example, there's nothing in it to protect you from typing the wrong declared variable in the wrong place. In fact, such an error can often be one of the most difficult bugs to discover. When dealing with large projects, many programmers like to consult cross-referencing programs that will go through their code and find every variable and the lines it's used in. Many such programs are commercially available, and they're often abbreviated as xref programs.

Logical Errors

Logical errors deal with the functionality of the program; that is, something is not occurring correctly or not happening at all. For example, perhaps you invoked the wrong procedure at the wrong time or passed the wrong information into a procedure. In other words, there's something faulty with the functional layout of the program. As scientific and engineering programmers, most of our applications are heavily mathematical, thus one of the best ways to detect a logical error in a program is to follow the math through in a step-by-step manner. I know this sounds like a truly horrendous and tedious measure for a long program, but it's probably not as bad as you imagine. While you might have to get out a calculator to solve some steps along the way, you don't have to solve all of the math in the program from beginning to end to isolate the errors—VB provides some debugging methods to aid you in these endeavors. These methods are part of VB's Debug object, and they allow you to print variable values to the Output window at specified points. (Note: For people used to earlier versions of VB, these methods work in a similar way to the Debug.Print method, except they don't write to the Immediate window. The Immediate window still exists in VB .NET and retains most of its other functions.)

The VB Debug object provides four possible methods you can use to accomplish debugging tasks. These methods are summed up in the sections that follow.

The Debug.Write Method

This method outputs the text specified to the Output window. You can type out the text string and place it in quotes or it can be a variable. Also, you may want to concatenate a typed-in message with a variable value to make it easier for you to figure out what value you're looking at and at what point during the run. This type of technique is recommended especially for longer applications with a large number of variables. The syntax of this method is as follows:

```
Debug.Write("The value of Y is " & Y)
```

The Debug.WriteIf Method

This method works in the same manner as the Write method, but it allows you to specify a conditional or some other type of Boolean expression as well. The specified text will only be written to the Output window if the Boolean expression evaluates to True.

The Debug.WriteLine Method

This method works in the same manner as the Write method with the only exception being that it writes a carriage return to the Output window as well as the specified text. This allows you to skip lines between important values and can make your outputs easier to read.

The Debug.WriteLineIf Method

This method is used in the same way as the WriteIf method, with the addition of writing a carriage return as well as the specified string to the Output window.

Debug Object Methods in Action

You're now going to examine how the Debug object methods work using an extremely simple example. However, as you'll see, these methods aren't difficult to employ and thus can be just as easily applied to a lengthy application. To start, add the following code to a form's Click event and execute it:

```
Dim X as Integer
X = 2
Debug.WriteLine(X)
X = X + 5
Debug.WriteLineIf(X > 2, X)
```

Now look at the bottom of your screen as you click on the form. You'll notice that every time you click on the form, a 2 will appear on one line and a 7 will appear on the line immediately following it, because your conditional (X > 2) was met. If you instead used the Write versions of these commands, the 2 and 7 would have appeared on the same line. Also, try changing the > sign to a < sign and you'll notice that only the 2 prints out because your condition is no longer met.

As you can see, the implementation of these debugging methods is quite easy. When you test out an application, I recommend placing one of these method commands after every major mathematical step is completed within your application. Employing this technique in such a way should greatly increase your speed at isolating errors and bugs. Also, one other suggestion I'd like to make is that you remember to remove these methods before distributing your application. Although theoretically you can leave them in with no harm to your application's performance, you wouldn't want to risk some unknown side effect over lines of code that have no purpose in the final compilation.

Before you move on to the next section, take a moment to examine Table 11-1. This table summarizes the three most common types of errors you'll encounter in scientific VB programming.

Table 11-1. Common Scientific VB Errors

ERROR	DESCRIPTION
Off by One	A common error associated with the counter variable in a loop structure being off by one increment
Type Mismatch	Occurs when you try to store a value in a variable that cannot hold data of that type
Divide by Zero	Occurs when the value of the denominator ends up equaling zero

VB Debugging Tools

VB comes with many useful tools on its Debug toolbar, so let's now take some time to go over them. You should be familiar with the first few tools on the toolbar already. As you know, you click the arrow to run your application, and you click the box to stop your application. The button that looks similar to the pause key on a tape or CD player is the Break button, and clicking it will send your application into Break mode. VB itself is also able to send your application into Break mode and does so when it's able to pick up an error. *Break mode* is a temporary suspension of the application, and within this mode, most of the other debugging tools come into play.

Step Into

Step Into is often referred to as "single stepping," because it allows you to execute your code in a line-by-line manner. You can access this feature either by continually clicking the appropriate icon or by repeatedly pressing the F11 key (F8 in VB 6.0). When you first press F11 to activate single stepping, you'll find that VB automatically highlights the first line of executable code found. This line is usually the beginning of the Form Class constructor (i.e., Public Sub New()). In VB 6.0, this line is usually present in a form's Load or Initialize event. If you press F11 again, this first highlighted line of code will execute and the next line of executable code will be highlighted. Repeated presses will allow you to continue to progress through the code in this manner.

If you get to a procedure or function call, you'll execute the function call and then jump over to the first line of code within the function/procedure. You'll then be able to single step through the entire procedure, and upon completion you'll return to the segment of code the call initiated from. One thing to take into consideration, however, is that single stepping does not simulate user events. As a result, if a certain event procedure requires a click to activate it, you won't be able to reach it just by single stepping.

Step Over

Step Over works in a similar manner to Step Into. The difference is that Step Over allows you to execute the code at the procedural level instead of the line-by-line level. This is often a great way to speed things along when you're going through your code and reach a procedure that you know works properly. You can access Step Over by either clicking its icon or by pressing F10 (Shift+F8 in VB 6.0).

Step Out

You use Step Out when you're inside a function call and you want to leave the function that was called. Step Out allows you to leave the function and continue the execution of your code.

Breakpoints

Clicking the Break icon on the Debug toolbar allows you to suspend the application and activate Break mode. However, this isn't a great method for stopping an application when you want it to go into Break mode at a certain point. Odds are you probably will never be lucky enough to click the icon at the exact moment necessary to suspend the application at line number 15 (or any other desired line, for that matter). This is where *breakpoints* come in. Breakpoints enable you to set places in the code where you want your application to suspend itself.

You can easily add breakpoints by selecting New Breakpoint from the Debug menu. When the New Breakpoint window appears, simply type in the name of the procedure and the code line number that corresponds to where you want the breakpoint to appear. From the New Breakpoint window, you can also specify the conditions, if any, that you want the application to break under. If no condition is specified, the program will always break at that point. Finally, when you've completely defined your breakpoint, click OK and you'll see a red "stop sign" appear next to the line of code you just specified.

Unconditional breakpoints are more easily set by clicking the left pane of the Code window in line with the line of concern. The red stop sign appears at the edge of the line of code you just chose. From this point on, when you run your code, the program will go into Break mode just before executing the line of code you specified. Also, keep in mind that you can enable and disable breakpoints from the Debug menu as well as clear all breakpoints. You can view the information that pertains to all of the breakpoints you set by opening the Breakpoints window.

Rather than use conditional breakpoints, some programmers prefer to use another method of the Debug object, the Debug.Assert method. This method allows you to write out a Boolean expression, and if this expression evaluates to False, the program will go into Break mode. The Debug.Assert method has the following syntax:

```
Debug.Assert(Boolean Expression)
```

The Immediate Window

The Immediate window (see Figure 11-1) serves two important purposes. The first use of the window is that it outputs the current value of a variable when you type **?** followed by the name of a variable or a property and press Enter. For example, to obtain the value of X, all you need to enter is **?X**. The second useful function of this window is that it allows you to change the value of a variable or a property. To accomplish this, all you need to do is type in the name of the variable or property followed by an equal sign (=) and the desired value. It's also possible to set a variable equal to a mathematical expression instead of just a value. For example, you could make X equal to $5 \times X$ by entering in the following: **X = 5 * X**. Of course, you can use more complicated expressions as well.

> **NOTE**   *The Immediate window is meaningful only when the application is in Break mode.*

Figure 11-1. The Immediate window

The Locals Window

The Locals window, shown in Figure 11-2, displays a listing of all of the variables that are local to the procedure you're currently executing. Thus the variables on this list will only be variables that were declared within that procedure. This window gives you the names of the variables, the type of each variable (e.g., Integer, Double, etc.), and the current value of each of the variables. You can, however, assign a new value to a variable you find within this window.

> **NOTE** *The Locals window is meaningful only when the application is in Break mode.*

Locals			
Name	Value		Type
⊞ Error1	{System.OverflowException}		System.
Num	9		Integer
Num2	0		Integer

📅 Call Stack | 🔲 Breakpoints | 🖵 Command Window | ▤ Output | 🖳 Autos | 🖳 Locals | 🖳 Watch 1

Figure 11-2. The Locals window

The Watch Window

If you checked out the Locals window I'm sure you noticed that it has two limitations. The first is that you can only see variables that are local to the procedure, and the second is that you can't specify which variables you want to monitor. VB automatically makes an unchangeable list of all local variables. The Watch window (see Figure 11-3) overcomes these limitations. You can view the current value of any property or variable by typing its name in the Name column. Also, as with the Locals window, you can change the value of a variable by double-clicking in the Value column, entering the new value, and pressing Enter.

NOTE   *The Watch window is meaningful only when the application is in Break mode.*

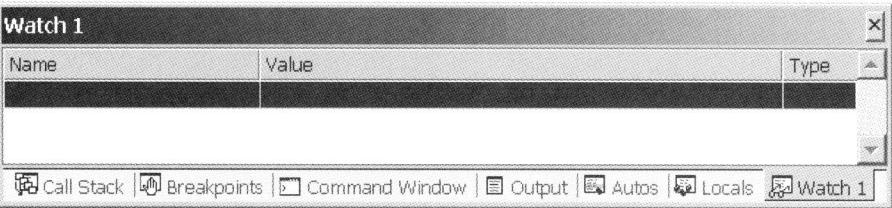

Figure 11-3. The Watch window

The QuickWatch Dialog Box

In the QuickWatch dialog box, you can enter the name of a variable or property, or an expression. The current value of the variable, property, or expression will then be displayed when you click the Recalculate button. While it may be quicker to use the QuickWatch dialog box to get the value of a single variable at a discrete point in time, you're better off using the Watch window to monitor variable changes as you step through the program. Because QuickWatch is a dialog box, you cannot leave it active in the background, as you can with the Watch window.

NOTE   *The QuickWatch dialog box is meaningful only when the application is in Break mode.*

The Call Stack Window

The Call Stack window, displayed in Figure 11-4, is another window that can often be of use when you debug a program, even though it doesn't yield any variable value information. As is the case with other debugging windows, this window is meaningful only when the application is in Break mode. If you open this window, you'll be presented with a listing of all of the procedure calls made up to this point, with the most recently called procedure listed on top. This type of information can often aid in the location of bugs. For example, suppose you have three procedures (A, B, and C) in your program, and when you go to run your program a conditional breakpoint tells you that something went wrong and suspends the execution. You then decide to view your Call Stack listing and discover that only procedures A and C were called up to this point. This means that this particular error is not in procedure B (although there may be others).

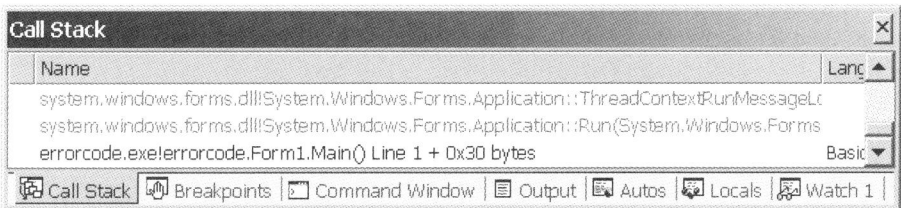

Figure 11-4. The Call Stack window

Dr. Watson

Dr. Watson is not a member of VB or VS; rather, it's a component of Microsoft Windows that can be of help in the debugging process. Dr. Watson is a program-error debugging tool that catalogs errors generated by applications running on the OS. Dr. Watson not only records the actual error that occurred, but also the system conditions that were present when the error occurred. In other words, it notes information about the system hardware and what other applications were running at the time. Thus, it can be an extremely useful tool when you test your applications on a variety of different machines to ensure the behavior of the program under different running conditions. You can access Dr. Watson by clicking the Start button, selecting Run, and typing **drwtsn32**. All errors are recorded in the file drwtsn32.log.

By this point you have a fairly good understanding of some of the different debugging tools that VB provides for you, because you've now been introduced to all of the commonly used ones. Don't get discouraged, though, if you encounter bugs that just seem to be elusive. Any experienced programmer will tell you that debugging can often be one of the toughest and most frustrating required tasks. In fact, some programmers claim that debugging is almost as much of an art form as it is a science. Just like everything else, though, the more programming and debugging you do, the better you become at them, so if you stumble across any hard-to-find bugs, just clear your head and get back to it. Before you know it, you'll have a working application.

Error Handling

Despite the most thorough debugging efforts, you'll find that no program will be completely bulletproof without some type of error handling. Let's consider a perfectly debugged mathematical routine that consistently gives the correct outputs over the full possible range of numerical inputs. Now picture the program user who inadvertently enters **I** instead of **1** and causes your mathematical routine to crash because the input was not numerical. Although this incident didn't result from a bug in the code, it was nevertheless just as disastrous. This is where error handling comes in.

Error handling enables you to code ways of dealing with these types of errors when they appear. Thus, rather than crashing your program, an error triggers the output of a warning message or some other preventative measure.

The IsNumeric Function

One of the best ways to deal with errors is to prevent them before they start. This is where the IsNumeric function often comes in handy, because it's able to make sure that a value can be interpreted as a number by VB. So if you want to avoid the previously mentioned I instead of 1 error, you can employ code such as the following:

```
Dim Num As Integer
        If IsNumeric(TextBox1.Text) Then
            Num = CInt(TextBox1.Text)
        Else : MsgBox("ERROR: Enter a number")
        End If
```

This code ensures that the value entered into TextBox1 is a numeric value prior to attempting to read it into the variable Num. If the function doesn't evaluate the entry to be numeric, an error message is displayed that prompts the user to correct the error. By using this technique, you don't have to worry about your application crashing if a text entry was mistakenly made.

> **NOTE** *In VB 6.0 there were a variety of other "Is functions," such as IsNull and IsMissing, that could check for Null strings or missing values, respectively. However, in VB .NET these functions are no longer supported.*

VB 6.0-Style Error Handling

You'll first examine VB 6.0 error-handling techniques because they're simpler and more straightforward than VB .NET's error-handling capabilities, and they can help you see how far error handling has progressed. VB 6.0 error handling was actually fairly limited and archaic for a modern programming language and, in fact, it didn't differ that greatly from error-handling techniques laid out in older versions of Basic such as Quick Basic. In VB 6.0, error handling basically consisted of trapping a fatal error with an On Error statement and then proceeding with either a Resume or a GoTo statement. In VB .NET, these types of error handling are referred to as *unstructured exception handling statements.* Let's examine what this means by using this type of error handling structure to output the same warning message in the preceding example. You'll do this by using the following VB .NET code:

```
Dim Num As Integer
On Error Goto NotNum
        Num = CInt(TextBox1.Text)
        Exit Sub
NotNum:
        MsgBox("ERROR: Enter a Number")
```

In this case, you don't take any preventive measures (using the IsNumeric function is a better way of handling this), but instead you'll only output your warning message in the event that an error occurs. If an error does occur, the GoTo statement directs VB to seek out the NotNum error label and execute the code contained under the label. In this case, it's to output your warning message. It's also important to note the Exit Sub directive placed before your error label. This is an important line of code, because without the Exit Sub statement, the warning message will be displayed even if there is no error. Thus, such a statement is a vital piece of code, unless you want your error message to display every time your code is executed, regardless of whether or not an error is present. If your error code was able to address the problem, you can use the Resume statement to go back to the line of code that brought on the error in the first place.

A variant of the Resume statement is the Resume Next statement, which doesn't return to the statement that caused the error, but rather begins re-executing code at the line immediately following the problematic line. When the Resume Next statement is used in conjunction with an On Error statement, a problematic line of code will simply be skipped. For example, if you executed the code

```
On Error Resume Next
Num = CInt(TextBox1.Text)
```

you would find that if an error did occur, Num would remain equal to its default value of zero.

Structured Exception Handling

Structured exception handling allows for much more robust error-handling techniques than unstructured exception handling because it gives the programmer the ability to treat different types of errors differently. In the unstructured exception handling you just witnessed, all errors would be handled in the same manner regardless of how they were generated. Structured exception handling is more complex, however, and it doesn't make use of the On Error statements previously covered.

Instead, structured exception handling is initiated with a Try statement. The Try statement signals the beginning of a Try block in which code that you suspect may cause an error is placed. If this code does result in an error, the program will throw an exception derived from the System.Exception class. The Try block will be coded to contain Catch statements that will evaluate the thrown exception. If one of the Catch statements matches the exception, the code in that particular Catch block will be executed and thus address the error. If there are no matching Catch statements, VB won't know how to deal with the error and an error will still be produced. This means that although structured exception handling is more powerful and versatile than unstructured exception handling, it's also more difficult to master because you must now explicitly account for all feasible errors in order to take full advantage of it and completely bulletproof your code. Before the Try block is terminated, a Finally statement can be made. This statement signals a section of code that will always execute last, whether or not one of the Catch statements is invoked. The code in this section is often used to clean up (e.g., close files, erase temporary files, etc.) prior to leaving the exception handling routine.

Before you can code an example to better understand the technique described in this section, you first need to understand the different exceptions (derived from the System.Exception class) that can be thrown. In the following sections, you'll examine some of the most commonly occurring exceptions.

> **NOTE** *For a complete listing of all possible exceptions, look in the VB Help under the System namespace.*

ApplicationException

This exception occurs when a nonfatal application error occurs. A *fatal* error is an error that would cause the program to completely crash out and lose all functionality.

ArgumentException

If you try to provide an invalid argument to one of the methods found within VB, you'll cause this exception to be thrown. In other words, if you needed to pass in an integer and you tried to pass in a string, you would cause this type of error to result.

ArgumentNullException

This is similar to the preceding exception, except it's a little more specific. This type of exception occurs when you try to pass a null reference into a method that's not equipped to accept null references.

ArgumentOutOfRangeException

This exception is caused when the value you try to pass in is out of the range of the variable set up to accept the argument. For example, this type of exception would occur if you tried to pass in the number 5345 to a variable set up to hold Byte values.

ArithmeticException

This type of exception will be thrown in two cases. The first case occurs when some type of error arises during some type of mathematical calculation. The second case is when a failed conversion occurs.

ArrayTypeMismatchException

As you should already know, arrays are declared in a way that specifies the type of data that they will hold. Thus, if you try to pass in data of another data type, you'll generate an array type mismatch and throw this exception.

DivideByZeroException

This type of exception should be obvious from the name, as it occurs when you try to divide a value by zero. This exception is often useful in cases where the denominator is a user-specified value.

ExecutionEngineException

This type of exception is thrown when something goes wrong with the functioning of the execution engine of the common language runtime (CLR).

IndexOutOfRangeException

This type of error occurs when you try to call up an element of an array that is outside the upper and lower index bounds of that array. For instance, if your array was dimensioned to hold 15 elements, and you tried to call upon an element in allocation unit 16, you would throw this type of exception.

NotFiniteNumberException

This exception occurs when a floating-point value (i.e., a Double or Single) becomes so large or small that it loses its finite nature and reaches positive or negative infinity. Because VB cannot generate discrete answers from calculations involving infinity, this type of exception will result. This type of exception can also be thrown if the value is not a number (NaN) value.

OutOfMemoryException

This exception is self-explanatory. It's thrown when your system runs out of memory and can no longer continue the execution of the program.

RankException

This type of exception occurs when you try to pass an array that contains the wrong number of dimensions. For example, you cannot pass a three-dimensional array into a method that calls for a two- or four-dimensional array—you can only pass it into a method that calls for a three-dimensional array.

A Structured Error-Handling Example

In this section, you'll code a brief example of structured error handling in which you declare two numbers and try to divide them. You will, however, arrange for an error to occur by making the denominator equal to zero. You can accomplish this with the following code:

```
Dim Num As Integer
Dim Num2 As Integer
Num = 9
Num2 = 0
Try
     Num = Num / Num2
Catch Error1 As OverflowException
     MsgBox(Error1.Message)
Catch Error2 As DivideByZeroException
     MsgBox(Error2.Message)
Finally
     TextBox1.Text = Num
End Try
```

As described previously, the statements whose execution may result in an error are placed in the first part of the Try block. In this case, your statement is engineered to fail and so you throw an exception. This particular example results in the Overflow error occurring first; thus, that is the exception thrown. This exception is then caught by your first Catch statement and outputted to a message box (see Figure 11-5). In case the DivideByZeroException happened to be thrown first, you include a Catch statement to deal with this error. Last, you display the value of Num into a text box. If you look in the text box, you'll see that the value of Num remains the same, because the division generated an error and thus the execution of the division was not completed.

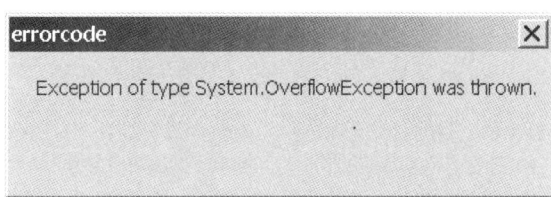

Figure 11-5. The error message box outputted by the Overflow error Catch statement

Now you've seen both the traditional unstructured exception handling and the more modern structured exception handling in action. If you incorporate these techniques into your applications, along with a rigorous debugging routine, you'll find that you can create highly stable and robust applications that are able to produce reliable results and withstand the majority of user mishaps, resulting in what is popularly known as a "well-behaved" application.

Packaging and Deploying Your Application

THIS CHAPTER IS THE SHORTEST ONE in this book, but in many ways, it's one of the most essential ones. Up to this point, you've read and learned about many of the basic building blocks you can utilize to create sound scientific utilities and applications. However, once you develop that "killer app," you need a way to distribute your application to other computers. There's no reason you should limit yourself to only running your application in the VB IDE—you should be able to create a software package that can run on any Windows-based PC (i.e., Windows 95/98/Me/NT/2000/XP). In this chapter, you'll examine how to package your applications and use the Setup Wizard to add deployment capabilities. So open up that newly finished program of yours and let's walk through the process of creating a finished user product.

First Steps

To begin the process of adding a deployment routine to your application, first click the File menu and go to Add Project. When you choose this option, a pop-up menu appears. Select the New Project option. You'll then see the New Project dialog box appear, from which you should select the Setup and Deployment Project category. Finally, select the Setup Wizard project type and proceed to add this to your current project (see Figure 12-1). The Setup Wizard is somewhat similar to the Package and Deployment Wizard found in VB 6.0, but it's not quite as straightforward to use.

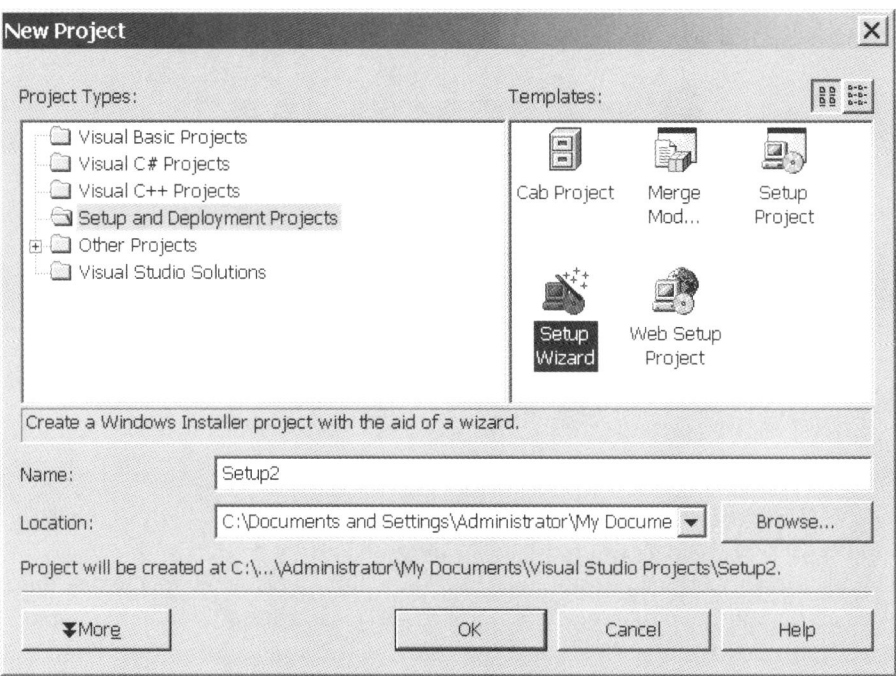

Figure 12-1. Choosing the Setup Wizard option from the New Project dialog box

> **CAUTION** *Before you continue further in this chapter, make sure that you've applied the techniques presented in Chapter 11 to check that you have a reliable and robust application.*

The Setup Wizard

Once you open the Setup Wizard, the first screen of the wizard appears. This screen's only purpose is to inform you that the Setup Wizard will help you add installation features to your application, as shown in Figure 12-2.

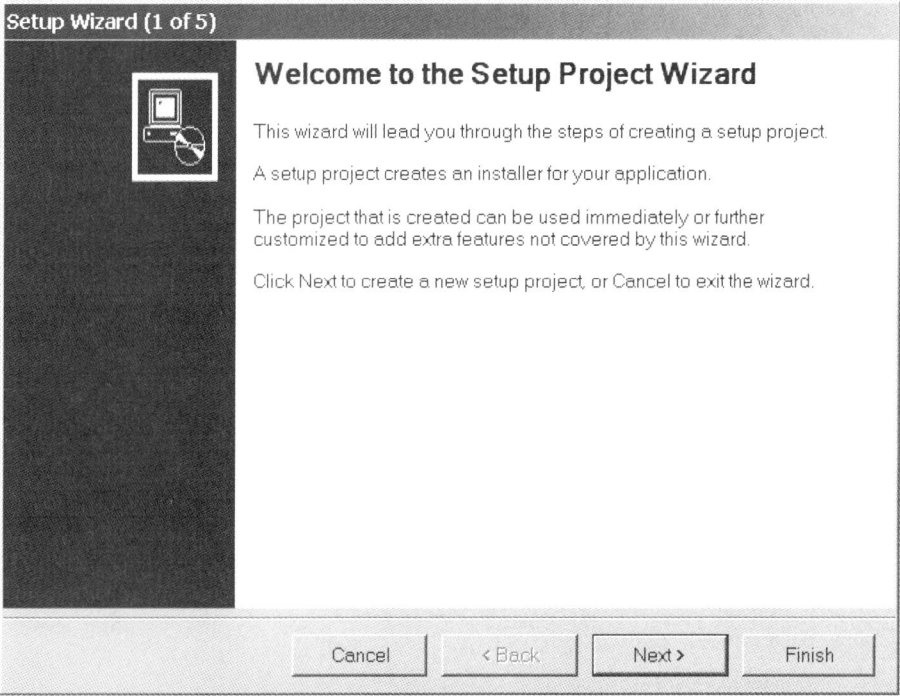

Figure 12-2. The initial Setup Wizard screen

Click the only real choice you have, the Next button, and move along. After you click Next, the introduction screen disappears, and you're presented with the second screen (screen 2 of 5) of the Setup Wizard, as shown in Figure 12-3. This screen is much more significant, because it allows you to choose from the different available deployment types. The type of deployment option you select determines how your application is packaged as well as how end users will get your application to run on their machines.

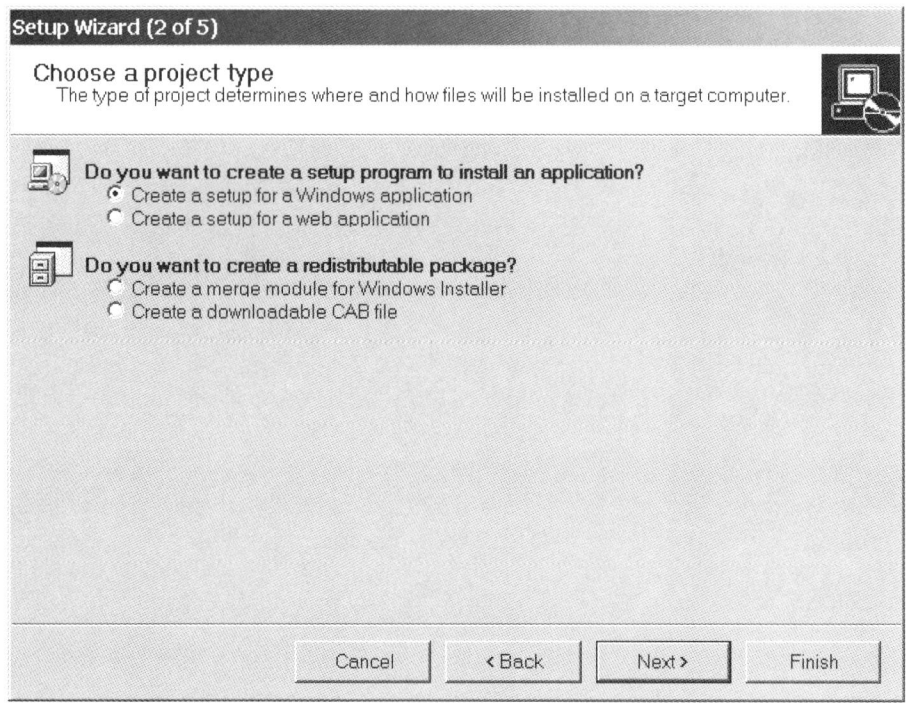

Figure 12-3. Using the Setup Wizard to choose a deployment type

The Windows Application Setup Option

You'll choose the Windows application setup option most frequently, because it adds the functionality required to set up your application on a standard desktop computer. Choosing this option results in the creation of a Windows Installer file (i.e., *.msi). This file contains the application executable as well as any other dependant files and the required registry information. When you activate this file, the Windows Installer loads and unpacks the contents of your file, and sets up your application on the target computer.

> **NOTE** *The Windows Installer comes with Windows 98, Me, 2000, and XP. However, it's not standard in Windows 95 or NT. Users of Windows 95 or NT can download the Windows Installer from Microsoft's Web site to gain the required functionality if they don't already have it.*

The Web Application Setup Option

This option is very similar to the previous one in that it creates a Windows Installer file that can be unpackaged and set up by the Windows Installer. The main difference is that an application packaged with this setup option will not be installed into the file system of a target computer; rather, it will be set up to be installed on a Web server. In other words, rather than being run off of a single desktop computer, this type of application can be accessed by multiple computers that have access to the applications contained on the Web server.

The Merge Module Option

Merge modules are a little different than the previous two options in that they don't consist of a full application you can install on a desktop computer or Web server. Instead, they're defined as reusable setup components whose functionality can be added to any Windows Installer installation file. You use merge modules (*.msm) when you have multiple applications that may need to share the same components. You can simply add those components by adding the merge module to the final *.msi file.

The CAB File Option

This option enables you to create a cabinet file (i.e., a type of compressed file) in which you can package ActiveX components. Once these components are packaged in a *.cab file, they can be downloaded into a Web browser, such as Internet Explorer. For a detailed description of cabinet files, read the MSDN article located at `http://msdn.microsoft.com/library/default.asp?url=/library/enus/vstool1/html/veovrcreatingcustompackages.asp`.

> **NOTE** *For even more control over how your application will be distributed, you can turn to third-party products, such as InstallShield, which enables you to generate your own custom installation scripts as well as build your application in a manner that's optimal for the distribution media (i.e., CD, DVD, disks, Web, etc.). To learn more about these and the other features of InstallShield, visit* `http://www.installshield.com`.

Once you've chosen your setup type, click Next and proceed to screen 3 of the Setup Wizard. This screen asks you about what types of project output you want to include and shows a listing of possible outputs, as displayed in Figure 12-4. The first item on the list is "Primary output," which is an option that you'll generally want to check, because it ensures that the application's executable (*.exe) file is included in your installation package. You're also given the option to add your debugging files, content files, and source files.

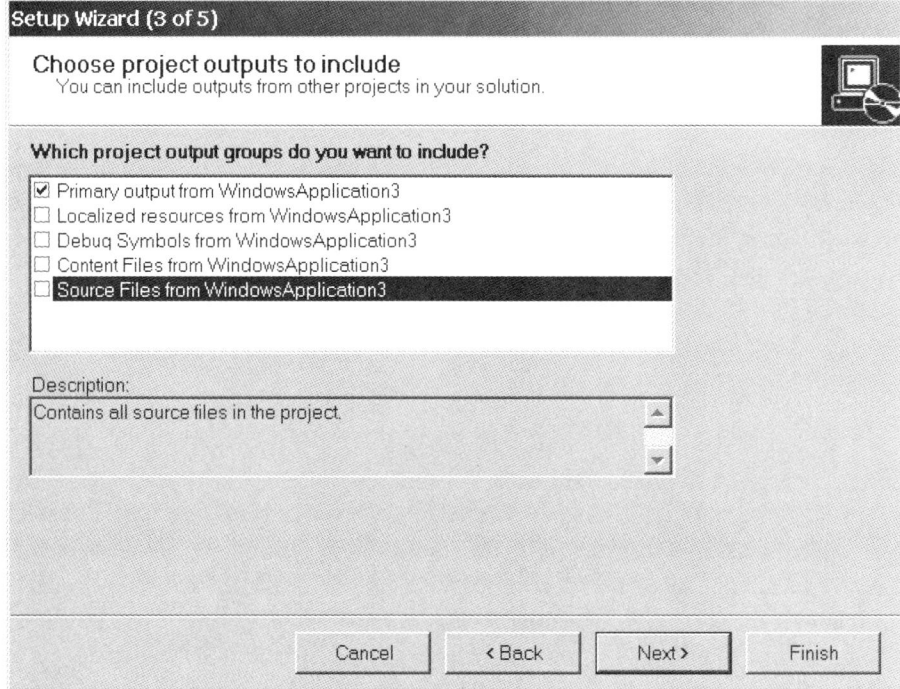

Figure 12-4. Selecting the project output types

After you check the items that you want included, click Next again to move to the next screen (see Figure 12-5). On this screen, you're given the option to add additional files to your installation. In other words, you may have written a handbook or some Help files that you want to accompany your application, or maybe you'd like to include the standard README.TXT file containing basic information. Adding the filenames to this screen ensures that those files get packaged along with your application and installed on the target computer or Web server. This is often important when you're dealing with third-party controls or projects involving ODBC drivers, because additional files that aren't always automatically incorporated into the setup package are often required for these components to run properly. This screen gives you the option of ensuring that these files are correctly transferred as well. For more information about which specific files are required, you should consult the vendor-supplied documentation that came with your product.

> **NOTE** *It's a good idea to consult the references section of your project to ensure that all files incorporated into the reference list have been incorporated into the setup package.*

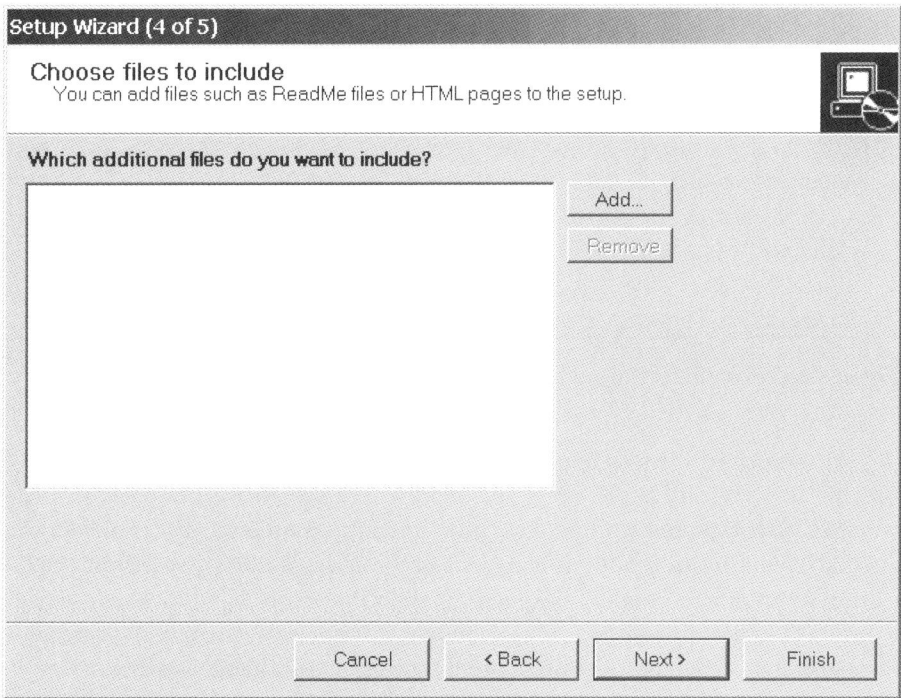

Figure 12-5. Adding additional files to the installation

Click Next one more time to reach the last screen of the Setup Wizard (see Figure 12-6). The purpose of this screen is quite simple: It's a summary screen. This screen gives you one last chance to review all of your selections and additions before you click Finish and add the setup project to your application.

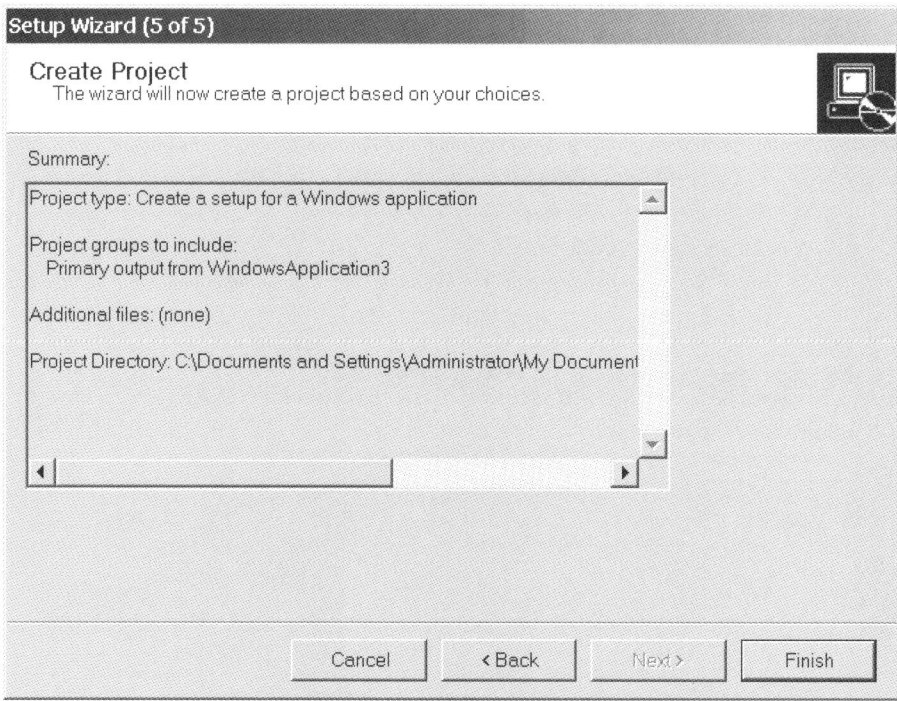

Figure 12-6. Reviewing the details of the selected setup options

When you've finished checking over your choices, click Finish. You'll notice that the Setup Wizard has disappeared and the setup project has been added to your Solution Explorer window. If you now go to the Solution Explorer window and make your recently added setup project the active project, you'll notice that a set of setup project properties appears in your Properties window. You're going to examine some of these properties now, so you can finish customizing your installation routine and move on to building your distributable product.

Deployment Properties

The deployment properties covered in the following sections allow you to customize your installation routine as well as personalize it. As you'll see, you can add company names and information, and you can have some control over how past installations are dealt with.

The Author Property

This property enables you to specify the company or individual responsible for writing this application. The user can view this information when he or she checks the properties of the installation file through Windows Explorer or some other means. The default for this property is the company name that was entered when Visual Studio was installed.

The Description Property

This property is also displayed when the installation file properties are examined, and it allows you to provide a brief description of what your program's capabilities are.

The DetectNewerInstalledVersion Property

If this property is set to True, Windows Installer searches for a newer version of the software that may be already installed on the target machine. If a newer version is found, installation will be aborted. If a newer version is not detected, installation will proceed as normal.

The Manufacturer Property

This property is generally the same as the Author property, and it has the same default setting. As with the Author property, this property is also viewable when the file properties are examined.

The ManufacturerURL Property

You probably guessed it. This property allows you to add your company's Web address to the File Properties listing.

The ProductName Property

This property allows you to specify a name for your product. This name will be used in the Add/Remove Programs menu as well as in the application's installation path. The default installation path for VS .NET applications is *C:\ProgramFiles\ManufacturerProperty\ProductNameProperty*.

The RemovePreviousVersions Property

If this property is set to True, the Windows Installer will look for a previous version of the same application. If no prior version is located, the installation will proceed as normal. If a prior version is detected, it will be uninstalled first and then the new version will be installed. If the property is set to False, the new version will be installed regardless of whether an older version is on the machine or not.

The SupportPhone and SupportURL Properties

These properties are both viewable on the File Properties screen and provide the user with a phone number and/or Web address he or she can use to help troubleshoot problems he or she may be experiencing with the application.

The Title Property

This property specifies the name of the installer used to set up the application. The default for this property is the name of the setup project (i.e., the name you chose when you added the Setup Wizard to your current project).

The Version Property

This property does just what its name implies: It stores the information that describes the version of the product about to be installed. Different versions are often necessary to account for upgrades and error fixes for a given software application.

Final Steps

Now that you've configured everything to match your preferences, it's time to build your application. You do this by changing the build configuration from Debug to Release. You then use the Build menu to build your project. After a few moments, the building will be complete. You can then go to your projects folder and look in the internal folder marked Release. Within this folder, you'll find a *.msi file that you can use to install your application. If you double-click this file you'll notice that the Windows Installer loads and begins to install your application. That's it. You've completed the packaging of your first program.

> **CAUTION**   *Although you've packaged your first program, before any public release of the packaged product occurs, you should install the package on a variety of machines running all feasible versions of the Windows OS to ensure compatibility. Likewise, testing various hardware configurations is also a good practice.*

CHAPTER 13

Mathematical Modeling

WITH THE ADVENT OF COMPUTERS, it's become increasingly possible to find mathematical solutions to "real world" problems. What's more, not only can these mathematical solutions help scientists and engineers design systems for experimentation or other uses, they can also help you simulate existing systems. Clearly, the ability to accurately create such models has changed the face of research and allows you to explore regions and situations that you otherwise might not have been able to. Mathematical models can also help you develop more accurate theoretical bases for experimentally derived results. Finally, such models are often great predictive tools that allow scientists and engineers to forecast the outcomes of certain events.

Most scientific programs generate their results based on a mathematical model of the system in question, so good mathematical modeling abilities are essential to scientific and engineering programmers. Mathematical models come in a variety of forms, and each of these forms can encompass overwhelming volumes of information on how to correctly proceed. Obviously, because of this factor, a single chapter won't be able to cover in depth all there is to know about mathematical modeling. However, the good news is that all mathematical models follow several basic principles. In this chapter, you'll have a chance to explore each of these principles and then use them to create a simple mathematical model of a chemical plant.

Defining the Problem

The first step towards creating any type of mathematical model is to define the problem that you're going to be looking at. For example, do you need a model that will predict the growth of a bacterial colony under given conditions, or are you interested in calculating the trajectory of a space shuttle, or anything in between? As you can clearly imagine, the mathematical models used to describe each one of these systems will be quite unique. The best way to proceed is first to figure out the answer to the question, "What type of system am I working on?"

Once you've established a clear picture of what it is you'll be modeling, you should next ask yourself, "What information do I need to generate from my model?" For instance, say that you did choose to monitor bacterial growth; do you want to know how long it will take the bacteria to reach a certain level, or are you interested in the level of bacteria after a certain amount of time? Even a subtle difference such as the one posed by this question will have some effect on how you structure your model, as obtaining each result will often require different inputs and/or different mathematical manipulations to calculate.

> **NOTE**   *Keep in mind that VB may not always be the best tool for mathematical modeling purposes. Programming languages like VB are often highly useful modeling tools, because they provide the greatest flexibility in how things can be accomplished, since everything can be custom coded. However, you shouldn't overlook many of the commercially available modeling packages, such as MATLAB with Simulink among others. Oftentimes the tried and true procedures and routines prewritten for use with these packages are well worth their limitations.*

Defining Variables and Parameters

Now that you've some sense of the subject and goal of your model, you must begin to add another layer of depth to your system definition. Before you proceed with this, take a minute to first define the meanings of variables and parameters in the context of mathematical modeling. You define parameters as intrinsic descriptors of the system, which remain constant throughout the process. For example, maybe the process is isobaric or isovolumetric. In either case, you'd define the pressure or the volume as an unchanging intrinsic property of the system. In other words, the pressure/volume is a preset value, which remains unchanged by the process. Variables, on the other hand, aren't constant, but rather relate interactions within the process. For example, adding X amount of heat might raise the temperature to Y, making both X and Y variable values. In turn, changes in Y might affect the system pressure P, demonstrating that variables are essential for establishing the interactions that occur within a process.

Next, ask yourself what variables and constants you need to define your system and its process. You should list all of the known parameters about the system. Following this, think about what information you want to obtain from your system in terms of variable quantities that you must evaluate. Also take into account the variable values that will be input into your system. For example, consider the following simple system. You have 1 mole of an ideal gas in a 5-liter isovolumetric container, and you want to examine the effects of changes in temperature on the pressure of the system (i.e., the pressure inside the container). For this type of system, your parameters would be $n = 1$ *mole* and $V = 5$ *liters*. Your input variable would be the temperature and your output value would be the pressure. You could then establish a relationship between T and P using the ideal gas law:

$$PV = nRT$$

Most of the time your models won't be this straightforward, and you'll need to calculate other variables in order to reach the final answer that you're looking for. For example, imagine that you work for a company that isolates, packages, and distributes different gases to research laboratories. A customer is working with some of your gases at a high temperature (573 K) and wants to know if your tanks will remain safe even with the increased pressure created by the high temperature. You know that your tanks will explode if they reach an internal pressure of greater than 3 atm. To determine if the tanks are safe at this temperature, you'd create a mathematical model using the preceding conditions. In this case, pressure wouldn't be your output variable, but rather the Boolean quantity *Safe=True* or *Safe=False*. However, you couldn't arrive at this Boolean quantity without first calculating the pressure and then entering the pressure into the relationship.

Is P<3atm?

Another factor that can help when trying to figure out the variable quantities needed to define your system is whether your system is a closed or an open system. In a closed system, the system is isolated and doesn't interact with the surrounding environment (i.e., everything else in the universe but the system). In other words, you must determine if changing any variables in the environment will result in a change in the system. If the answer is no, then your system is closed. An open system, on the other hand, does interact with the environment, so changes in environmental conditions can lead to changes in system conditions. Recall the last example. A change in the temperature of the area surrounding the tank would lead to a change in the tank temperature over time (according to Newton's law of cooling), and this change in tank temperature would in turn lead to a change in tank pressure. This system thus qualifies as an open system.

Relating Variables and Parameters

This topic, touched on slightly in the last section, is probably the most critical part of the mathematical modeling process, because this is where you call upon mathematical equations to define relationships between variables. For example, in the scenario presented in the last section, you saw how you could use the ideal gas law to relate the tank temperature to the pressure, and you could relate the environmental temperature to the tank temperature at a certain point in time through Newton's law of cooling. Real-world mathematical models are rarely this simple, however, with most models involving a much larger number of variable quantities than just two or three. Some models even make use of thousands of different variables. As you can imagine, picking the appropriate equations and the proper order in which to apply them isn't always the most straightforward process. For this reason, model building is oftentimes an iterative process in which you set up your model and compare its output to an experimentally determined value. If the model doesn't predict the experimentally determined value to the desired level of accuracy, then you revise your mathematical relations until you reach your desired level of accuracy.

It's also important to choose the correct equations for the job at hand. Revisiting the gas tank scenario, if the tank contained a real gas instead of an ideal gas, using the ideal gas law would be a bad approximation—real gases only approach ideality at high temperatures and low pressures, which isn't the case in this problem. You'd therefore want to use a more appropriate mathematical relation, such as a gas law that involves a compressibility factor or a real gas adjustment factor. As you can see, when choosing your mathematical relations, it's crucial that you take into account the system conditions to which you're going to apply these equations.

Using Flowcharts

One great way to aid in the development of mathematical models is to create flowcharts (or flow diagrams) of the system you're modeling. Flowcharts are diagrams that consist of boxes representing the different steps your model will be required to take in order to go from the information input into the model to the desired output. For example, look at Figure 13-1 and see how the diagram clearly shows the logical workings behind the gas tank safety problem.

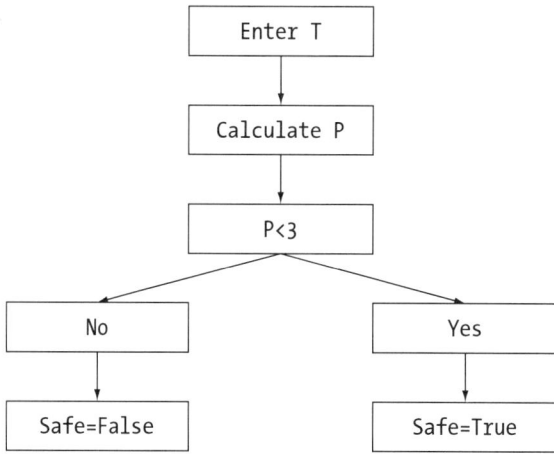

Figure 13-1. The flowchart for the gas tank safety problem

This is a simple example of the use of flowcharts, and they can get much more elaborate. In fact, in many larger applications each box might represent a whole procedure instead of just a single line of code, and each procedure in turn might have its own flowchart.

> **NOTE** *One commonly used tool for creating flowcharts you might want to try is Microsoft Visio.*

The time it takes to construct a flowchart, however, is often well worthwhile, because it can help you to clearly lay out the logic of your program. Once a flowchart has been constructed, you know which variable quantities to calculate first and what order to call procedures. This makes coding larger applications much more manageable; instead of representing these huge abstract tasks, they become a series of smaller tasks with clearly laid out written guidelines. Another great aspect of flowcharts is that they force you to work through the program logic before you begin coding. This means that you're likely to weed out a good portion of logical errors early on and end up with fewer hard-to-find bugs later on.

The Black Box Approach

Sometimes you can simplify mathematical models by treating certain parts of a system as a "black box." This means the inner workings of that particular part of the system are ignored, and the subsystem is just viewed as a relationship between what goes in and what comes out. Here's an example situation that you'll see modeled in detail at the end of the chapter where the system is a chemical plant. In this plant, there's a chemical reactor that is involved in converting your reactants into the product of interest. Through experimentation, you know that 90 percent of the limiting reagent will be converted into product at the specified reaction conditions of the plant. With this information, you could easily relate the reactor inlet streams to the outlet streams by using just the stoichiometry of the chemical reaction and this relationship; you don't need to know how the reactor operates as a function of temperature, pressure, catalyst concentration, and/or other pertinent factors. This makes your reactor a so-called black box and greatly simplifies your task of generating a model.

As you can clearly see, the black box approach can be quite useful when you're dealing with complex multicomponent systems. However, before going with such an approach, you should verify that the use of black boxes is appropriate. For example, the preceding reactor model cannot account for changes in reaction conditions; if conditions did change, the model would no longer be accurate. As the modeler, you have to weigh the complexity of the model versus the accuracy of the model and the model's ability to deal with variations in conditions. Usually the more robust a model, the more complex it is, and because of this factor you must make the decision as to which is most appropriate for your particular needs.

Degree of Freedom Analysis

As you can imagine, it can often be a daunting task to properly define a large system with the correct number of mathematical relations. In fact, to ensure that the model functions properly, you need to take care that you don't underdefine or overdefine your model. Luckily, there's a relatively simple technique that can help you to ensure your models are perfectly defined (in terms of number of mathematical relations) before you begin to use them to evaluate your system. This technique is known as *degree of freedom analysis*.

Degree of freedom analysis shows the number of variables that must be specified in order for all of the other variables to be calculated. This analysis is based on the principle of needing n equations to solve for n unknowns, and you can perform the analysis by using the equation

$$df = V - V_k - E$$

where df is the degrees of freedom remaining. V represents the total number of variables, and V_k represents the number of known (specified) variables. E represents the number of mathematical equations. Thus, if you had a system with 5 unknown variables, 1 known variable, and 3 equations, you'd have 1 degree of freedom in your system. In degree of freedom analysis, there are three possible resulting cases, as described in the following sections.

Case 1

If the value of df is equal to zero, no degrees of freedom remain within the system. The number of equations equals the number of unknown variables, and therefore the system is perfectly defined. This is the scenario that you must aim for in order to have a solvable model, because it ensures that one unique solution exists for each variable.

Case 2

If the value of df is greater than zero, your system is underdefined. In this case, there are more unknown variables than equations, making the system unsolvable. Having too few equations means that a number of unknown variables equal to df would have to be arbitrarily specified in order to solve the problem. These arbitrarily assigned values indicate that an infinite number of solutions would be possible for all remaining unknown variables, which is obviously not a desirable situation.

Case 3

If the value of *df* is less than zero, there are more equations than unknown variables, which also results in an unsolvable solution. In this case, the system is overdefined and no solution exists for the equation set.

To best understand how degree of freedom analysis works, you really need to see it in action, so the next section moves on to the example system for this chapter, in which you'll see how to create a model of a simplified chemical plant.

Mathematical Modeling of a Chemical Plant

Imagine you're a scientific programmer working for a chemical corporation that wants to build a new chemical plant. This plant will take oxygen and methane gases in stoichiometric quantities and output carboxyl as the product stream and water as a waste stream. Here's the equation:

$$2CH_4 + 3O_2 \rightarrow 2CHOOH + 2H_2O$$

Figure 13-2 illustrates the plant's basic design.

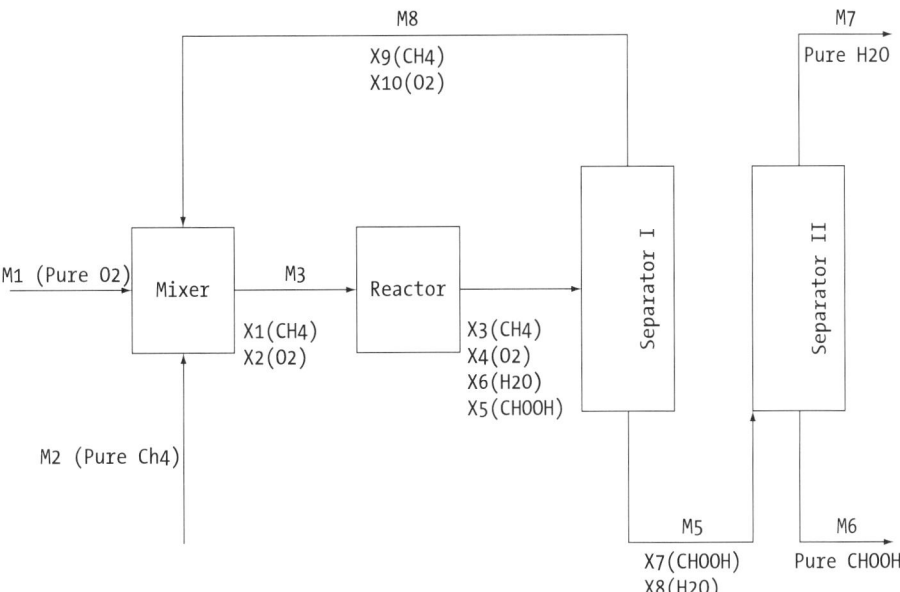

Figure 13-2. Schematic representation of your chemical plant

The engineers who are busy designing the plant provide you with details about the industrial design. For example, you know that the raw materials will be added in their stoichiometric ratios and that this raw material input will be combined with raw materials found in a recycle stream, prior to being fed to the reactor. The engineers also tell you that the reactor is being constructed to yield a 90 percent conversion of methane to product. The product-containing stream that leaves from the reactor will then be fed to a separator, which will remove all (100 percent) of the methane and oxygen gases from the stream and send them back to the mixer via the recycle stream. After the first separation, the water product mixture passes through a second separation phase, which will remove 100 percent of the water and yield a pure product stream and a water waste stream. It's your job to create a model of this plant that will allow you to specify the amount of product you want to make, and based on this amount determine the amount of raw materials that you need to add.

To get started, first look at the flowchart in Figure 13-2 and find the total number of variables within the model. As you can see, there are 18 variables present, including the total molar flow rates of each stream (M1 to M8) and the mole fractions of each component (X1 to X10). However, only 14 independent variables occur within the system. For example, take a look at the reactor feed (stream 3), which has three variables. Only two out of these three variables are needed to define the system, because if you know the mole fraction of methane, you also know the mole fraction of oxygen is one minus the mole fraction of methane. The mole fraction of oxygen is thus not independent, but instead dependent on the mole fraction of methane. You only need to worry about independent variables, so declare your independent variables as follows:

```
Private X1 As Double
Private X3 As Double
Private X4 As Double
Private X5 As Double
Private X7 As Double
Private X9 As Double
Private M1 As Double
Private M2 As Double
Private M3 As Double
Private M4 As Double
Private M5 As Double
Private M6 As Double
Private M7 As Double
Private M8 As DoublePrivate M6desired As Double
```

NOTE *All variables are declared as Doubles to ensure the accuracy of the model to the highest degree of precision possible. Accuracy is crucial to all models, but especially to many engineering design models, where safety considerations weigh in on the proper functioning of the system.*

Now that you know you're dealing with 14 independent variables, you also know that the *V* term for the degree of freedom analysis is 14.

You've determined how many independent variables you're dealing with, so next you need to concern yourself with the number of independent mathematical relationships you can draw up between these variables. In the case of a chemical plant, this is done through material balances. For example, if stream 5 goes in and streams 6 and 7 go out, then the number of moles in stream 5 must be equal to the number of moles in streams 6 and 7 combined. You can also create relationships based on your percent conversion and the stoichiometry of the chemical equation. In the following sections, you'll examine all of these relationships in depth, but for now just consider the fact that you can only create 13 such relationships. This means that you still have one degree of freedom to worry about before you're able to solve your model.

Setting a Basis

Because you have one degree of freedom remaining, you have to specify one variable before you can proceed with solving the problem. The most obvious variable to specify is the product stream molar flow rate; however, this variable isn't advantageous from the point of solving the problem. You should instead specify the molar flow rate of the reactor feed stream (M3) to the arbitrary value of 100. You then use this value to solve for the value of all the other variables and compare the resulting value of M6 to the desired value. Using this discrepancy, scale up the value of M3 to a value that will yield the desired value of M6 and solve again for all of the other variables. Set up this basis using the following code:

```
Private Sub SetBasis()
  M3 = 100
  X1 = 2 / 5
End Sub
```

You also take advantage of your first relationship in this routine by setting the mole fraction of X1 equal to 2/5. You're able to do this because the raw materials were fed into the mixer at stoichiometric conditions. You also know that the reactants in the recycle stream should be in stoichiometric proportions as well, since they were 100 percent recovered from the reactor product stream.

The Reactor

Now that you've set your arbitrary basis, you're able to solve the material balances that occur across the chemical reactor. The conversion rate is 0.9, so you can ignore the inner workings of the reactor and treat it as a black box. Here's the code for the material balances across the reactor:

```
Private Sub Reactor()
 M4 = ((1 - 0.9) * M3 * X1) + (0.9 * M3 * X1) + (0.9 * M3 * X1) + _
((1 - 0.9) * M3 * (1 - X1))
 X3 = (((1 - 0.9) * M3 * X1) / M4)
 X4 = ((1 - 0.9) * M3 * (1 - X1)) / M4
 X5 = ((0.9 * M3 * X1) / M4)
End Sub
```

The first balance you perform results in the molar flow rate of stream 4 (M4) by determining how much water and product is produced (middle terms) and how much methane and oxygen remains after the reaction (end terms). You next determine the mole fractions of methane, water, and product found in stream 4. It's also important to remember that when dealing with chemical reactions, you must incorporate the reaction stoichiometry. In this case, there's a one-to-one correlation between the number of moles of methane and the number of moles of water and product, so you need to adjust for differing coefficients. Also, the different coefficient found before the oxygen in the reaction is taken into account by the mole fraction of the oxygen. However, in many other reactions, that one-to-one ratio doesn't always exist.

Separators I and II

The part of the process where the unused oxygen and methane are removed and placed in a recycle stream occurs at separator I, while the remaining water and product mixture continues on to the second separator. The balances constructed around this piece of equipment are as follows:

```
Private Sub Sep1()
 M8 = (M4 * X4) + (M4 * X3)
 M5 = M4 - M8
 X7 = ((M4 * X5) / M5)
 X9 = ((M4 * X3) / M8)
End Sub
```

First, you know that 100 percent of all of the oxygen and methane are entered into the recycle stream (M8), so the recycle stream is equal to the total moles of these two components found in stream 4. Stream 5 is what remains of stream 4 after the components that make up stream 8 have been removed. Finally, now that you've defined the total molar flow rates of the two streams, you determine the necessary mole fractions of the components found within the streams.

You then take the information you calculated about stream 5 and use that information in the relationships that describe what occurs at separator II. These relationships are given by the following code:

```
Private Sub Sep2()
 M6 = M5 * X7
 M7 = M5 - M6
End Sub
```

The first balance takes advantage of the fact that you know 100 percent separation occurs between water and product, and therefore stream 6 is equal to the product component of stream 5. Likewise, the remainder of stream 5 corresponds to the water component and is equivalent to stream 7.

The Mixer

The recycle stream you calculated (stream 8) is fed into a mixer, which adds the recycled reactants to streams of raw materials. The mixer then combines all of these different streams to yield stream 3, which you used as your basis. You were told that streams 1 and 2 would be found in stoichiometric ratio, so you can solve for these two input streams using the following material balances:

```
Private Sub Mix()
 Dim M1M2 As Double
 M1M2 = M3 - M8
 M1 = (2 * M1M2) / 5
 M2 = (3 * M1M2) / 5
End Sub
```

As you look at the equations used in this example, it's important to note that the routine only really makes use of two independent equations, since you can substitute M3 - M8 every place M1M2 is used. Also, remember that at this point you've defined every independent variable within the system, so now it's time to examine what you calculated and make the necessary scaleup.

The Scaleup

In order to initiate your scaleup procedure, you must first compare the value you obtained for your product stream with the value you actually desire. Accomplish this as follows:

```
Private Sub ScaleUp()
    Dim S As Double
    S = M6desired / M6
    M3 = M3 * S
    Call Reactor()
    Call Sep1()
    Call Sep2()
    Call Mix()
End Sub
```

You perform this comparison by dividing your target value by your actual value. This will tell you how many times greater your target value is than your actual value and will enable you to scale up your basis number by this much. This new scaled-up basis number will produce a product stream that is equivalent to the target product stream. You then employ this new scaled-up basis in the recalculation of all your variables, and from this recalculation you'll learn the values of raw materials that you require in your inlet streams.

Now that you have the mathematical logic worked out for your chemical plant, add an interface, as shown in Figure 13-3, and a command button to initiate the calculation.

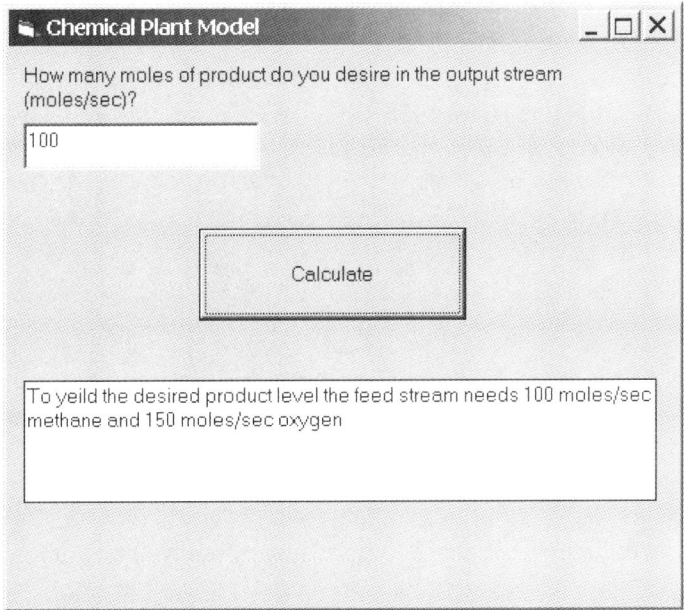

Figure 13-3. The GUI to your chemical process simulator

The code for the command button's Click event is as follows:

```
Private Sub Command1_Click(ByVal eventSender As System.Object, ByVal _
eventArgs As System.EventArgs) Handles Command1.Click
    M6desired = CSng(Text1.Text)
    Call SetBasis()
    Call Reactor()
    Call Sep1()
    Call Sep2()
    Call Mix()
    Call ScaleUp()
    Text2.Text = "To yield the desired product level the feed stream needs " & _
M1 & " moles/sec methane and " & M2 & " moles/sec oxygen"
End Sub
```

Now you're set to execute your model and determine the values of your inlet streams (Figure 13-3).

NOTE *In designing this model, almost all variables were declared as Private (module scope) to give them more globalized access from the different procedures. It's generally better to use local variables when possible and pass values to procedures as parameters in order to prevent accidental changes to key quantities. However, here this practice wasn't used in order to lessen the number of variable declarations and produce a shorter and easier-to-follow example.*

In the real world, however, you should remember that at this stage your model isn't truly complete. Now that you've developed your model, a testing phase would begin, which generally encompasses using the model to predict known quantities. Then, based on how the model performs, you make refinements to improve the accuracy and the usefulness of the model. You'd also have to incorporate some of the error handling capabilities discussed in Chapter 11. That way if your model misbehaves or receives any faulty input parameters, you can be instantly informed, rather than presented with a faulty result.

Hopefully by this point, you have a basic understanding of how mathematical modeling works and what it entails. The techniques discussed in this chapter are useful guidelines for creating mathematical models and will serve you well for constructing many different types of basic mathematical models. This subject is one of the most crucial to the scientific programmer, and anyone who is seriously pursuing a career in any type of scientific or engineering programming discipline should read even more on the intricacies of mathematical modeling.

CHAPTER 14

Bioinformatics

BIOINFORMATICS IS CURRENTLY ONE of the hottest fields in scientific computing, and the need for skillful bioinformaticists is only expected to grow in the coming years. As a result of the amazing success of genomics projects like the Human Genome Project and the recent interest in the field of proteomics, the biological sciences have been amassing tremendous amounts of data. The enormity of this data, being much too large to analyze by hand, has given rise to a union between biological sciences and computer-based data analysis, which in turn has led to the birth of the field of bioinformatics.

The field of bioinformatics is constantly striving to create more powerful and more efficient algorithms to analyze gene and protein sequence data. While the methodologies used to develop such algorithms are well beyond the scope of this book, you'll get an introduction to bioinformatics by examining the code of several applications, presented in this chapter, that are quite useful to molecular biologists in the laboratory setting. First, you'll look at a way to predict possible protein sequences when presented with a gene sequence, and then you'll learn how to create restriction maps for a segment of DNA.

Predicting Protein Sequences

Odds are that not everyone who bought this book has a background in the biological sciences, so this section starts off by providing a very brief introduction to the molecular biology topics of transcription, translation, and the genetic code. Having a basic knowledge of these topics is essential for understanding the protein sequence prediction program, so anyone who is not familiar with them should read this entire section. If you have a background in molecular biology and hence an understanding of these topics, feel free to skip ahead to the actual applications. However, if you desire a more complete understanding of the topics touched on in this chapter, you may be interested in the following resources:

- Griffiths, A. J. et al. 1996. *An Introduction to Genetic Analysis, Sixth Edition.* New York City: W.H. Freeman and Company—This book is a great text, providing a concise but thorough introduction to the field of genetics and molecular biology. The book will supply you with much of the needed biological background required by the field of bioinformatics.

- Waterman, M. S. 1995. *Introduction to Computational Biology: Maps, Sequences, and Genomes.* New York City: Chapman and Hall/CRC—You'll need some of the background knowledge found in the previous text in order to make this reference easily understandable, but with the necessary background, it does provide a good introduction to some of the basic algorithms employed by bioinformaticists.

If you want to keep abreast of recent developments in bioinformatics, you'll want to check out the Bioinformatics.Org Web site (`http://www.bioinformatics.org`). The site also features links to bioinformatics tools and resources that may aid you in your own projects.

DNA

Deoxyribonucleic acid (DNA) is a molecule, double helical in structure, that serves as the information storage center for biological life forms. You can think of it as the hard drive for your body's cells. Only instead of storing information in binary units, such as sequences of zeroes and ones, DNA uses repeating units of the molecules adenine (A), guanine (G), cytosine (C), and thiamine (T). Different sequences and lengths of these repeating units make up the different genes necessary for cellular functioning. Genes, however, aren't directly involved in these cellular functions; they instead contain the information required to make the appropriate proteins. Proteins are a form of cellular machinery, and genes are like files that contain the blueprints needed to make this cellular machinery. DNA sequences can't be directly translated into protein structures, however, so some prior processing is required, the first of which is transcription. Also, remember that because DNA has a double-helical structure, it consists of two complementary strands. That is, the As and Cs in one strand will be base paired with the Ts and Gs in the other strand, and vice versa (see Figure 14-1).

5'-ATTGCTA-3'
3'-TAACGAT-5'

Figure 14-1. A sample DNA sequence

However, you're able to deal with just a single strand, since genes are encoded by a single strand of DNA and not by the base-paired complements.

Transcription

The first step involved in gene expression is the transcription of gene-encoding DNA into ribonucleic acid, or RNA. This particular type of RNA is known as *messenger RNA,* or mRNA, because it carries the necessary information about the gene that is going to be expressed out of the nucleus (the part of the cell that stores the DNA) and into a region of the cell that allows for the production of proteins. mRNA forms a complementary strand with the gene-encoding piece of the DNA strand (see Figure 14-2). The only exception is that RNA doesn't contain the nucleotide thiamine, but instead contains uracil (U), which substitutes for T in positions complementary to A.

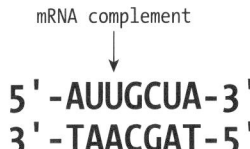

```
        mRNA complement
               ↓
     5'-AUUGCUA-3'
     3'-TAACGAT-5'
```

Figure 14-2. A DNA strand and its mRNA complement

Another important fact to consider is the end of the DNA and RNA strands. If you look at the strand segments shown in Figures 14-1 and 14-2, you'll see that the strands all have a 5' end and a 3' end, which are based on the chemical composition of the molecule's backbone at the end point. Although the exact chemical structures aren't important for developing your computer program, you do need to understand that DNA and RNA can only be synthesized from the 5' end to the 3' end. This means you must keep track of the various ends in your code so you arrive at the right protein, and not a protein that begins in the wrong place (i.e., one that was translated backwards).

Translation

Translation is exactly like it sounds: it's the process by which the information storage medium, mRNA, is translated from a sequence of nucleotides into a sequence of amino acids. Amino acids are the building blocks of proteins, which play a major role in the structure and function of biological cells. It turns out that every three nucleotides form a unit called a *codon,* and every codon codes for one amino acid. This translation utilizes an adaptor molecule, transfer RNA (tRNA), which is able to "read" the nucleotide sequence with one end and has an amino acid attached to the other end. Many different types of tRNAs exist, and each type of tRNA can only read and interact with certain codons. The tRNAs thus function as the adaptors that make sure the correct amino acids end up in the right places in the protein sequence, in much the same way as you can only fit a square peg into a square hole. The codon sequences that call for the various amino acids are referred to as the *genetic code*. In your application, you want to use this genetic code to translate your mRNA into possible amino acid sequences (see Table 14-1).

Table 14-1. The Genetic Code

UUU-	Phe	UCU-	Ser	UAU-	Tyr	UGU-	Cys
UUC-	Phe	UCC-	Ser	UAC-	Tyr	UGC-	Cys
UUA-	Leu	UCA-	Ser	UAA-	Stop	UGA-	Stop
UUG-	Leu	UCG-	Ser	UAG-	Stop	UGG-	Trp
CUU-	Leu	CCU-	Pro	CAU-	His	CGU-	Arg
CUC-	Leu	CCC-	Pro	CAC-	His	CGC-	Arg
CUA-	Leu	CCA-	Pro	CAA-	Gln	CGA-	Arg
CUG-	Leu	CCG-	Pro	CAG-	Gln	CGG-	Arg
AUU-	Ile	ACU-	Thr	AAU-	Asn	AGU-	Ser
AUC-	Ile	ACC-	Thr	AAC-	Asn	AGC-	Ser
AUA-	Ile	ACA-	Thr	AAA-	Lys	AGA-	Arg
AUG-	Met	ACG-	Thr	AAG-	Lys	AGG-	Arg
GUU-	Val	GCU-	Ala	GAU-	Asp	GGU-	Gly
GUC-	Val	GCC-	Ala	GAC-	Asp	GGC-	Gly
GUA-	Val	GCA-	Ala	GAA-	Glu	GGA-	Gly
GUG-	Val	GCG-	Ala	GAG-	Glu	GGG-	Gly

Within the genetic code, however, are some special sequences that are important in their functionality. For instance, the codon AUG codes for the amino acid methionine, and is known as the Start codon, because every protein sequence must begin with AUG. This means translation doesn't necessarily start with the first few nucleotides, but rather won't begin until an AUG is detected in the sequence.

A protein sequence without the first codon also raises further issues with regards to reading frame: does the first codon begin with the first nucleotide on the mRNA strand, the second one, or the third one? In essence, there are three possible reading frames, and you've no real way of predetermining which reading frame is correct, as it can vary from mRNA strand to mRNA strand. So you must search for AUGs in all three possible reading frames before you can begin your translation. More likely than not, there will only be one reading frame in which you find an AUG, but you can't eliminate the possibility of an AUG arising in more than one frame (see Figure 14-3).

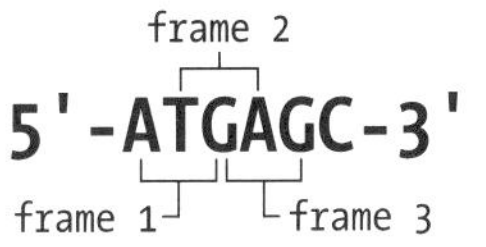

Figure 14-3. The three possible reading frames

In addition to the Start codon, however, you need to take into account three additional codons that don't code for any amino acids. These codons are called Stop codons, and they consist of the sequences UAA, UGA, and UAG. When one of these codons is reached in your mRNA sequence, they terminate the translation process, and therefore specify the end point of your amino acid sequence.

Protein Sequence Prediction Program

You'll begin this example application by starting with a blank form and adding three rich text boxes to the form along with a command button (see Figure 14-4). You want to use rich text boxes instead of standard text boxes in this situation because rich text boxes can display a greater number of characters, which means you aren't limited to the sizes of sequences that you're able to work with.

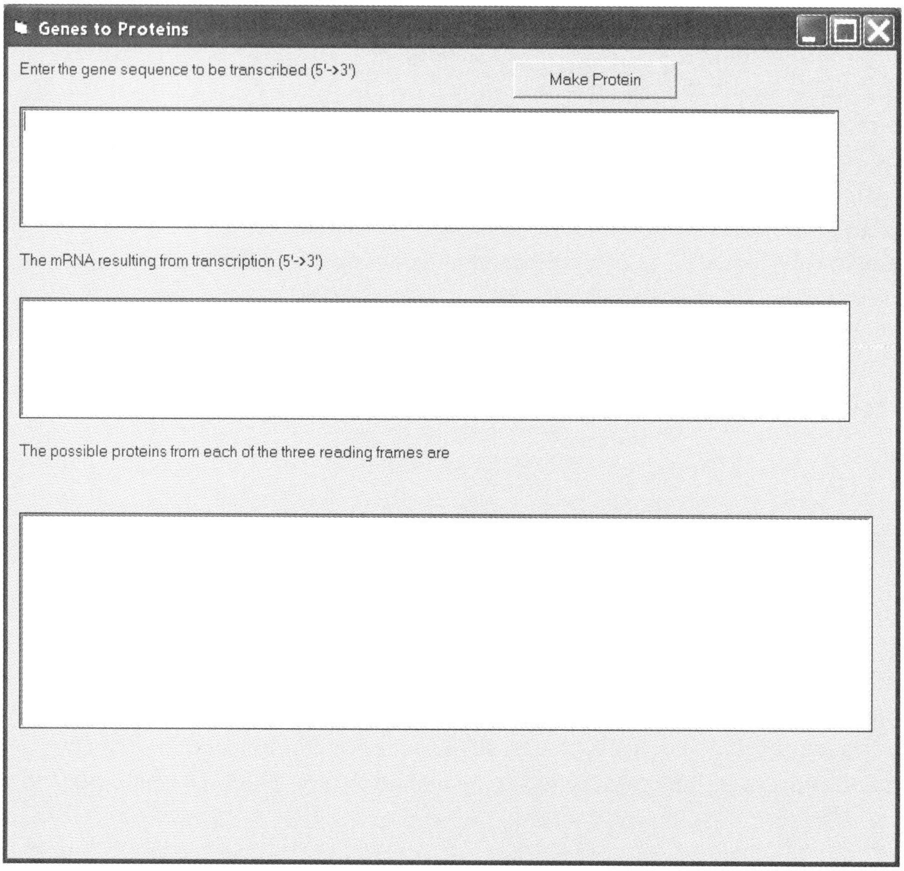

Figure 14-4. The GUI for your protein sequence program

Once you've completed setting up your form, add the following code to your command button's Click event:

```
Private Sub Button1_Click(ByVal eventSender As System.Object, ByVal _
eventArgs As System.EventArgs) Handles Button1.Click
        Dim DNA As String
        Dim RNA As String
        Dim RF1 As String
        Dim RF2 As String
        Dim RF3 As String
        DNA = RichTextBox1.Text
        RNA = Transcribe(DNA)
        RichTextBox2.Text = RNA
        RF1 = Translate(RNA, 1)
        RF2 = Translate(RNA, 2)
```

```
        RF3 = Translate(RNA, 3)
        RichTextBox3.Text = "Reading Frame 1" & ControlChars.CrLf & _
ControlChars.CrLf & RF1 & ControlChars.CrLf & ControlChars.CrLf & _
"Reading Frame 2" & ControlChars.CrLf & ControlChars.CrLf & RF2 & _
ControlChars.CrLf & ControlChars.CrLf & "Reading Frame 3" _
& ControlChars.CrLf & ControlChars.CrLf & RF3
End Sub
```

As you can see by examining the code, the first step that you take is to define several string variables. One variable holds your DNA sequence, while a second variable holds your mRNA sequence. Finally, the last three variables that you declare will hold your protein sequences in each of the three possible reading frames. After declaring your variables, you then read in your DNA sequence from RichTextBox1 and call upon your Transcribe function. You pass your DNA sequence into the Transcribe function in the procedure call. The code for the Transcribe procedure is as follows:

```
Private Function Transcribe(ByVal DNA As String) As String
        Dim I As Integer
        Dim mRNA As String
        DNA = UCase(DNA)
        For I = 1 To Len(DNA)
            If Mid(DNA, I, 1) = "A" Then
                mRNA = "U" & mRNA
            ElseIf Mid(DNA, I, 1) = "T" Then
                mRNA = "A" & mRNA
            ElseIf Mid(DNA, I, 1) = "G" Then
                mRNA = "C" & mRNA
            ElseIf Mid(DNA, I, 1) = "C" Then
                mRNA = "G" & mRNA
            Else : MsgBox("Error in gene sequence")
            End If
        Next I
        Transcribe = mRNA
  End Function
```

In this procedure, you first apply the UCase function to your DNA data in order to ensure that all letters are uppercase. This is just meant as a form of error handling, because it helps to ensure that your code will still function properly if the user enters a, g, c, or t, instead of A, G, C, or T. Next, you use a loop structure that contains a block If inside to read the string of DNA characters. If you look closely, as you choose the appropriate base pair for the mRNA sequence, you add it to the beginning of the RNA string that you're building. This is because the RNA is synthesized from 5' to 3', as stated earlier. Since you also want to display your RNA strand in the same orientation, your final RNA strand should therefore be in the reverse order when compared to your DNA strand. You should also note that in the Else condition you output an error message if a character other than A, T, C, or G was input. This step also ensures the reliability and accuracy of your program's output. Once the function is complete, you send the results back to the Click event procedure, where they are output in RichTextBox2.

The next lines of code found in the Click event call upon the Translate procedure three times: once to calculate the sequence in reading frame 1, once to calculate the sequence in reading frame 2, and once to calculate the sequence in reading frame 3. This reuse of the same procedure demonstrates the convenience of using procedures as well. Imagine having to duplicate the same code three different times. The code for this procedure is as follows:

```
Private Function Translate(ByVal RNA As String, ByVal RF As Short) As String
        Dim STP As Boolean
        Dim Start As Boolean
        Dim Prot As String
        Dim Codon As String
        Dim StartNum As Integer
        Dim RFV As Short
        STP = False
        Start = False
        RFV = RF
        Do Until Start = True Or RFV > (Len(RNA) - 2)
            If Mid(RNA, RFV, 3) = "AUG" Then
                Start = True
                StartNum = RFV
            End If
            RFV = RFV + 3
        Loop
        RFV = StartNum
        If Start = True Then
            Do Until STP = True Or RFV > (Len(RNA) - 2)
                Codon = Mid(RNA, RFV, 3)
                Select Case Codon
                    Case "AUG"
                        Prot = Prot & "M"
                    Case "UGA", "UAA", "UAG"
                        STP = True
                    Case "UUU", "UUC"
                        Prot = Prot & "F"
                    Case "UUA", "UUG", "CUU", "CUC", "CUA", "CUG"
```

```
                        Prot = Prot & "L"
                Case "AUU", "AUC", "AUA"
                        Prot = Prot & "I"
                Case "GUU", "GUC", "GUA", "GUG"
                        Prot = Prot & "V"
                Case "UAU", "UAC"
                        Prot = Prot & "Y"
                Case "UCU", "UCC", "UCA", "UCG"
                        Prot = Prot & "S"
                Case "CCU", "CCC", "CCA", "CCG"
                        Prot = Prot & "P"
                Case "ACU", "ACC", "ACA", "ACG"
                        Prot = Prot & "T"
                Case "GCU", "GCC", "GCA", "GCG"
                        Prot = Prot & "A"
                Case "CAU", "CAC"
                        Prot = Prot & "H"
                Case "CAA", "CAG"
                        Prot = Prot & "Q"
                Case "AAU", "AAC"
                        Prot = Prot & "N"
                Case "AAA", "AAG"
                        Prot = Prot & "K"
                Case "GAU", "GAC"
                        Prot = Prot & "D"
                Case "GAA", "GAG"
                        Prot = Prot & "E"
                Case "UGU", "UGC"
                        Prot = Prot & "C"
                Case "UGG"
                        Prot = Prot & "W"
                Case "CGU", "CGC", "CGA", "CGG", "AGA", "AGG"
                        Prot = Prot & "R"
                Case "AGU", "AGC"
                        Prot = Prot & "S"
                Case "GGU", "GGC", "GGA", "GGG"
                        Prot = Prot & "G"
            End Select
            RFV = RFV + 3
        Loop
    Else : Prot = "No Start Codon in reading frame"
    End If
    Translate = Prot
End Function
```

The Translate procedure starts off with the RNA sequence and the reading frame information, passed from the procedure call. The function then uses this information to search through the mRNA sequence, in the specified reading frame, and locate the start codon, if any. If a Start codon is found, the Boolean variable Start is set equal to True and the indeterminate loop structure is exited. The procedure then uses a second loop, which continues to read through the sequence, three characters at a time, and adds the appropriate amino acid (single letter notation) to the string named Prot. If a Stop codon is located instead, the variable STP is set equal to True and the loop structure is exited. If a proper amino acid sequence was created (i.e., a start codon was found in the reading frame), the procedure will return this sequence. If an amino acid sequence was not generated, then the procedure returns the string "No Start Codon in reading frame." The procedure is repeated for each of the three reading frames, and the results are output in RichTextBox3 (see Figure 14-5).

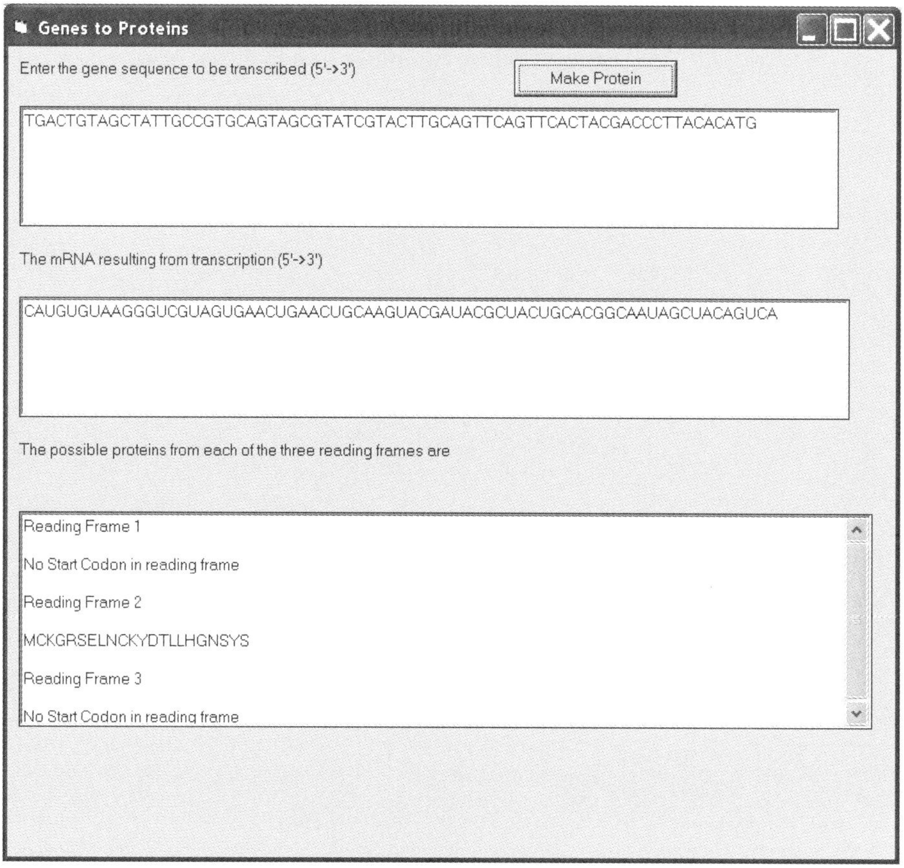

Figure 14-5. A sample output of the protein sequence prediction program

Restriction Mapping

Restriction mapping is a commonly used technique in molecular biology that establishes reference points along a strand of DNA, such as a plasmid or chromosome. You create this type of map by cutting the DNA strand at certain sites and then determining the order in which the cut sites were located. A computer program that could automate the process of this ordering technique would be very useful. However, before getting into the specifics of ordering the cut sites, you should take a look at how you'd accomplish the initial steps of restriction mapping.

Restriction Enzymes

The first part of the technique you must consider is how you cut your DNA strand. This cutting action is accomplished by using an enzyme (a specialized protein catalyst) that can cleave DNA. Restriction enzymes are enzymes that can recognize specific DNA sequences and, upon recognition, cleave the DNA strand somewhere within the target site. Each of these enzymes recognizes unique DNA sequences that tend to be palindromic. For example, a commonly used restriction enzyme isolated from *E. coli* bacteria is EcoRI, which recognizes the following sequence:

> 5'-GAATTC-3'

> 3'-CTTAAG-5'

The Mapping Technique

Restriction mapping generally involves using two different restriction enzymes. For illustration purposes, say that these are called restriction enzymes 1 and 2. First, a sample of your DNA is cleaved using restriction enzyme 1. Next, a sample of your DNA is cleaved using restriction enzyme 2. You then take a third sample of your DNA and cleave it with both restriction enzymes 1 and 2. This last step is referred to as a *double digest*, because two enzymes are cleaving the DNA at the same time.

These digested samples then undergo a technique called *gel electrophoresis*, in which you position DNA fragments at the edge of a gel-like mesh of agarose and expose the gel to an electric field. DNA has a fairly uniform negative charge/size ratio, and thus the DNA fragments will travel through the gel toward the more attractive pole of the electrical field. The larger fragments of DNA, however, have a harder time of navigating their way through the gel matrix, so they travel slower than their smaller counterparts. This leads to a separation of the DNA fragments based on size. Biologists can then figure out the size of the fragment by comparing its migration distance to the migration distances of known standards. Let's consider the following example found in Figure 14-6.

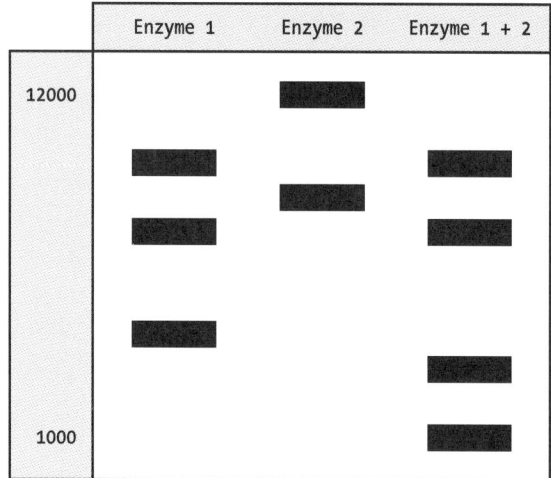

Figure 14-6. Fragment migration from gel electrophoresis

If you look at the first column, where enzyme 1 is used to digest a DNA strand, you'll see three bands appearing on the gel. These bands correspond to fragments of 9000, 7000, and 4000 bases, respectively. In the second column in which the strand was digested by enzyme 2, fragments appear that correspond to 8000 and 12,000 bases. In the Double Digest column appear four fragments of lengths 9000, 7000, 3000, and 10,000 bases.

From this data you can create a restriction map that shows the cut sites in the sequence in which they occur in the DNA strand (see Figure 14-7).

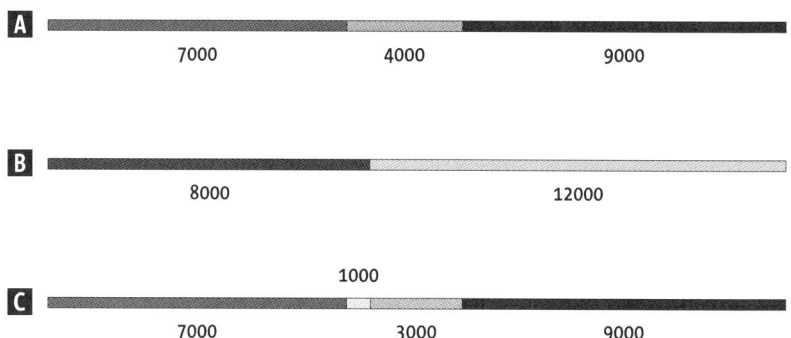

Figure 14-7. A) Ordered sequence from digest with enzyme 1. B) Ordered sequence from digest with enzyme 2. C) Ordered sequence from double digest (restriction map). The boundaries between color segments represent the cleavage sites.

You create this restriction map by trying to overlap fragments in the double digest with fragments from the single digests. For example, since a 7000 base piece appears in the double digest and one of the single digests, you know that it's likely an end piece. You would begin with this piece and add other double digest fragment lengths to it to try to re-create other single digest fragments. For example, 7000 + 1000 = 8000, so it's likely the 8000 base fragment encompasses both of these fragments. Therefore, enzyme 1 cuts the strand after 7000 bases from the end piece and enzyme 2 cuts the strand after an additional 1000 bases. If you now repeat this process with the 1000 base piece, you see that 1000 + 3000 = 4000, from which you can conclude that if you travel down the strand an additional 3000 bases, you'll encounter an enzyme 1 cut site again. Continue to repeat this process until you have used up all of the fragments. This type of technique can break down if a restriction enzyme has 2 or more consecutive cut sites, however, since you won't be able to distinguish the resultant fragment from an end piece. In this situation, scientists often change enzymes or turn towards more complex triple digests. For the purposes of simplifying the example application by eliminating the error handling code required to deal with this situation, assume this is not the case for your restriction mapping program. Again, for the sake of simplicity, also assume that your fragments add up perfectly. In actuality, size measurement by gel electrophoresis is not an ultra precise process; measurements are approximate, so fragments may not always add up exactly. It is left up to you, however, to add this capability after you've mastered the basic routine.

The Restriction Mapping Program

Begin your application by adding a MSFlexGrid control to your form along with a text box and a command button control. Next, add the following code to lay out your grid and add the data entry functionality:

```
Private Sub Form1_Load(ByVal sender As System.Object, ByVal e As _
System.EventArgs) Handles MyBase.Load
        TextBox1.Visible = False
        TextBox1.Font = AxMSFlexGrid1.Font
        With AxMSFlexGrid1
            .Cols = 5
            .Rows = 10
            .FixedCols = 0
            .FixedRows = 1
            .Row = 0
            .Col = 0
            .Text = "Digest 1"
            .Col = 1
```

```
                    .Text = "Digest 2"
                    .Col = 2
                    .Text = "Double Digest"
                    .Col = 3
                    .Text = "Ordered Cuts"
                    .Row = 1
                    .Col = 0
            End With
            DimTextBox()
        End Sub


Private Sub DimTextBox()
        With AxMSFlexGrid1
            TextBox1.Location = New Point(TwipsToPixelsX(.CellLeft) _
+ .Location.X, TwipsToPixelsX(.CellTop) + .Location.Y)
            TextBox1.Size = New Size(TwipsToPixelsY(.CellWidth), _
TwipsToPixelsY(.CellHeight))
            TextBox1.Visible = True
            TextBox1.Focus()
        End With
    End Sub
    Private Sub AxMSFlexGrid1_EnterCell(ByVal eventSender As System.Object, _
ByVal eventArgs As System.EventArgs) Handles AxMSFlexGrid1.EnterCell, _
AxMSFlexGrid1.Enter
        TextBox1.Text = AxMSFlexGrid1.Text
        DimTextBox()
    End Sub
    Private Sub TextBox1_TextChanged(ByVal eventSender As System.Object, _
ByVal eventArgs As System.EventArgs) Handles TextBox1.TextChanged
        AxMSFlexGrid1.Text = TextBox1.Text
    End Sub
    Private Sub TextBox1_KeyDown(ByVal eventSender As System.Object, ByVal _
eventArgs As System.Windows.Forms.KeyEventArgs) Handles TextBox1.KeyDown
        Dim KeyCode As Short = eventArgs.KeyCode
        Dim Shift As Short = eventArgs.KeyData \ &H10000
        With AxMSFlexGrid1
            Select Case KeyCode
                Case  Keys.Down
                    If .Row < .Rows - 1 Then .Row = .Row + 1
                Case Keys.Up
                    If .Row > 1 Then .Row = .Row - 1
                Case Keys.Right
                    If .Col < .Cols - 1 Then .Col = .Col + 1
```

```
                Case Keys.Left
                    If .Col > 0 Then .Col = .Col - 1
            End Select
        End With
    End Sub
    Private Sub TextBox1_KeyPress(ByVal eventSender As System.Object, ByVal _
eventArgs As System.Windows.Forms.KeyPressEventArgs) Handles TextBox1.KeyPress
        Dim KeyAscii As Short = Asc(eventArgs.KeyChar)
        With AxMSFlexGrid1
            If KeyAscii = Keys.Return _
And .Row < .Rows - 1 Then
                .Row = .Row + 1
            End If
        End With
        If KeyAscii = 0 Then
            eventArgs.Handled = True
        End If
    End Sub
```

You've seen most of this code before, so it won't be described in detail here. However, notice the Load event, which lays out the properties of your grid control. You give your control 5 columns and 10 rows. The first row is a fixed row in which you enter the titles "Digest 1" and "Digest 2" in the first two columns. The third column is labeled "Double Digest" and forms the last of the columns required for data entry. The fourth column is titled "Ordered Cuts" and it's in this column you place the ordered fragments. In the fifth column, you place the name (i.e., Enzyme 1 or 2) of the enzyme responsible for creating a fragment of that length.

> **NOTE** *You must also remember to import the Microsoft.VisualBasic. Compatibility.VB6 namespace, as described in Chapter 9, to ensure proper functioning of the MSFlexGrid 6.0 control.*

Now, you need to develop a way to get the data you enter into your application in a format that you can mathematically manipulate. Accomplish this using the GetData procedure that is coded here:

```
Private Sub GetData(ByRef C1() As Integer, ByRef C2() As Integer, ByRef DD() _
As Integer)
        Dim I As Short
        Dim null As Boolean
```

```
With AxMSFlexGrid1
    .Col = 0
    .Row = 1
    I = 0
    null = False
    Do Until null = True
        If .Text <> "" And IsNumeric(.Text) Then
            I = I + 1
            C1(I) = CInt(.Text)
            .Row = I + 1
        Else : C1(0) = I
            null = True
        End If
    Loop
    .Col = 1
    .Row = 1
    I = 0
    null = False
    Do Until null = True
        If .Text <> "" And IsNumeric(.Text) Then
            I = I + 1
            C2(I) = CInt(.Text)
            .Row = I + 1
        Else : C2(0) = I
            null = True
        End If
    Loop
    .Col = 2
    .Row = 1
    I = 0
    null = False
    Do Until null = True
        If .Text <> "" And IsNumeric(.Text) Then
            I = I + 1
            DD(I) = CInt(.Text)
            .Row = I + 1
        Else : DD(0) = I
            null = True
        End If
    Loop
End With
End Sub
```

This procedure uses an indeterminate loop (Do Loop) structure to read through each of the first three columns in your grid control. The loop continues to cycle through the routine until a null string or nonnumeric text is reached. The IsNumeric function ensures that the program won't crash when using the CInt function to enter the data into an array. The reason for stopping when a null string is reached is that you want to get an accurate count of how many pieces of data are in each column. You don't want to waste time processing nonexistent data. In this case, you use the zero position to store the number of elements in each array, and use the 1 to upper bound to store the actual data. In this application, array C1 corresponds to the data in column 1, while C2 and DD correspond to columns 2 and 3 (the Double Digest column), respectively. It's also important to note that the values that you read in are retained after the procedure is exited, because of the ByRef declaration.

Now that you have your data entered into your application, you need to develop a way to find an end point in your sequence so that you have a place to begin your mapping process. Accomplish this by using the FindEnd procedure, which works as follows:

```
Private Sub FindEnd(ByVal C1() As Integer, ByVal C2() As Integer, _
ByVal DD() As Integer, ByRef row As Short, ByRef col As Short)
        Dim I, J, K As Short
        For I = 1 To DD(0)
            For J = 1 To C1(0)
                If C1(J) = DD(I) Then
                    row = I
                    col = 1
                    C1(J) = 0
                    Exit Sub
                End If
            Next J
            For K = 1 To C2(0)
                If C2(K) = DD(I) Then
                    row = I
                    col = 2
                    C2(J) = 0
                    Exit Sub
                End If
            Next K
        Next I
    End Sub
```

This procedure uses the same criteria as the example problem. You define an end piece as a piece that appears in the same band in both the double digest and one of the single digests. As a result, you search through the data from both column 1 and 2 until you find a fragment that matches one of the double digest fragments. You then output the corresponding coordinates of this fragment and set the fragment equal to zero to ensure that you don't make use of the same fragment twice.

Once you have established an end piece, it's time to begin the rest of the ordering process, so you now code the Order procedure. The code for this procedure is as follows:

```
Private Sub Order(ByVal C1() As Integer, ByVal C2() As Integer, ByVal DD() _
As Integer, ByVal Row As Short, ByVal col As Short)
        Dim Temp As Integer
        Dim ordered, I, J As Short
        With AxMSFlexGrid1
            .Col = 2
            .Row = Row
            Temp = CInt(.Text)
            .Col = 3
            .Row = 1
            .Text = Temp
            .Col = 4
            If col = 1 Then
                .Text = "Enzyme1"
            ElseIf col = 2 Then
                .Text = "Enzyme2"
            End If
            DD(Row) = 0
            ordered = 1
            Do Until ordered = DD(0)
                For J = 1 To C1(0)
                    For I = 1 To DD(0)
                        If DD(I) <> 0 And (DD(I) + Temp) = C1(J) Then
                            .Col = 3
                            ordered = ordered + 1
                            .Row = ordered
                            Temp = DD(I)
                            .Text = DD(I)
                            DD(I) = 0
                            .Col = 4
                            .Text = "Enzyme1"
                            C1(J) = 0
                            Exit For
                        End If
```

```
                    Next I
               Next J
               For J = 1 To C2(0)
                    For I = 1 To DD(0)
                         If DD(I) <> 0 And (DD(I) + Temp) = C2(J) Then
                             .Col = 3
                             ordered = ordered + 1
                             .Row = ordered
                             Temp = DD(I)
                             .Text = DD(I)
                             DD(I) = 0
                             .Col = 4
                             .Text = "Enzyme2"
                             C2(J) = 0
                             Exit For
                         End If
                    Next I
               Next J
          Loop
     End With
End Sub
```

This procedure enters your end piece fragment into the first cell of column 4 and then enters the enzyme that cut the fragment into the first cell of column 5. The routine then sets that double digest fragment equal to zero as well to once again ensure that no fragment is used more than once. Next, you use a nested loop structure to try to add this fragment (now called Temp) to other double digest fragments in order to re-create a fragment equivalent in size to one of the single digest fragments. When this process occurs, the fragment, whose addition successfully re-created a single digest fragment, is entered in the next column of the flex grid. This fragment then becomes the new Temp value and is set equal to zero in the double digest fragment list. The single digest fragment it helped re-create is also set equal to zero. This process then continually repeats until all of the fragments have been ordered.

Before you can execute this application, however, you need to add some code to your button's Click event in order to ensure that all of the preceding procedures are called in the correct order. To do this, add the following code and run your restriction mapping application. Your results should resemble Figure 14-8.

```
Private Sub Button1_Click(ByVal sender As System.Object, ByVal e As _
System.EventArgs) Handles Button1.Click
        Dim C1(11) As Integer
        Dim C2(11) As Integer
```

```
        Dim DD(11) As Integer
        Dim row, col As Short
        GetData(C1, C2, DD)
        FindEnd(C1, C2, DD, row, col)
        Order(C1, C2, DD, row, col)
End Sub
```

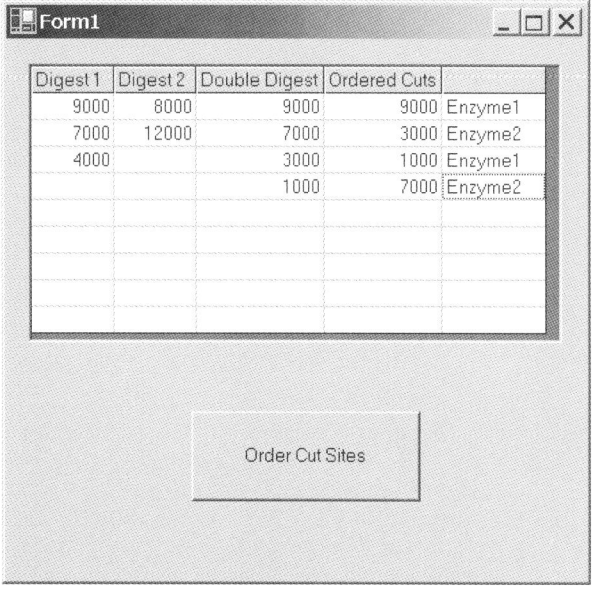

Figure 14-8. The results of your restriction mapping program

TIP   *Try to combine this routine with the graphics capabilities that you learned in Chapter 10 to actually draw the restriction map.*

This concludes the chapter in bioinformatics. Although this chapter only scratches the surface of what bioinformaticists actually do, hopefully it gave you a better understanding of how bioinformatics works, as well as helped you learn how to code two useful laboratory utilities.

Web-Based Applications

Up to this point, you've dealt solely with desktop applications that could be installed and run on any Windows PC. However, while the new .NET platform does offer a multitude of enhancements for desktop programming, the most revolutionary advancements occur in the area of Web-based applications and Web services. Web services are basically programmed protocols that allow programs to share information; in other words, they allow data sharing through interprogram communication. These Web services generally take advantage of XML and the Simple Object Access Protocol, or SOAP. Although XML-based data formats don't seem to be catching on in science and engineering as quickly as they are in business, various scientific communities are developing a host of special-purpose extensions. You should monitor your professional organizations to keep up to date on scientific XML specifications, such as the ones listed in the sidebar "Scientific XML Specifications Under Development."

Scientific XML Specifications Under Development

- **Instrument Markup Language (IML):** An XML specification being developed for use in instrument monitoring and control

- **Chemical Markup Language (CML):** An XML specification for storing 2D and 3D chemical structure information

- **Mathematical Markup Language (MathML):** An XML specification for storing mathematical equation data

---

Web services won't become widespread in science, however, until these specifications are better refined and more widely adopted. Thus, the focus of this chapter will instead be on Web-based applications, which are beginning to slowly emerge within the scientific and engineering communities. This is especially true in the field of biotechnology; for example, from the National Center for Biotechnology Information Web site (among others) you can perform Blast searches on gene and protein sequences (see Figure 15-1). To learn more about these searches, visit http://www.ncbi.nlm.nih.gov/. These searches allow you to enter a sequence and will compare your sequence to tens of thousands of other sequences to try to find similar ones.

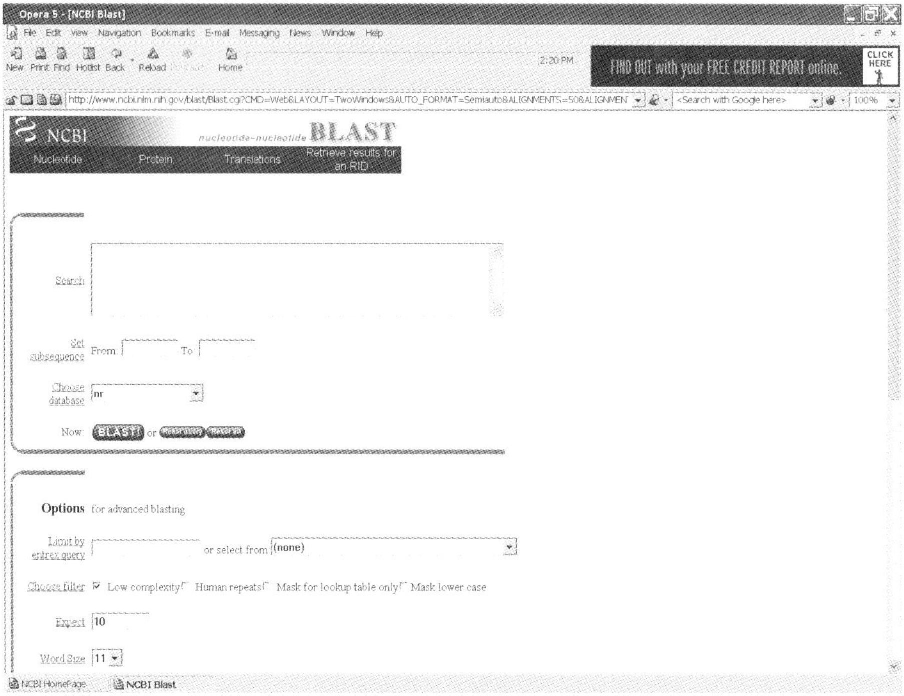

Figure 15-1. The Blast interface

In fact, this type of application illustrates one area in which Web-based applications can provide key scientific technologies. If you take a minute to think about the heavy-duty processing and storage requirements needed to perform Blast searches, you'll realize that it would be far too impractical for every biologist to have his or her own Blast setup. However, since Blast searches can be performed through a Web-based application, anyone with access to a Web browser can easily use this powerful application to carry out their own Blast searches. As you can see, Web-based applications are ideal for situations in which resources would prohibit the widespread dissemination of a desktop version.

Even for simpler computations, Web-based applications offer unique advantages to field researchers and analysts as well. This becomes especially true as the capabilities of handheld devices like Pocket PCs and cell phones continue to grow, along with the wireless Web infrastructure. It's not so hard to imagine a scientist in a remote location collecting some data with his or her Palm or Pocket PC, transferring the data to a Web Form, and submitting the data to the main office via a modem or even a wireless connection. His or her desktop setup could then crunch the numbers and report back the results without the scientist having to leave the work site. Furthermore, as Web-based applications continue to mature and grow, more and more uses will surface and whole new doors will be opened to investigators.

Web Forms and the .NET Framework

Web Forms, a new addition to VB .NET, are designed to simplify the development of Web-based applications. As you'll see in upcoming sections, you can develop Web Forms in much the same manner as more traditional Windows Forms–based applications, since at design time you still have the ability to draw out your controls and then add the required code. This is a major advancement in developing Web applications, because it allows programmers to leverage one set of skills to design both Web and desktop programs.

You'll find the base functionality for Web-based applications in the System.Web namespace, which includes classes that allow for the use of different HTTP-based protocols. In addition, you'll also find classes that can manipulate cookies, aid in file transfers, and work with cached files. These classes are inherited by the System.Web.UI namespace, which provides the functionality required to create Web Forms and also lays out the base functionality of their corresponding controls. If you continue to look up the hierarchy, you'll see that two more namespaces inherit the functionality of the System.Web namespace: System.Web.UI.HtmlControls and System.Web.UI.WebControls. The WebControls namespace fully lays out the functionality behind the new ASP .NET (Active Server Pages) Server Controls or Web controls. You'll learn more about ASP .NET and Web controls in a minute, but for now, just keep in mind that these controls are much more similar to the ActiveX controls that you use in desktop development than to traditional client-side HTML controls. The HtmlControls namespace, on the other hand, lays out the remaining functionality required to use HTML server controls.

Web Form Properties

Before delving into the different types of server controls available to you, here's a closer look at the actual properties of Web Forms themselves. Since it's probably a good idea to try experimenting with some of these new properties as they are discussed, begin by creating your first Web project. Bring up the New Project dialog box, only this time don't select Windows Application, but instead select ASP .NET project.

Normal desktop-based applications make direct use of the common language runtime (CLR)—notably the System.Windows.Forms namespace—in order to execute compiled Windows Forms code. Web Forms, however, are more complex in that they contain an HTML-based component (i.e., the layout the user sees, based on System.Web.UI.Page) as well as the code that makes up the program logic. Because of the dual component nature of these forms, Web Forms use ASP .NET as a runtime engine to process the HTML components and call upon the CLR to process the logical code. This logical code can be written in VB, C#, or any other .NET language, and thus ASP .NET functions as an almost universal Web-based runtime engine for the Visual Studio languages.

Once your new ASP .NET project is created and up on your computer, take a look at your IDE; it should resemble Figure 15-2. You'll notice that the form window no longer contains the standard gray WinForm in the top-left corner, but instead the whole form window contains a blank HTML document (WebForm1.aspx). You'll also notice that the controls in your toolbox are different. These controls are either unique Web controls or Web controls that are the counterparts of the standard Windows application controls. For now, click the blank HTML document and examine some of the novel properties that you encounter in the Properties window.

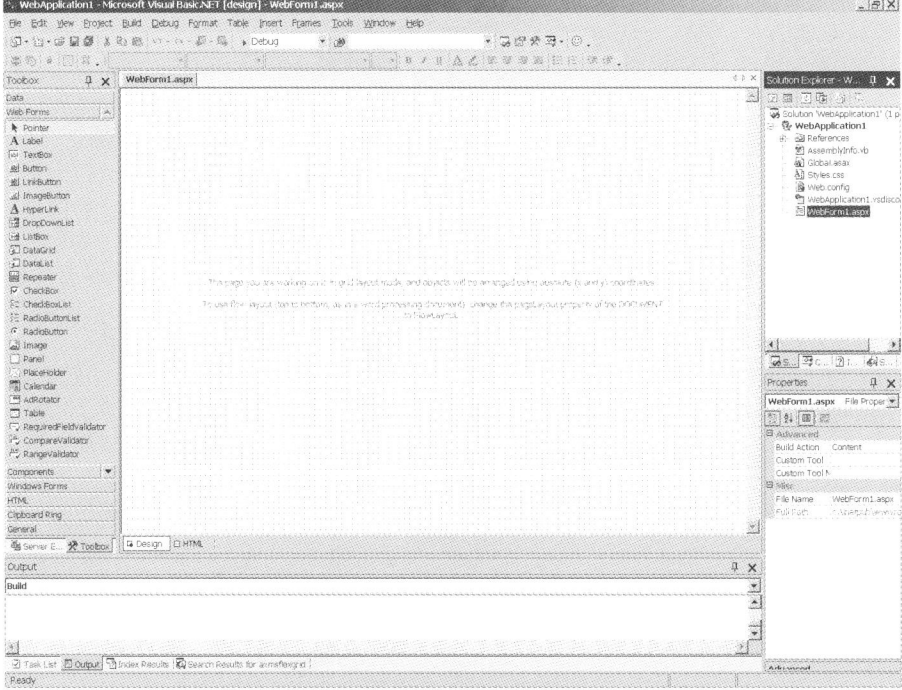

Figure 15-2. The altered VB .NET IDE

NOTE   *In addition to viewing the blank Web Form, you might also want to look at the HTML code behind the interface if you're familiar with HTML. You can examine this by looking at the bottom of the form window, where you'll find two buttons that allow you to switch back and forth between the form's design view and its HTML code.*

The language Property

As mentioned earlier, the ASP .NET runtime engine, which is designed to work with multiple Visual Studio languages, processes the document. This property allows you to specify which language your logical code will be written in—VB, C#, or JScript. For the purposes of this example, choose VB.

The link Property

This property sets the color of unvisited hyperlinks that are contained within the document. It's often a good idea to distinguish between visited and unvisited links, because it helps to make your Web page more user friendly.

The pageLayout Property

If you want to lay out the different controls on your Web Form in the same way as you would on a WinForm, leave this property set to its default, GridLayout. This setting allows you to position controls at any X,Y coordinate on the form. The other setting, FlowLayout, functions more like many traditional HTML editors in that it only allows you to insert items at the cursor's current position, much like in a word processor.

The targetSchema Property

Anyone who has worked in Web design before knows that not all browsers handle HTML in exactly the same way. Thus, certain HTML flavors work better with certain browsers. With this property, you can optimize your HTML for use in certain browser types. As of the writing of this book, you could choose between Internet Explorer 5 (the default), Netscape Navigator 4.0, or Internet Explorer 3.02/Netscape Navigator 3.0. With the recent releases of Netscape 6 and Internet Explorer 6, however, it's likely that additional options may later be incorporated.

The vLink property

The key to recalling what this property does is to remember that *v* stands for *visited*. This property works in exactly the same way as the link property in that it sets hyperlink color, only this property controls the color after the link has been visited.

Server Controls

What makes *server* controls unique is that they are in a sense a hybrid between traditional VB form controls and client-side HTML controls. Standard HTML controls are able to furnish a graphical interface component that you can load into a browser window via an HTTP protocol, provided you perform all state management manually. Server controls overcome this limitation by taking the graphical aspect of HTML controls and combining it with a server-based component that is capable of managing properties and states. This allows events to be used in conjunction with these controls and greatly simplifies the task of making a Web program responsive.

> **NOTE** *In order for these applications to work properly, the server side must be able to support these controls, therefore they only run under Microsoft's IIS-based servers.*

HTML Controls and HTML Server Controls

If you look in your toolbox, you'll notice that one of the menu options is HTML. Selecting this menu option brings up a listing of different HTML controls, which you can add to your Web Form. If you add these controls to your form, you'll see that they are normal client-side HTML controls, with no special server-side capabilities. Keep in mind that a lack of server-side capability isn't necessarily a downside. If a component of your program doesn't need event handling or other server-side capability, you don't have to use a server control. For instance, a label that contains static text wouldn't look or behave any differently in a server control or client-side control.

> **NOTE** *If you are familiar with HTML, you can edit the tags by switching from Design view to HTML view.*

In order to add server-side capabilities to your controls, you must first place one of these controls on your form and right-click. A pop-up menu appears to offer you a list of options. Select the Run As Server Control option, as shown in Figure 15-3, and VB .NET will configure the control as Server Control. Once you have established your control as a server control, you're able to use it in conjunction with events. HTML server controls have limited functionality, since they are nothing more than client-side controls with limited server-side capabilities. These types of controls were designed to primarily add server control capabilities to existing Web applications.

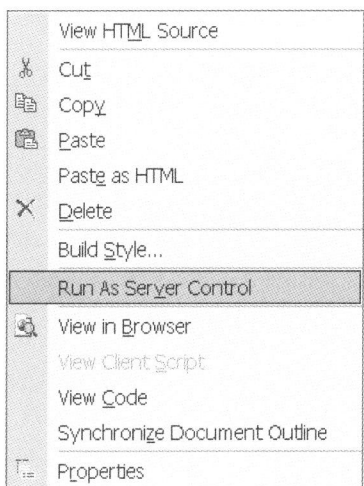

Figure 15-3. Setting up your control to work as a server control

ASP .NET Server Controls

While the HTML server controls just discussed do represent an improvement over more traditional client-side controls, the major advance in Web application programming is in the form of ASP .NET controls. In fact, you'll focus on these controls in depth and use them to code your simple Web application later in the chapter. Although ASP .NET server controls do rely on HTML to create their user interface, they have a more flexible and robust object model than the HTML server controls. In addition to making these controls behave more like Windows Form–based controls, this object model allows for advanced features such as data binding and the ability to detect the type of Web browser being employed by the end user. These controls are then able to dynamically adjust their output in a way that is optimized for the browser type.

Now that you know what ASP .NET server controls are, take a look in the tool-box and examine exactly what controls are available to you. As you look down the list, you'll see that many controls have exact counterparts in the Windows Forms toolbox menu, such as labels and button controls. Other controls have a name that may be foreign to you, but are almost exactly equivalent to a Windows Forms control that you have already worked with. For example, DropDownList is the same as a combo box control. These controls are summarized in Table 15-1.

Table 15-1. ASP .NET Server Controls and Their Windows Forms Equivalents

ASP .NET CONTROL	WINDOWS FORMS EQUIVALENT	FUNCTION
Label	Label	Displays textual information
TextBox	TextBox	Displays text or allows user to enter text
Button	Button	Initiates an action
Hyperlink	LinkLabel	Links together Web pages by permitting URL navigation
DropDownList	ComboBox	Presents users with a list and displays the selection in a box
ListBox	ListBox	Allows users to select an item from a list of items
CheckBox	CheckBox	Allows users to select one or more options when used in conjunction with other check boxes
RadioButton	RadioButton	Allows users to select only one option when used in conjunction with other radio buttons

In addition to these familiar controls, you'll have a chance in the following sections to examine other useful new controls, since they have no equivalent Windows Form–based counterparts.

The CheckBoxList and RadioButtonList Controls

These controls work exactly the same way as their single counterparts (i.e, a RadioButton or CheckBox), only you don't have to manually group them. The difference with the *List versions of these controls is that they come pre-grouped—a feature especially useful when it comes to working with RadioButtons, because it frees you from having to perform extra steps to ensure that the RadioButtons behave in a mutually exclusive manner. The downside to these grouped controls is that you don't have much control or flexibility with how you position them on your Web Form.

The Validator Controls

The Validator controls provide a great way to eliminate potential errors by ensuring that all inputted data is in the correct format. Each one of the Validator controls can't function as a lone entity, but instead must be tied to an input control such as a text box. You'll probably find that you have one or more Validator controls for each input control in your project. You tie the Validator controls to a specific input control by referencing the input control in the ControlToValidate property. If the input control's information doesn't meet the criteria laid out in the Validator control, the ErrorMessage property will output an error message. To gain a better understanding of what types of validation criteria are available, take a look at the different types of Validator controls in the following sections.

The RequiredFieldValidator Control

This is the simplest of all of the validation controls, because this control doesn't try to verify any of the information entered into the input control. This control's sole purpose is to ensure that some form of data was entered into the control. In order to use more specific criteria, you need to turn to one of the other types of validation controls.

The RangeValidator Control

This validation control will check to see if the information within the input control lies within a specified range of acceptable values. This range of values is established using the MaximumValue and MinimumValue properties. You must also set the data type of the input data you're validating using the Type property whose default setting is String. This control won't validate data that doesn't fit into the specified data type.

> **NOTE** *The established range of acceptable values is inclusive of the end points.*

The CompareValidator Control

This control allows you to perform comparisons between the data in the input control and a value specified in the ValueToCompare property. The Operator property dictates the type of comparisons, and the comparisons are based on the different numerical operators. For example, you could check to see if the values are equal to one another or if one value is greater than the other.

The RegularExpressionValidator Control

This type of validation is basically a formatting check. It's most commonly used to verify fixed format data like those of phone numbers that you want entered in a particular format—for example, (XXX) XXX-XXXX; but you could just as easily use this control to validate dates, times, or some other type of entry that needs to be formatted in a special way, such as ensuring that a protein or DNA sequence only contains the correct alphabetic characters. This formatting standard is referred to as a *regular expression,* and can be set up by using the ValidationExpression property. The syntax for setting up these expressions is found in VB's Help section under the term "Regular Expressions."

The CustomValidator Control

This control does just what you would guess by its name: It allows you to set up a custom criterion that your data must meet in order to pass the validation test. Perhaps you only want users to enter even numbers or meet some other criterion that the other Validator controls don't allow you to account for. In these cases, this control will allow you to perform either client-side or server-side validation of the inputted data.

The ValidationSummary Control

This control doesn't do any validation itself, but instead it displays the error messages generated by all of the other validation controls on the form. This control can be quite helpful if you want to display all your error messages in one location (set Visible = False on all other Validator controls), since it's easier to place this single control at the desired location than to arrange all of the other Validator controls in a precise manner.

Validating Data with Validator Controls

In order to gain a better understanding of exactly how to use these Validator controls, try coding a simple example program. First, add a text box and a button control to your Web Form. Next, add a RangeValidator control to your form and enter the string "ERROR: out of range" into the ErrorMessage property. Now set the Type property to Integer, the MaximumValue property to 100, and the MinimumValue property to 0. Also make sure that the Validator control is going to check the data entered into your text box by setting the ControlToValidate property equal to TextBox1. You can now enter the following few lines of code into your command button's Click event to initiate the validity check and complete the sample application.

```
Private Sub Button1_Click(ByVal sender As System.Object, ByVal e As _
System.EventArgs) Handles Button1.Click
        If RangeValidator1.IsValid Then
            'Take Action
        End If
    End Sub
```

As you can see, it's quite simple really. All you do is construct a simple If-Then statement that checks the IsValid property of the RangeValidator control. This causes the Validator control to perform its validity check. If the check determines the IsValid property to be True, then the specified action will be taken. If you placed a number in the text box that was outside the range, the validity check would fail, and the error message you specified would appear in the location you placed the Validator control. Executing this application should launch the browser, which shows the HTML form in Figure 15-4.

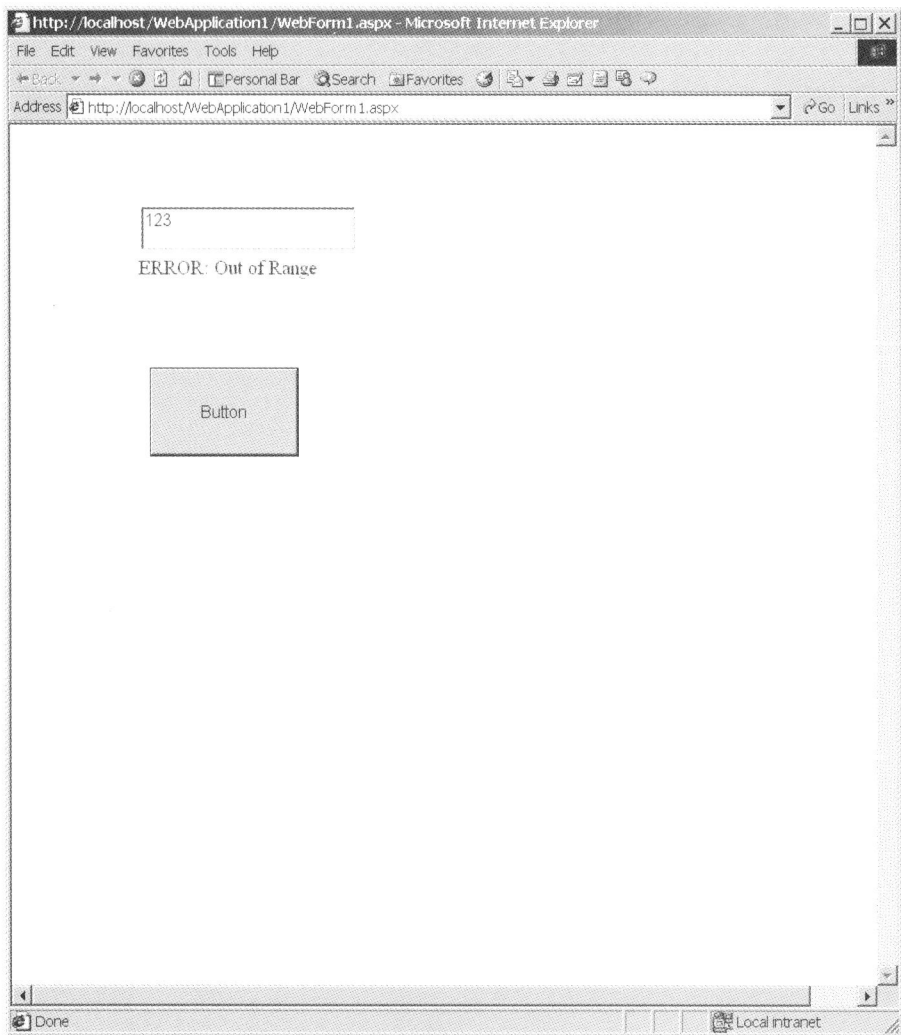

Figure 15-4. A Validator control in action

Events and Web-Based Applications

Events in Web-based applications are handled by the ASP .NET runtime engine, which ensures that the client-side user interface objects are tied to the correct server-side program logic. In other words, a click of a command button that was loaded into a user's browser page executes the Click event code found on the server. It isn't necessary to know exactly how this is accomplished, as the ASP .NET runtime engine does this in a completely behind-the-scenes manner. However, it's important to know that because of this client-server setup, the repertoire of events present in Web-based applications is limited.

This is because Web events require what is known as a *server round-trip*. When you start your Web-based application, a Web page based on a Web Form is constructed on the server and sent to the client's Web browser. At this point, the user can enter data and the like, but will then have to click a button or take some other type of action that will cause the page to be posted back to the server. The server processes the changes and creates a new updated version of the page to send back to the client. This type of setup makes it very impractical to use certain types of events, like MouseMove events, because undertaking this round-trip every time the mouse moves would be a horrendous experience. Therefore, Web events are basically limited to your Click-type events and Changed events that will trigger when the control is left—something to consider when you decide on what type of application to code. The smaller the dependence on events, the better your Web application will function.

> **NOTE** *You still can simulate MouseMove-type events and other events using VBScript or other scripting languages like JavaScript, JScript, etc., since these will execute on the client.*

A Simple Web-Based Application

You are now going to code a simple Web-based application that will allow you to use Newton's Universal Law of Gravitation to calculate the force of gravity between two objects. This application is straightforward and designed to illustrate how similar coding a Web Form–based application is to coding a normal Windows Forms–based application. Of course, you can implement much more complex program logic, using all of the skills that you have learned throughout this book. Coding those more awe-inspiring applications, however, will be left up to you and the skills that you have acquired.

Newton's Universal Law of Gravitation is simple. It states that the gravitational force between two objects is affected by the masses of the objects and their proximity to one another. This relationship is defined by the following equation:

$$F = G\frac{M_1 M_2}{r^2}$$

M_1 and M_2 represent the masses of the two objects and r represents the distance between the two objects. G is the universal gravitational constant, which is equal to $6.672 * 10^{-11}$ N*m^2/kg^2 and F is the resultant force.

You'll begin your application by adding four labels and three text boxes to your blank Web Form. Next, you add three RequiredFieldValidator controls and a button control. The layout should look something like that shown in Figure 15-5.

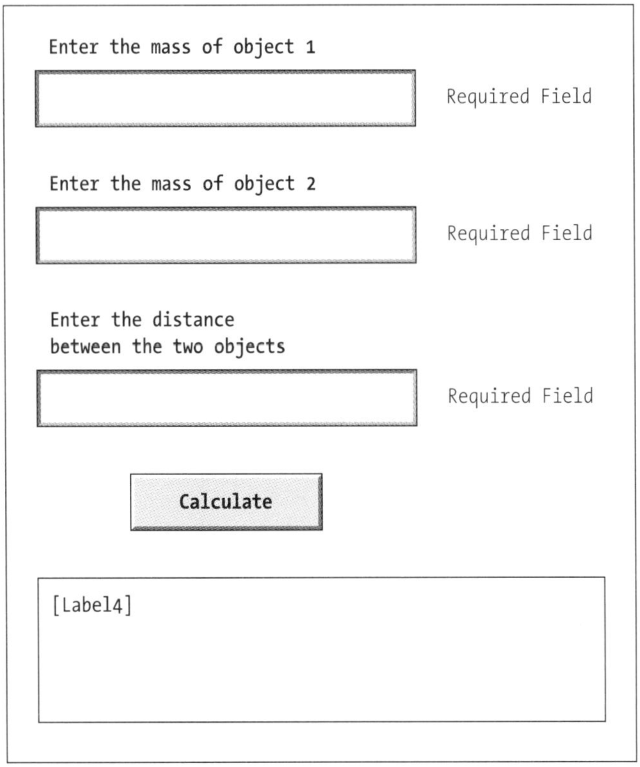

Figure 15-5. Setting up your Web-based application

Once the layout is complete, make sure that each Validator control is linked to the text box that it's positioned next to. You'll then add the following code to your command button's Click event.

```
Private Sub Button1_Click(ByVal sender As System.Object, ByVal e As _
System.EventArgs) Handles Button1.Click
        Dim M1, M2, r, G, F As Double
        G = 6.672 * (10 ^ -11)
        If RequiredFieldValidator1.IsValid And RequiredFieldValidator2.IsValid
And RequiredFieldValidator3.IsValid Then
            M1 = CDbl(TextBox1.Text)
            M2 = CDbl(TextBox2.Text)
            r = CDbl(TextBox3.Text)
            F = ((M1 * M2) / (r ^ 2)) * G
            Label4.Text = "The Force of gravity is " & F
        End If
    End Sub
```

As you can see, the code doesn't look any different from the code that would be used to write an equivalent desktop application. As usual, you first declare your variables. Next, you try to ensure that all of the proper data entry requirements are satisfied by using the Validator controls. You then read in your data using a conversion function and perform your calculation. Lastly, you output your data. Notice that even though you have some restrictions in terms of lack of events and the like, you can still leverage most of your skills to easily create Web-based applications. Executing this application should launch the browser, which shows the HTML form in Figure 15-6.

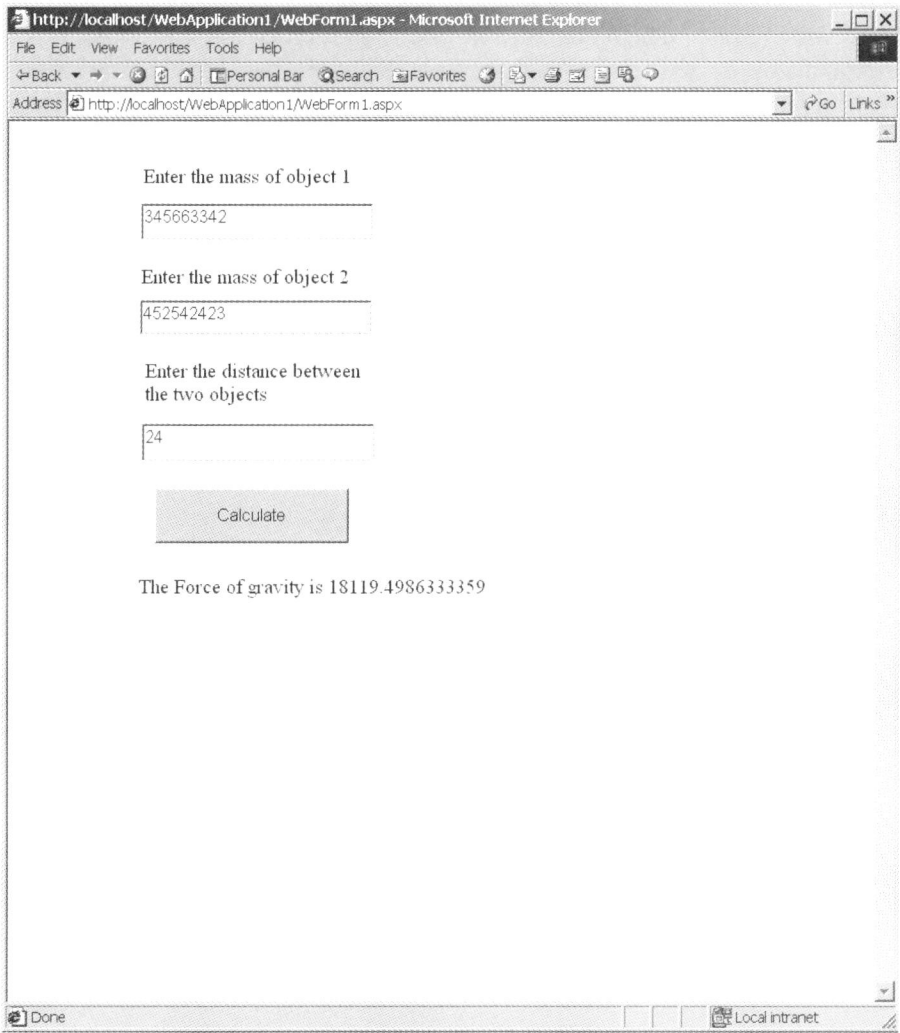

Figure 15-6. Executing your Web-based application

Conclusion

Congratulations, you have just finished *Visual Basic and Visual Basic .NET for Scientists and Engineers.* By now, you should have a firm understanding of all of the concepts required to effectively use VB in the scientific world. From this point on, you're limited only by your own imagination, as you now possess the skills required to program solutions to the majority of scientific problems. This doesn't mean that you should stop learning about VB or programming in general, however. Anyone who is seriously thinking of pursuing a career in scientific programming should seek out more advanced methodologies and tools and learn about them as well. Both science and computing are rapidly changing fields, with newer and better technologies constantly emerging, and in order to stay on top of your field you need to stay on top of these technologies as well. Thus, in many ways the completion of this book isn't an ending but rather a beginning—a foundation to build your future endeavors and skills upon.

Index

Announcing *About VS.NET*—
the *free* Apress .NET e-newsletter with great .NET news, information, code—and attitude

We guarantee that this isn't going to be your typical boring e-newsletter with just a list of URLs (though it will have them as well).

Instead, *About VS.NET* will contain contributions from a whole slate of top .NET gurus, edited by award-winning, best-selling authors Gary Cornell and Dan Appleman. Upcoming issues will feature articles on:

- Best coding practices in ADO.NET

- The hidden "gotchas" in doing thread programming in VB.NET

- Why C# is (not) a better choice than VB.NET

- What Java can learn from C# and vice versa

About VS.NET will cover it all!

This *free* e-newsletter will be the easiest way for you to get up-to-date .NET information delivered to your Inbox every two weeks—more often if there's breaking news!

Apress Titles

ISBN	PRICE	AUTHOR	TITLE
1-893115-73-9	$34.95	Abbott	Voice Enabling Web Applications: VoiceXML and Beyond
1-893115-01-1	$39.95	Appleman	Appleman's Win32 API Puzzle Book and Tutorial for Visual Basic Programmers
1-893115-23-2	$29.95	Appleman	How Computer Programming Works
1-893115-97-6	$39.95	Appleman	Moving to VB. NET: Strategies, Concepts, and Code
1-893115-09-7	$29.95	Baum	Dave Baum's Definitive Guide to LEGO MINDSTORMS
1-893115-84-4	$29.95	Baum, Gasperi, Hempel, and Villa	Extreme MINDSTORMS: An Advanced Guide to LEGO MINDSTORMS
1-893115-82-8	$59.95	Ben-Gan/Moreau	Advanced Transact-SQL for SQL Server 2000
1-893115-48-8	$29.95	Bischof	The .NET Languages: A Quick Translation Guide
1-893115-67-4	$49.95	Borge	Managing Enterprise Systems with the Windows Script Host
1-893115-28-3	$44.95	Challa/Laksberg	Essential Guide to Managed Extensions for C++
1-893115-44-5	$29.95	Cook	Robot Building for Beginners
1-893115-99-2	$39.95	Cornell/Morrison	Programming VB .NET: A Guide for Experienced Programmers
1-893115-72-0	$39.95	Curtin	Developing Trust: Online Privacy and Security
1-59059-008-2	$29.95	Duncan	The Career Programmer: Guerilla Tactics for an Imperfect World
1-893115-71-2	$39.95	Ferguson	Mobile .NET
1-893115-90-9	$44.95	Finsel	The Handbook for Reluctant Database Administrators
1-893115-42-9	$44.95	Foo/Lee	XML Programming Using the Microsoft XML Parser
1-893115-55-0	$39.95	Frenz	Visual Basic and Visual Basic .NET for Scientists and Engineers
1-893115-85-2	$34.95	Gilmore	A Programmer's Introduction to PHP 4.0
1-893115-36-4	$34.95	Goodwill	Apache Jakarta-Tomcat
1-893115-17-8	$59.95	Gross	A Programmer's Introduction to Windows DNA
1-893115-62-3	$39.95	Gunnerson	A Programmer's Introduction to C#, Second Edition
1-893115-30-5	$49.95	Harkins/Reid	SQL: Access to SQL Server
1-893115-10-0	$34.95	Holub	Taming Java Threads
1-893115-04-6	$34.95	Hyman/Vaddadi	Mike and Phani's Essential C++ Techniques
1-893115-96-8	$59.95	Jorelid	J2EE FrontEnd Technologies: A Programmer's Guide to Servlets, JavaServer Pages, and Enterprise JavaBeans
1-893115-49-6	$39.95	Kilburn	Palm Programming in Basic
1-893115-50-X	$34.95	Knudsen	Wireless Java: Developing with Java 2, Micro Edition
1-893115-79-8	$49.95	Kofler	Definitive Guide to Excel VBA

ISBN	PRICE	AUTHOR	TITLE
1-893115-57-7	$39.95	Kofler	MySQL
1-893115-87-9	$39.95	Kurata	Doing Web Development: Client-Side Techniques
1-893115-75-5	$44.95	Kurniawan	Internet Programming with VB
1-893115-46-1	$36.95	Lathrop	Linux in Small Business: A Practical User's Guide
1-893115-19-4	$49.95	Macdonald	Serious ADO: Universal Data Access with Visual Basic
1-893115-06-2	$39.95	Marquis/Smith	A Visual Basic 6.0 Programmer's Toolkit
1-893115-22-4	$27.95	McCarter	David McCarter's VB Tips and Techniques
1-893115-76-3	$49.95	Morrison	C++ For VB Programmers
1-893115-80-1	$39.95	Newmarch	A Programmer's Guide to Jini Technology
1-893115-58-5	$49.95	Oellermann	Architecting Web Services
1-893115-81-X	$39.95	Pike	SQL Server: Common Problems, Tested Solutions
1-893115-20-8	$34.95	Rischpater	Wireless Web Development
1-893115-93-3	$34.95	Rischpater	Wireless Web Development with PHP and WAP
1-893115-89-5	$59.95	Shemitz	Kylix: The Professional Developer's Guide and Reference
1-893115-40-2	$39.95	Sill	The qmail Handbook
1-893115-24-0	$49.95	Sinclair	From Access to SQL Server
1-893115-94-1	$29.95	Spolsky	User Interface Design for Programmers
1-893115-53-4	$39.95	Sweeney	Visual Basic for Testers
1-59059-002-3	$44.95	Symmonds	Internationalization and Localization Using Microsoft .NET
1-893115-29-1	$44.95	Thomsen	Database Programming with Visual Basic .NET
1-893115-65-8	$39.95	Tiffany	Pocket PC Database Development with eMbedded Visual Basic
1-893115-59-3	$59.95	Troelsen	C# and the .NET Platform
1-893115-26-7	$59.95	Troelsen	Visual Basic .NET and the .NET Platform
1-893115-54-2	$49.95	Trueblood/Lovett	Data Mining and Statistical Analysis Using SQL
1-893115-16-X	$49.95	Vaughn	ADO Examples and Best Practices
1-893115-68-2	$49.95	Vaughn	ADO.NET and ADO Examples and Best Practices for VB Programmers, Second Edition
1-59059-012-0	$34.95	Vaughn/Blackburn	ADO.NET Examples and Best Practices for C# Programmers
1-893115-83-6	$44.95	Wells	Code Centric: T-SQL Programming with Stored Procedures and Triggers
1-893115-95-X	$49.95	Welschenbach	Cryptography in C and C++
1-893115-05-4	$39.95	Williamson	Writing Cross-Browser Dynamic HTML
1-893115-78-X	$49.95	Zukowski	Definitive Guide to Swing for Java 2, Second Edition
1-893115-92-5	$49.95	Zukowski	Java Collections

Available at bookstores nationwide or from Springer Verlag New York, Inc. at 1-800-777-4643; fax 1-212-533-3503. Contact us for more information at sales@apress.com.

Apress Titles Publishing SOON!

ISBN	AUTHOR	TITLE
1-893115-91-7	Birmingham/Perry	Software Development on a Leash
1-893115-39-9	Chand	A Programmer's Guide to ADO.NET in C#
1-59059-009-0	Harris/Macdonald	Moving to ASP.NET
1-59059-016-3	Hubbard	Windows Forms in C#
1-893115-38-0	Lafler	Power AOL: A Survival Guide
1-59059-003-1	Nakhimovsky/Meyers	XML Programming: Web Applications and Web Services with JSP and ASP
1-893115-27-5	Morrill	Intermediate Linux
1-893115-43-7	Stephenson	Standard VB: An Enterprise Developer's Reference for VB 6 and VB .NET
1-59059-007-4	Thomsen	Building Web Services with VB .NET
1-59059-010-4	Thomsen	Database Programming with C#
1-59059-011-2	Troelsen	COM and .NET Interoperability
1-59059-004-X	Valiaveedu	SQL Server 2000 and Business Intelligence in an XML/.NET World
1-893115-98-4	Zukowski	Learn Java with JBuilder 6

Available at bookstores nationwide or from Springer Verlag New York, Inc. at 1-800-777-4643; fax 1-212-533-3503. Contact us for more information at sales@apress.com.

About Apress

Apress, located in Berkeley, CA, is an innovative publishing company devoted to meeting the needs of existing and potential programming professionals. Simply put, the "A" in Apress stands for the "Author's Press™." Apress' unique author-centric approach to publishing grew from conversations between Dan Appleman and Gary Cornell, authors of best-selling, highly regarded computer books. In 1998, they set out to create a publishing company that emphasized quality above all else, a company with books that would be considered the best in their market. Dan and Gary's vision has resulted in over 30 widely acclaimed titles by some of the industry's leading software professionals.

Do You Have What It Takes to Write for Apress?

Apress is rapidly expanding its publishing program. If you can write and refuse to compromise on the quality of your work, if you believe in doing more than rehashing existing documentation, and if you're looking for opportunities and rewards that go far beyond those offered by traditional publishing houses, we want to hear from you!

Consider these innovations that we offer all of our authors:

- **Top royalties with *no* hidden switch statements**
  Authors typically only receive half of their normal royalty rate on foreign sales. In contrast, Apress' royalty rate remains the same for both foreign and domestic sales.

- **A mechanism for authors to obtain equity in Apress**
  Unlike the software industry, where stock options are essential to motivate and retain software professionals, the publishing industry has adhered to an outdated compensation model based on royalties alone. In the spirit of most software companies, Apress reserves a significant portion of its equity for authors.

- **Serious treatment of the technical review process**
  Each Apress book has a technical reviewing team whose remuneration depends in part on the success of the book since they too receive royalties.

Moreover, through a partnership with Springer-Verlag, one of the world's major publishing houses, Apress has significant venture capital behind it. Thus, we have the resources to produce the highest quality books *and* market them aggressively.

If you fit the model of the Apress author who can write a book that gives the "professional what he or she needs to know ™," then please contact one of our Editorial Directors, Gary Cornell (gary_cornell@apress.com), Dan Appleman (dan_appleman@apress.com), Karen Watterson (karen_watterson@apress.com) or Jason Gilmore (jason_gilmore@apress.com) for more information.